Swallows, Amazons and Coots

There is always more in life than meets the eye. The delightful and unique Arthur Ransome stories from *Swallows and Amazons* to *Great Northern?* have captivated us over the years. But now we learn, thanks to this fascinating book, that there are more aspects and depths to the stories than we ever imagined. In no way does this diminish them – on the contrary. By giving us a more profound understanding of the author, the adventures and exploits of his characters take on an extra depth and dimension. These are stories for children that no adult should miss.

Virginia McKenna, O.B.E.,
portrayed Mrs Walker in *Swallows & Amazons* (1974)

An admirable introduction for newcomers to the *Swallows and Amazons* novels, written with detailed and expert knowledge. Julian Lovelock clearly has a deep affection and admiration for Ransome's writing, and places the books in a rich and complex context. This is an elegant and leisurely guide through the books in the company of an amiable and well-informed companion.

Peter Hunt,
Professor Emeritus in Children's Literature at Cardiff University
and co-author of *How Did Long John Silver Lose His Leg?* (2013)

This is a splendid and timely book. Julian Lovelock restores Arthur Ransome to his rightful place on one of the peaks of children's fiction. Perhaps even more importantly, he reminds us, by way of a plainly and grippingly told tale, of the pleasure to be had when, returning as an adult to books treasured in childhood, we are seized once again by Ransome's moral strength, his technical command whether of seafaring, copper-mining, birdlore or Arctic exploration, and the cordial power of his story-telling.

Fred Inglis,
Emeritus Professor of Cultural Studies at the University of Sheffield

Lest we forget, what Rowling did for magicians in the noughties, Arthur Ransome did for sailing holidays in the 1930s and '40s. In this charming but exacting study, Lovelock brings vividly alive the world of *Swallows and Amazons* and the intriguing character of its creator. Here is a real 'spot in time' of English culture. Lovelock presents the first serious study of the whole oeuvre, an apparently lost world of the certainties of Empire and the patriarchal family.

Stefan Hawlin,
Professor in English Literature, University of Buckingham

For Pat —

Swallows, Amazons and Coots

A Reading of Arthur Ransome

With all good wishes,

Julian Lovelock

Julian Lovelock

With a Foreword by
Sophie Neville

The Lutterworth Press

The Lutterworth Press
P.O. Box 60
Cambridge
CB1 2NT
United Kingdom

www.lutterworth.com
publishing@lutterworth.com

ISBN: 978 0 7188 9436 8

British Library Cataloguing in Publication Data
A record is available from the British Library

Copyright © Julian Lovelock, 2016

First Published, 2016

Extracts from Ransome's works © Arthur Ransome Literary
Estate, by permission Penguin Random House.

Contents

For the officers and crew of
Margaret Mary III
wherever they may now be sailing

List of Illustrations

Note: *All of the Ransome illustrations listed below are copyright © Arthur Ransome Literary Estate, by permission Penguin Random House.*

Foreword

How many of us have grown up under the strident crossed flags of the Swallows and the Amazons? How many children have gazed at line drawings that rarely show faces and yet immerse them in a world they can map out for themselves as they let their imaginations run free?

Arthur Ransome's well-loved series of classic books about the Swallows, Amazons and Coots, along with a few Eels, have graced the shelves of bookshops since the 1930s. As a child, my father looked forward to the publication of each new hardback almost every Christmas. Oh, that he had kept those first editions! Instead he bought Puffin paperbacks for me. I devoured them all, ever-eager to go camping and explore wild places, imagining myself sometimes as Susan, sometimes as Nancy or Peggy. Ransome literally taught me to sail a small boat and camp effectively, just as he taught so many others. He wrote as if he himself were living the adventures, which of course he was. The only thing he failed to describe was the reality of outdoor temperatures. It seems he was quite impervious to the cold.

Although I never saw myself as a competent able-seaman, I was fortunate enough to play Titty Walker in the 1974 feature film of *Swallows and Amazons*, with Virginia McKenna as 'the best of all natives'. Since the Blu-ray has been re-mastered for cinemas, I can still be seen rowing *Amazon* across Derwentwater as a shivering twelve-year-old, wearing no more than a cotton dress, grey cardigan and an enormous pair of navy blue gym knickers. I clearly remember filming this sequence, since the director, the cinematographer and a sizeable 35mm Panavision camera were also in the dinghy. As children, living out the drama in the Lake District, collecting firewood, making patterans and catching perch, we became intimately involved in the story and developed a meaningful association with the imaginary landscape carefully pieced together over seven weeks of filming.

Ten years later, I was able to work on the BBC television serial of *Coot Club* and *The Big Six*, made entirely on location in East Anglia under the generic title of *Swallows and Amazons Forever!* I was given the task of finding a boy to play Tom Dudgeon and children with Norfolk accents to play the Death and Glories, together with the baddies, George Owdon, Ralph Strakey and Rodley's sons. We spent three months filming on the Norfolk Broads, calling out, 'Coots Forever! And Ever!' with Rosemary Leach who played Mrs Barrable, Patrick Troughton in the guise of Harry Bangate, the Eel Man, and Julian Fellowes, who led the Hullabaloos across Breydon Water with a narrow moustache flickering in menace on his upper lip.

It wasn't until another thirty years passed, when I was asked by members of The Arthur Ransome Society how the books were adapted for the screen, that I read these stories more deeply and began to research into Ransome's life. I discovered glimpses of his own history in the characters – Captain Flint, junketing about overseas; Captain John, responsible for his three younger siblings; Dick, the boy with round glasses who loved bird-watching; and his sister, the lyrical author Dorothea. The Swallows were originally based on the children of Ransome's old friends, the Altounyans (though he was later hotly to deny it): Taqui, Susie, Titty, Roger and Brigit, whom he met when they came to visit their grandparents in 1928 and stayed at Holly Howe, the real Bank Ground Farm, above Coniston Water.

Of course, not all Ransome's characters are human. The yacht *Nancy Blackett*, bought with 'Spanish gold', as he was wont to call publisher's royalties, was used as his model for *Goblin* in *We Didn't Mean to Go to Sea* and *Secret Water*. You can sail her across the North Sea today. *SL Esperance* and *SL Gondola*, his models for Captain Flint's houseboat, can still be found in Cumbria. Indeed, you can take a trip down Coniston Water on the National Trust's replica of the *Gondola*, just as the Ransome family did when they spent summer holidays on a farm beneath knickerbockerbreaker rocks at Nibthwaite. Keep a sharp lookout for Secret Harbour at the southern end of Peel Island. You might even spot a cormorant. 'They've got india rubber necks.'

It is wonderful now to have Julian Lovelock's *Swallows, Amazons and Coots*, a new full-length critical study that provides further background to Ransome's well-loved tales, as a travelling companion. In it, we learn how Ransome agonised over his plots 'in the cider press', despite the tyranny of stomach ulcers and his demanding Russian wife. We find out how Evgenia Petrovna Shelepina, the girl he whisked away from Trotksy's office in Petrograd and the dangers of the Bolshevik revolution, became his harshest critic and yet made useful, if not brilliant, suggestions. Although she proved an edifying editor, her comments were harsh enough to have me weeping with laughter. We learn that Susie Altounyan thought it was Evgenia who best represented Mate Susan, willing to go anywhere and cook anything, but not without insecurities when it came to strangers appearing in the Lake District. Her bad-tempered potatoes are the give-away. And, in many ways Ransome's writing did depend on Evgenia, who took care of meals and practicalities as the couple endlessly moved house despite Jonathan Cape's deadlines. David Wood experienced her firm hand on his neck as he crafted the screenplay to the 1974 *Swallows and Amazons* film. 'Susan wouldn't say that,' Evgenia told him emphatically, although David managed to find the page in the novel that proved her wrong.

But while *Swallows, Amazons and Coots* offers a brief introduction to Ransome's life and times, showing how these are often the starting-point for his writing, it warns against 'biographical reductionism'. Instead it focuses on the themes woven through the *Swallows and Amazons* novels, looking at how his characters develop as well as revealing the complexities that lie beneath Ransome's simple but sparkling prose. It highlights the 'explorers' and 'savages' imagery of a colonial world, celebrates the threatened beauty of rural England and points to the unease of the 1930s that lies only just beneath the surface. It questions the role of women in an ingrained patriarchal culture while highlighting the class divisions which would be challenged when the Second World War was over.

I was, in fact, re-reading *Peter Duck* when the manuscript of *Swallows, Amazons and Coots* arrived in the post and I immediately discovered a fresh perspective on Ransome's treasure island fantasy. It started life as a pirate story told by the Swallows and Amazons when they are holed up on a winter cruise on the Norfolk Broads – a story in which they make themselves the main characters. But in the story, an old sea-dog spins his own yarn in which the children are somehow also caught up as they sail with him to the Caribbees, fight with real pirates and discover hidden pearls. 'It is,' says Julian Lovelock, 'a story within a story within a story; a metafictional delight.'

As I read *Swallows, Amazons and Coots*, my eyes grew accustomed to looking towards distant horizons, my understanding developed and I walked forward in anticipation. It occurred to me some time ago that Ransome must have thought the Lakeland rush-bearing festivals made Bowness seem like Rio, but I had not taken in other obvious references to South America: stout Cortez on the Peak in Darien, the anticipated armadillo, the River Plate and the Spanish Main, not forgetting Cape Horn and the Magellan Straits in *Secret Water*. I've been inspired to think more critically about the novels, about the people, the places and their origin.

Recently I stepped into a carriage of the steam locomotive that takes a new film adaptation of *Swallows and Amazons* into the next generation of children's lives and wondered what the future will hold. Thankfully Ransome's wilderness is still there to be found and with it, freedom. Bobby McCulloch, who plays Roger in the movie, said, 'I really want to sail to an island with my brothers and survive without my parents, just like the Swallows.' One of the other young actors said, 'Sailing on the lake, sleeping under the stars, who wouldn't want that?'[1] We just have to make our own decisions and take the practical steps to embark on voyages of exploration and discovery. It's not out of reach.

As President of The Arthur Ransome Society, I come across people everywhere who not only admire Ransome but readily tell me how his stories have influenced their lives. They always strike me as having become remarkably good decision-makers who delight in their own tales of outdoor life and nautical accomplishments. How many sailors do you know who happen to be called Roger? I've met a number who admit to being given certain books at an impressionable age that gave them direction and encouragement to last a lifetime. My own list is endless. During the pirate feast aboard Captain Flint's houseboat Titty declared she would like to go to Africa and see forests full of parrots. And some years later I did just that. I found myself drawing a number of charts in Botswana as Meyer's parrots swooped down from the palm trees. I cooked on camp fires, slept in a tent and travelled by dug-out canoe. The most serendipitous occurrence was that, along with the girls playing the Amazons, I learnt how to shoot with a bow and arrow under the gaze of Old Man Coniston. As a result, I went on to play an archery champion in another movie and ended up meeting my husband at a longbow tournament. Our arrows should be fletched with green parrots' feathers, only I fear we'd never find them in the grass.

I'm sure that Arthur Ransome enthusiasts and students of children's literature will enjoy and appreciate *Swallows, Amazons and Coots*. It's the first book devoted wholly to a critical reading of the twelve *Swallows and Amazons* novels that introduce the young to adventure and bring solace to adult readers. Without in any way detracting from the magic of Ransome's well-loved stories, it offers new insights into his skill as a writer – a skill that led him to be awarded the first Carnegie Medal in 1936, an honorary Doctor of Letters in 1951 and a CBE in 1953 as his books were translated and enjoyed all over the world. I wish *Swallows, Amazons and Coots* 'God speed', and all the success it deserves.

Sophie Neville
President of The Arthur Ransome Society

---

1. Melissa Brobby, 'Swallows and Amazons Cast Q&As', *Visit England*, 5 July 2016: https://www.visitengland.com/blog/july-2016/quotes-cast-swallows-and-amazons.

Acknowledgements

In my reading of Arthur Ransome I have inevitably been influenced by the many people who have already written and talked about the *Swallows and Amazons* novels. In particular, I am indebted to Professor Peter Hunt (*Approaching Arthur Ransome*), Professor Fred Inglis (*In Pursuit of Happiness*) and Professor Victor Watson (*Reading Series Fiction*), who are, I think, the doyens of Ransome criticism; although I have not always agreed with them, they have influenced and challenged my thinking. There are many other critics who have had their say, all listed in the Select Bibliography, as well as numerous contributors over the years to *Mixed Moss*, the Journal of The Arthur Ransome Society, and some inspiring speakers at The Arthur Ransome Society's Literary Weekends. *The Best of Childhood*, edited by Roger Wardale and others, is a treasure trove of information, as are Christina Hardyment's *Arthur Ransome and Captain Flint's Trunk* and the beautifully written and produced *The World of Arthur Ransome*. Roger Wardale's series of publications on Arthur Ransome and the settings of his novels, lavishly illustrated with photographs old and new, provide further fascinating background. Winifred Wilson, the Society's librarian, and Paul Wilson have been immensely helpful.

I am grateful to the executors of Arthur Ransome's Literary Estate and to Random House for permission to quote from Ransome's novels, letters and diaries, and to use a number of Ransome's own inimitable illustrations.

I am also grateful to Professor Stefan Hawlin of the University of Buckingham for his help and encouragement when I embarked on this project, and to Professor Peter Hunt and Mr Geraint Lewis for taking the trouble to read through a draft of the text and for their wise advice. I want to thank especially Dr Hazel Sheeky Bird for being a perceptive and challenging critical friend, and Sophie Neville for her support and for writing the Foreword.

Finally, my thanks to everyone at The Lutterworth Press for believing in the book and turning it into reality.

Julian Lovelock
Buckingham, 2016

Introduction:
'The Romantic Transfiguration of Fact'

This is not so much a book about Arthur Ransome, whose life and complex character have been explored in every detail, but about his *Swallows and Amazons* novels (though the author and his work are more than usually intertwined). There are twelve books in all, written between 1930 and 1947: *Swallows and Amazons* (1930), *Swallowdale* (1931), *Peter Duck* (1932), *Winter Holiday* (1933), *Coot Club* (1934), *Pigeon Post* (1936), *We Didn't Mean to Go to Sea* (1937), *Secret Water* (1939), *The Big Six* (1940), *Missee Lee* (1941), *The Picts and the Martyrs* (1943), and *Great Northern?* (1947). Fragments of a further novel with the working title *Swallows & Co,* started and abandoned after *The Picts and the Martyrs,* were discovered among some of Ransome's papers lent to the Lakeland Museum at Abbot Hall, Kendal. They were edited by Hugh Brogan and published as *Coots in the North* (1988).

It was, I think, in 1960 that I began reading the *Swallows and Amazons* novels – first in a hospital bed, and then curled each night in my bunk on the sort of boating holiday that Ransome's characters would have enjoyed. By then I knew Pin Mill and the River Orwell, which are the starting point for both *We Didn't Mean to Go to Sea* and *Secret Water.* Like Ransome's Swallows I had made the crossing, described so vividly in *We Didn't Mean to Go to Sea,* to Flushing (Vlissingen) in Holland. So I thought myself an adventurer too, and shared their nautical world and language, though in my case there were adults to keep us out of danger – or at least to take us out of danger when the sea turned rough or the old Atlantic paraffin engines of *Margaret Mary III,* the 1930s motor yacht on which we were able-seamen, broke down (which they frequently did).

Looking back, there was also another way in which I came close to sharing the world of the Swallows and Amazons. It was only fifteen years after the end of the Second World War and the British Empire was

in the death throes that Ransome had half foreseen and half lamented.
The Sussex preparatory school which I attended (and which was a far
happier place than Ransome's school, Windermere Old College) still
seemed to be preparing us boys to administer the fast disappearing
colonies. In Geography, half the world was coloured a fading red in
our atlases; we collected stamps from Gold Coast, Tanganyika and
Zanzibar, and from Rhodesia and Nyasaland; we were Baden-Powell's
Scouts, when Scouting was still about serving God, Queen and Country.
In History we learned of breath-taking victories at Crécy, Poitiers
and Agincourt; of Drake and Raleigh; of Nelson and Wellington; of
Livingstone and Rhodes. Out of class, we revelled in victories against
German and Japanese foes, vividly illustrated in tasteless comic books,
which we re-enacted with armies of plastic *Airfix* soldiers. My father,
who would have been a near contemporary of Ransome's Commander
Walker, had evacuated troops from the beaches of Dunkirk before
spending the war sweeping mines in the Indian Ocean. But whatever
the triumph of the allied forces over Hitler's axis of evil, these were the
dog days of *Great* Britain.

It was not long afterwards that the innocent but precarious era that
Ransome so vividly evokes, and which I had at least partly experienced,
was over. In 1965 I was one of a group of schoolboys – we were aged
fifteen and sixteen – who ventured onto the Norfolk Broads for our
own holiday, and explored for myself the rivers and villages that are
the setting of *Coot Club* and *The Big Six*. By then the 1960s were
swinging, the Beatles and the Rolling Stones were symptomatic of a
new and exciting youth culture, and (according to Philip Larkin) sex,
which largely passed the Swallows and Amazons by, had begun.[1] We
were discovering girls and beer, and our exploits, though tame, were
somewhat different from those of Ransome's Norfolk Coots.

It was more than forty years later – after a number of sailing holidays
on the Norfolk Broads on board the *Perfect Lady* and *Leading Lady*
yachts from Herbert Woods's yard at Potter Heigham – that I finally
drove north to explore Windermere and Coniston Water. But I'm not
sure that the delay mattered more than symbolically, because (unlike the
wholly real Norfolk settings) Ransome's Lake is neither Windermere nor
Coniston Water, nor even a simple mixing of the two, but an imaginative
transformation of the Lake District landscape (Derwentwater is
another particular source). Indeed, seeing Windermere's Blake Holme
and Coniston's Peel Island was an anti-climax: Wild Cat Island is much
larger and more exciting than its actual precursors.

---

1. Philip Larkin, 'Annus Mirabilis' (1967).

Russia in particular, written in collaboration with Karl Radek, was an open letter canvassing support from the American people by appealing to their own revolutionary history and instincts. On the surface, at least, Ransome saw the Bolshevik revolution against the Tsar as a people's justifiable overthrowing of tyrannical oppression. He went as far as apparently accepting Bolshevik atrocities as a necessary evil, remaining on the British government's list of suspected Bolshevik activists until 1937, but this is unlikely to have been his real opinion and a later MI5 file note is probably right: 'S.76 is not a Bolshevik. His interest in, association with various Bolshevik leaders has always been literary rather than political. He has, I think, no special political views.'[1]

For another five years, Ransome and Evgenia were based in the Baltic (first in Reval, Estonia; then in Riga, Latvia), where Ransome continued to work as a journalist, now for the *Manchester Guardian*. Political tensions eased and he made regular trips back to Moscow. They both enjoyed sailing a series of boats: *The Slug, Kittiwake*, and *Racundra*. *Kittiwake* was a small 16-foot dinghy, to which Ransome added a tiny cabin, and perhaps there is something of her in *Coot Club*'s *Death and Glory*. *Racundra* was built in Riga and the story of her maiden voyage is told in Ransome's yachting classic, *Racundra's First Cruise* (1923); the escapist world it describes is part reality, part fiction, and foreshadows the utopia of the children's novels. It was only in 1924, with the British government's grudging recognition of the Russian Revolutionary government, that Ransome claimed that he had at last been vindicated and that 'his war was over'. He and Evgenia, now his new wife, sailed for England in November 1924 and settled at Low Ludderburn, a cottage near Ambleside in the Lake District.

Ransome and Evgenia were devoted to each other, but it was never an easy marriage. Evgenia had a domineering personality and seems to have taken or influenced most of the decisions that affected their married life, not always to her husband's benefit, and in old age Ransome was frightened of her. She was invariably an unkind (though sometimes accurate) critic of his books. This uncomfortable personal life (when taken with the disaster of his first marriage and his sad estrangement from his daughter) was a likely factor in his seeking solace in seemingly escapist stories.

Ransome continued to write for the *Manchester Guardian*. He was sent to report on elections in Egypt and to investigate the extent of Russian

1. National Archive, released March, 2005. Quoted in David Pallister, 'Still our enigma, our Petrograd correspondent', in theguardian.co.uk, 1 March, 2005.

influence in China (commissions which he accepted reluctantly); the unsuccessful *The Chinese Puzzle* (1927) was to be his final political book. In February 1928, he made his last visit to Moscow in order to cover the exile of Trotsky. He also wrote a regular column on fishing, later collected and published as *Rod and Line* (1929). But, now in his mid-forties, he was feeling increasingly trapped on the treadmill of journalism and worried that his original desire to write novels was still being shouldered out.

In 1915 Dora Collingwood had married her long-time suitor, Ernest Altounyan. They lived in Syria, but every few years they returned with their young family to holiday in the Lake District. It was thus that in 1928 Ernest spent the summer teaching their children to sail on Coniston Water in the dinghies *Swallow* and *Mavis*, with Ransome as an enthusiastic spectator. When the time came for the Altounyans to return to Syria, the children gave Ransome a pair of scarlet slippers as a birthday present. The following year Ransome began to turn the inspiration of that summer, and the experiences of his own childhood summers, into *Swallows and Amazons*, which was originally dedicated to 'THE FOUR FOR WHOM IT WAS WRITTEN IN EXCHANGE FOR A PAIR OF SLIPPERS' (for some reason the youngest of the five Altounyan children, Brigit, was left out). Later the number was increased to SIX, to include their parents. Sadly, Ransome was soon to fall out with the Altounyans and in his *Autobiography* he ignores the part they played in the conception of the *Swallows and Amazons* novels.

In 1929, the *Manchester Guardian*'s editor, C.P. Scott, offered Ransome a large salary to become the resident correspondent in Berlin. After discussing the matter with Evgenia, who hated the idea of being uprooted from the garden she was creating at Low Ludderburn, he rejected the offer (which would have meant financial security), resigned from the *Guardian* and started work on *Swallows and Amazons*. He had served a long apprenticeship as a writer. The discipline of writing dispatches had shorn his prose of its early excesses and it was now a model of clarity, ideal for a children's novelist. However, he had become so accustomed to writing short articles that constructing a full-length novel was to prove difficult for him. His mind was filled with episodes and characters, but organising them into a fictional narrative was usually a struggle.

In 1935 the Ransomes decided to leave Low Ludderburn. Although they could have enlarged and improved the property, the lack of sanitation and a mains water supply, as well as the damp Lake District atmosphere which was affecting Evgenia's health, were insuperable problems. More significantly, they were missing the thrill they had experienced sailing *Racundra* at sea. Thus they headed for the Suffolk coast, a popular yachting centre and close to the Norfolk Broads where they had enjoyed sailing holidays since 1931. They rented Broke Farm, on the north side of the River Orwell opposite the yachting village of Pin Mill, and bought the *Nancy Blackett*, which, as *Goblin*, was to feature in *We Didn't Mean to Go to Sea* and *Secret Water*. For Ransome, the *Nancy Blackett* was the best ship he ever had, but Evgenia found her too cramped, and so she was sold and a new yacht, the *Selina King*, was built at Harry King's yard at Pin Mill and launched in September 1938. After an enjoyable season of sailing in 1939, Ransome made a very stormy passage to Lowestoft where she was laid up in a boat-shed on Oulton Broad for the duration of the war; he was never to sail her again. In that same year the Ransomes moved to Harkstead Hall on the Shotley Peninsula, on the south side of the Orwell. It was a solid red-brick farmhouse with a garden that Evgenia loved, so it should have made a perfect home, but the outbreak of war meant that it could have been commandeered at any time and the frequent air-raids made sleep difficult. As a result, in October 1940 they moved back to the Lake District and to The Heald, a seventeen-acre estate on the banks of Coniston Water (Heald Wood features in the episode of Roger's night with the charcoal burners in *Swallowdale*). In Suffolk Ransome had written the East Anglian novels *We Didn't Mean to Go to Sea*, *Secret Water*, and *The Big Six*; at The Heald he wrote his last three novels, *Missee Lee*, *The Picts and the Martyrs*, and *Great Northern?* (which he was to complete in London).

Evgenia found The Heald cramped and isolated, and in 1945, with the war in Europe over, the Ransomes were on the move again. Failing to find a suitable house in Suffolk, they settled on a flat in London's Marylebone. Ransome finished *Great Northern?*, his last significant book, in 1947. Then the noise of urban life and the lure of the Lakes proved too much and in 1948 the Ransomes bought the near derelict Lowick Hall, just south of Coniston. Much as they loved the house, the project was beyond them and two years later they were back in London beside the Thames at Putney. They continued to move between London (the sensible choice) and the Lake District (where their heart lay) until Ransome's death. They rented, then bought, Hill Top Cottage in Haverthwaite. After *Selina King*, Ransome bought and sailed three further yachts, coming ashore for the last time in 1954 after an especially rough channel crossing.

In spite of Ransome's failing health, there was a return to the Lake District in November 1963, but this last port of call for the Ransomes was as impractical as it was inevitable. After a fall which led to a failed operation on his back, Ransome was soon confined to a wheelchair and they simply could not cope. With senility closing in on him, he was moved to the Cheadle Royal Hospital, Manchester, where he died in June 1967. He is buried in the churchyard at Rusland, near the lakes of both Coniston and Windermere. Evgenia died in 1975 and is buried beside him.

This brief account of Ransome's life has deliberately focused on the areas that help us to contextualise the *Swallows and Amazons* novels: his difficult relationship with and early loss of his father; his unhappiness at school; his troubled marriages; his years as a journalist which shaped his lucid prose and his idiosyncratic creative process; his love and intimate knowledge of both the Lake District and East Anglia, which provide the settings for all but three of his novels. For those wanting to delve further into Ransome's life, there are three major biographies. Hugh Brogan's authoritative *The Life of Arthur Ransome* (1984) is a well-researched and largely sympathetic portrait. Roland Chambers's more recent and controversial *The Last Englishman* (2009) concentrates wholly on Ransome's years in Russia and Eastern Europe, examining the myths that have grown up around him, but in the end failing to establish where his political sympathies lay. Most enthralling, though less detailed, is Christina Hardyment's *The World of Arthur Ransome* (2012), a beautifully written and illustrated book that is a mine of information. There are also Ransome's *Autobiography* (1976) and his letters, but their author is sometimes an unreliable witness and they have to be read with caution.

Playing Politics

For the reader, however, it is Ransome's politics which remain the most problematic element of his life, and in particular the apparent disjunction between the Ransome of 1913 to 1924 and the Ransome of post-1929, the Ransome of the novels. As well as the Bolshevik insider, there is the resolutely middle-class writer of what can seem to be resolutely middle-class and often imperialist tales.

It is arguable that the constant is the naïvety of Ransome's character, which showed itself in his penchant for sensation and melodrama. Robert Bruce Lockhart describes him as 'a sentimentalist, who could always be relied on to champion the under-dog . . . an incorrigible

romanticist who could spin a fairy-tale out of nothing'.[1] Whether in
'bohemia' or in Russia, it was as much the thrill of the life and the events
that drove Ransome as it was the ideals behind them. He loved the
anarchy and adventure; he loved the daring, excitement and ambition
of the Russian revolution – whatever side he was on – and he loved
being in the spotlight. It was mainly the romance of the revolution that
was important to him, not whether it succeeded or failed. As he wrote
in *On Behalf of Russia*:

> These men who have made the Soviet government in Russia,
> if they must fail, will fail with clean shields and clean hearts,
> having striven for an ideal which will live beyond them. Even if
> they fail, they will none the less have written a page of history
> more daring than any other which I can remember in the history
> of humanity.[2]

Above all, it massaged Ransome's ego – always a fragile one, whatever
the outward appearance – to be at the centre of a world-important
event and to be fêted by its principle players. Paul Foot concurs with
this argument, suggesting in his introduction to Ransome's writings on
Russia that it was not that Ransome had no interest in politics, but that
he had no serious ideological commitment.[3] Ransome himself admits
to an 'ineradicable tendency to disagree with any majority wherever I
happened to be'.[4] We do not know if anything more than Ransome's
original ambition to be a novelist rather than a journalist caused him to
retire from the political arena. Certainly he gives no other explanation,
though Foot suggests that his silence on Russia after 1924 may have
been partly to protect Evgenia's family and partly because of his
eventual disgust at Stalin's crimes against his people. Yet retire he did.
So Foot writes:

> Even the most pedantic Ransome addict would be hard pressed to
> find in any of these children's books a single word about politics.
> The subject simply doesn't arise. There is nothing even of the
> implied radicalism of that other great children's story-writer,
> whom Arthur Ransome much admired, E. Nesbit. The children's

---

1. Robert Bruce Lockhart, *Memoirs of a British Agent* (London: Putnam,
   1932), pp. 266-67.
2. Arthur Ransome, *On Behalf of Russia* (1918), in Arthur Ransome, *Arthur
   Ransome in Revolutionary Russia*, with Introductory Essay by Paul Foot
   (London: Redwords, 1992), p. 51.
3. *Arthur Ransome in Revolutionary Russia*, p. 11.
4. *Autobiography*, p. 23.

world in Ransome's books is, quite deliberately, hived off from the adult world outside. Though all the famous books were written in times of slump, war or post-war reconstruction, there is hardly a whisper of any of this in any of them.[1]

But although it is true that Ransome's novels make no explicit statement about politics and they are an escape from 'the adult world outside', I think Foot misses an important element. On a superficial reading of the *Swallows and Amazons* novels, Ransome seems to reveal himself not as apolitical but as conservative. Back in England he was saddened by the threat to the old colonial way of life, with all its traditional values. Thus, as well as an escape, his fictional world epitomises (though sometimes with more than a hint of irony) Britain as it had been and as he wanted it to remain; buffeted by events, yet always surviving through the strong personal morality of his characters.

However, I believe there is another twist, because balanced against Ransome's love of the colonial way of life, and the hierarchical and patriarchal society it implies, are his championing of the Bolsheviks and the Russian poor in their struggle against autocracy; his championing in the novels of ordinary, rural people; his championing of piracy and savagery; his discussion of the nature of girlhood and by implication the changing place of women in society. So within the apparently conservative society of *Swallows and Amazons*, I think there is in fact also the 'implied radicalism' that Foot denies – a deliberate challenging of the distinctions between naval seamen and pirates, between explorers and savages, between male and female.

It is not that Ransome ignored (as Foot suggests) the troubled times in which he lived. He had, after all, witnessed first-hand not only the exhilaration of the Russian revolution but also its depressing aftermath. In January 1918 he had suffered the loss of his brother, Geoffrey, in the trenches of the Great War. He had seen the unrest in North Africa in 1924-1925 and the dangers brewing in the Far East in 1926-1927. Rather, he created – for himself and for his readers – a fictional world, both as a refuge and as a symbol, which is at once secure and free; where the conservative and the radical are held in tension; where, whatever the troubles, things turn out right in the end. But of course it was a world that was collapsing. By the time Ransome wrote his last novel, there had been another global conflict and things had changed irrevocably.

---

1. *Arthur Ransome in Revolutionary Russia*, p. 9.

'The Romantic Transfiguration of Fact'

Imagine for a moment the excitement on the lawn of Holly Howe, the Walkers' holiday home in the Lake District, as the Swallows and Amazons (which is what the Walker and Blackett children respectively name themselves, after the dinghies which they sail) explore a dressing up box. Urged on by Titty, who has been reading Defoe's *Robinson Crusoe* (1719), the Swallows dress up as explorers. The Amazons, always less conventional and more daring, become pirates. Their friends, the Callums, join in, though for the moment they are somewhat overawed and excluded. Later they will all delve deeper among the costumes, and in wild flights of imagination will climb Kanchenjunga, visit the 'Caribbees' on a treasure voyage, join Arctic expeditions, survey 'Secret Water', sail the China Seas, become Picts and martyrs, and foil villains in the Hebrides. Mrs Walker, who normally thinks it best to leave her children to play by themselves, is persuaded to become Queen Elizabeth, then Man Friday (though Commander Walker is away, playing another part and wearing his own naval dress). The children's games are usually either of imperial exploits or of families ('Mothers and Fathers', though they would not admit it). Ransome, who always likes to be the centre of attention, is directing operations. He dresses up as a bohemian writer, as a spy, and even as some of his own characters: Captain Flint; John and Titty Walker; Dorothea and Dick Callum.

And in a shed in Tom Dudgeon's garden, a group of Norfolk children, also joined by the Callums, engage in the same play. Here Dorothea, the aspiring novelist, takes charge, and in her fertile imagination her friends become outlaws and detectives, though the stolid Tom is reluctant to take part. The younger children are also somewhat sceptical. They prefer to remain in the real world – as pirates aboard the *Death and Glory*, and river inspectors, and salvage men. Ransome is here as well, pulling the strings, disguised as 'Admiral' Barrable, or the anonymous skipper of the *Cachalot*, and sharing his enthusiasms of sailing and fishing, ornithology and photography.

Ransome describes the method of his novels as 'the romantic transfiguration of fact': in other words, the transforming of the ordinariness of the real world into romantic adventures through the imagination and specifically through the playing of imaginative (though deadly serious) games.[1] In an important essay, Jerry Phillips

1.   Letter to Helen Ferris, 18 March 1937, reproduced in Roger Wardale et al., eds, *The Best of Childhood* (Kendal: Amazon Publications, 2004), p. 184.

and Ian Wojcik-Andrews offer further insight into the nature of such games, and thus into the nature of the Swallows and Amazons:

> Play is a politics – it inculcates gender, class, ethnicity, and their attendant codes of social behaviour. . . . In the sense that *Swallows and Amazons* mimics or repeats the colonialist topos of adventure (the notion of discovery, the notion of proprietorial settlement, and the notion of utopia) in a familiar domestic setting, the book is concerned with representing a politics of play.[1]

In the two Norfolk Broads novels, the games are, in fact, somewhat different to those on the lake, mimicking in particular the struggle against the urban values of the 'Hullaballoos' and the injustices meted out by bullies and tyrants. It is only in the first of the Suffolk novels, *We Didn't Mean to Go to Sea*, that the children are swept out into a stormy North Sea and are forced briefly to confront reality.

It is widely acknowledged that Arthur Ransome is one of the most influential children's writers of the twentieth century. In particular, he is credited with changing the direction of children's fiction from the school story, which had been fashionable in the early years of the century, to the holiday story. Victor Watson writes (in *Reading Series Fiction*):

> Arthur Ransome's *Swallows and Amazons* was a move in a new direction – out of school and into the holidays – and it led eventually, alongside the many series of schoolgirl stories, to an astonishing growth in camping and tramping adventure stories.[2]

However, this is only partly true. Percy Westerman, for example, wrote fourteen novels about holiday adventures with the Boy Scouts, beginning with *Sea Scouts of the Petrel* (1914), and including *A Mystery of the Broads* (1930); in all, Westerman wrote more than 150 novels for boys. In similar vein were the Girl Guide novels of Dorothy Osborn Hann (from 1921) and Frances Nash (from 1922). But the point about Ransome's novels is that his child characters are normally free from adult authority (though adults are never far away), and wholly liberated from the sort of imposed rules, regulations, and godliness that characterise the Scout and Guide movements. Thus Juliet Dusinberre is nearer the mark when she reminds us that Ransome's children 'owe

---

1. Jerry Phillips and Ian Wojcik-Andrews, 'History and the Politics of Play in T.S. Eliot's "The Burial of the Dead" and Arthur Ransome's *Swallows and Amazons*', in *The Lion and the Unicorn* 14.1 (1990), pp. 54–55.
2. Victor Watson, *Reading Series Fiction* (London and New York: Routledge Falmer, 2000), p. 76.

their literary ancestry and freedom to Mark Twain's *The Adventures of Tom Sawyer* (1876), to Richard Jefferies's *Bevis* (1882), and above all to R. L. Stevenson's *Treasure Island* (1883)'.[1] Dusinberre goes on to place them in 'a tradition of dispensing with parents which began with Carroll's *Alice in Wonderland* (1865) and reached its apotheosis in Kenneth Grahame's *The Golden Age* (1895)'.[2]

Ransome was followed and sometimes imitated by the many writers who concerned themselves with what children get up to out of school. There were, for example, his schoolgirl protégées, Katharine Hull and Pamela Whitlock (*The Far Distant Oxus*, 1937, and its successors); there was Aubrey de Selincourt (like Ransome, a former pupil of Rugby School), with a series of family sailing stories, including *Three Green Bottles* (1941) and *Family Afloat* (1944); there was David Severn, in particular his tales of 'Crusoe' Robinson (1942-1946) and the Warner family (1947-1952); there was Enid Blyton churning out the adventures of the Famous Five (from 1942) and the Secret Seven (from 1949); and, later in the twentieth century, Marjorie Lloyd's *Fell Farm* novels (from 1951) returned for their subjects to camping adventures in the Lake District. But what singles out Ransome from all these authors is his ability to create a world of childhood escape which is so close to reality that it is utterly believable. Hugh Brogan writes:

> The essence of the child, he [Ransome] held, is its imagination, the way in which, left to itself and not withered by obtuse or manipulative adults, 'it adopts any material at hand, and weaves for itself a web of imaginative life', building the world again into a splendid pageantry: and all without ever (or hardly ever) blurring its sense of the actual.[3]

Two exceptions to such 'sense of the actual' are *Peter Duck* and *Missee Lee*, which are both fantasies, but still made almost credible by the realism within the fantasies. For example, in *Peter Duck*, as the *Wild Cat* is pursued down channel by the evil pirate Black Jake, every navigation mark, every landfall, every change of tide and weather, is entirely accurate – not surprisingly, since Ransome wrote with the standard mariners' guide, the *Channel Pilot*, beside him.

*

---

1. Juliet Dusinberre, *Alice to the Lighthouse* (Basingstoke: Macmillan, 1987; revised edition 1999), p. 90.
2. Dusinberre, p. 90.
3. Hugh Brogan, *The Life of Arthur Ransome* (London: Hamish Hamilton, 1985), pp. 313-14.

Although in actual time the twelve *Swallows and Amazons* novels were written over a seventeen-year span, in the internal time of *Swallows and Amazons* the period only lasted from summer 1930 to summer 1934 (six novels, from *Winter Holiday* to *The Big Six*, are squeezed into 1932 alone).[1] This fictional chronology means that the characters age comparatively little during the series and are never allowed to enter adolescence. However, contrary to what some critics argue, they do learn from their experiences and change, and Chapters 8 and 9 will consider how *We Didn't Mean to Go to Sea* and *Secret Water* in particular are about the difficult business of growing up. It also means that the first readers of Ransome's early novels would have outstripped their heroes and heroines and become adults by the time the final novels were written.

More significantly, it means that by the time Ransome drew the *Swallows and Amazons* series to a close in 1947, Britain had lived through the Second World War and the way of life that he depicts, and that in the stories resists the symbolic storms beating against it, had already disappeared. But this did not stop the novels from continuing to enjoy huge popularity well into the 1950s and even beyond: they enabled children in the immediate aftermath of the war to escape from the austerity that resulted from the struggle, just as earlier readers had escaped from the unease of the 1930s or from their own wartime privations, and adult readers could look back nostalgically to the way things had once been. However, the cultural upheaval of the 1960s led to a new social inclusiveness in children's literature, a willingness to confront adolescent emotions more directly, and a usually frenetic pace more in tune with modern life. In the twenty-first century, the experiences of children in an increasingly urban, technological and consumer-orientated era, who are far more sexually aware than previous generations, may have too few points of contact with Ransome's characters to empathise wholly with them. So to be properly appreciated today, the *Swallows and Amazons* novels must, I think, be read as products of their era; not as dead period pieces, but as exciting and relevant adventures which propound a strong personal morality and a love of nature and outdoor life, turning to advantage their setting in an increasingly distant past.

---

1. Probably. See Chapter 12 for a discussion of the date of *Great Northern?*, the final novel in the series. The treaty in *Swallows and Amazons* is actually signed in summer 1929, so arguably the setting of subsequent novels should shift a year earlier, but *Swallowdale*, the next summer, is set in 1931 and a later note from Ransome gives 1930 as the start of the series.

This reading of Ransome's novels will concentrate on both the means by which Ransome transfigures fact – how he transfigures his own experience and memories into the worlds of the Swallows, Amazons, and Coots – and how the children, in turn, transfigure those worlds into something different again through the playing of games. It will also show how the novels, through their symbolism, tell other, deeper stories. Thus it will investigate the language through which Ransome creates his other world, just as different as Carroll's Wonderland or Lewis's Narnia, but far more believable and so far more accessible. It will show how the novels are nevertheless bound up with Ransome's life and times, especially the loss of his father, and how he was something of a 'last romantic', conscious that the countryside which he so lovingly describes, and the innocence of his characters, were under mortal threat. Above all, it will argue that the novels reflect the dying British Empire and its values whilst recognising its precariousness and its absurdities in a changing world. If you listen hard, you will hear amid the escape, exuberance and adventure an elegiac note, as childhood, Empire and the rural idyll all come to an end.

1.
Swallows and Amazons:
Explorers, Pirates and Savages

'Began *S and A*', wrote Ransome in his diary entry for 24 March 1929, and thus he 'caught his typewriter on the other side' and the *Swallows and Amazons* series was under way at last – four years after he had returned from overseas hoping to fulfil his ambition to become a novelist instead of a journalist and foreign correspondent. The novel describes a series of nautical adventures played out on the Lake in the North, with the Swallow explorers colonising an island, befriending the local Amazon pirates, capturing an enemy ship, and discovering stolen treasure.

In later years Ransome was to have considerable difficulty in constructing his plots, but there appears to have been no such problem with *Swallows and Amazons.* He wrote mainly chronologically (something that was not true of most of his subsequent books) and managed to complete 253 pages in less than two months. He then had to turn his attention to newspaper articles and it was not until November 1929, when he was sent by the *Manchester Guardian* to report on the general election in Egypt, that he had time to revise his first draft (he was taken ill and a spell in bed afforded him the opportunity he needed). Embarrassingly, Ransome rejected the proposed illustrations for the book produced by the leading illustrator Steven Spurrier for being too stylised and sentimental (only the map of the Lake in the North and the dust jacket were used), so the first edition, published in July 1930, is without pictures. In 1931 an edition was published with illustrations by Clifford Webb, but eventually Ransome insisted on drawing all his own illustrations, sometimes 'with help from Miss Nancy Blackett', and their ability to portray action from the characters' point of view, their avoidance of facial detail (Ransome's limitations as an artist have the happy result that child readers can imagine themselves as one of the characters) and their sense of space are part of the attraction of the books. Ransome's illustrations for *Swallows and Amazons* were first published in the 1938 reprint.

Places and People

It is the realistic description of places and people that grounds Ransome's fiction and makes it believable and accessible. *Swallows and Amazons*, and its successor *Swallowdale*, draw most from memories of his own childhood holidays at the end of Victoria's reign and from the visits of the Altounyan family in 1928-1929.

Swallows and Amazons is set in the Lake District, and the same setting is shared by *Swallowdale*, *Winter Holiday*, *Pigeon Post*, and *The Picts and the Martyrs*. The 'Lake in the North' is created from a collage of accurate descriptions of the real places on Windermere and Coniston Water that Ransome knew and loved, as one might expect from a correspondent who had displayed an unerring eye for detail, and, more importantly, an ability to convey vividly atmosphere and feeling (for example, in *Six Weeks in Russia* and *Racundra's First Cruise*). 'I just bagged the bits I liked best from both of them,' he wrote to an enquiring reader, Miss Simpson, in May 1932.[1] But he moulded these bits into somewhere new and universal. As he wrote in the same letter:

> To tell you the real (& secret) truth. I wanted everybody to feel that the lake was their own lake no matter what lake that was. . . . I had a letter from a little girl (very little) from Africa who thought it must be her lake, Nyanga.

In the same way the four Swallows were at the start based loosely on the Altounyan children, Taqui, Susan, Mavis (nicknamed Titty in real life), and Roger. They are organised as a ship's crew: John (Captain, serious-minded though occasionally reckless, aged twelve); Susan (Mate, practical and even more serious-minded, aged eleven); Titty (Able-seaman, imaginative and courageous, aged nine); and Roger (Ship's Boy, mischievous and chocolate-loving, aged seven).[2] While most children's novels of the

---

1. Letter to Miss Simpson, 10 May 1932, reproduced in Roger Wardale et al., eds, *The Best of Childhood* (Kendal: Amazon Publications, 2004), p. 70.
2. Ransome could be inconsistent on detail. The ages I suggest are from his 'Chronology' (1943), reproduced in *The Best of Childhood*, p. 303; Nancy is shown as twelve and Peggy as eleven. A note written before he started on *Swallows and Amazons* gives the ages as John – twelve, Susan – ten, Titty – nine, Roger – six, Nancy (Jane) – thirteen, and Peggy (Mary) – twelve; but

period were aimed specifically at either boys or girls, Ransome's decision to feature both genders as main characters meant a potential doubling of his audience. However, he knew that a preponderance of girls in his cast would be off-putting to young male readers, so Taqui, the eldest Altounyan and the leader, had to become a boy. She seems to have been untroubled by her sex change and for a time joined in her transformation, signing her letters to 'Uncle Arthur' from 'Captain John'.

In an early note on the novel, Ransome lists the fictional surname of the Swallows as Smith, but this was subsequently changed to Walker, the maiden name of Ransome's first wife. Perhaps this is in part the family Ransome never enjoyed, estranged as he was from his only daughter. Certainly the Swallows were quickly to become more important to him than their real-life Altounyan counterparts, whom he came to resent and ultimately to disown. Ernest Altounyan, who should have known more about the creative process and Ransome's sensitivity, did not help matters by suggesting that the Swallows were no more than portraits of his own children and that he might be the model for their absent father:

> What I most especially like and marvel at is your extraordinary accurate characterisation of the kids. Each is just right – as far as I know them – and each has got a really good look in, and though Titty is the heroine, all the others get a really good share . . . I am personally quite content to go down to posterity as the author of the famous Duffer telegram.[1]

Whatever the original similarities between Altounyan's family and Ransome's Swallows (and in *Swallows and Amazons* there are many), Altounyan failed to understand that it is the novelist's job to transform fact into fiction, and that Ransome shapes the raw materials of experience into another world that is his own. However realistic that world appears, too much can be made of the possible connections between real places and people and their fictional counterparts. The fascination with Ransome's own extraordinary life has inevitably meant that the *Swallows and Amazons* series has suffered more than most from what the novelist Sebastian Faulks terms 'biographical reductionism', not least in recent years.[2]

---

as the characters turned out it seems right that the two Captains should be about the same age and that Susan should be at least as old as Peggy.

1. Letter from Ernest Altounyan, 20 July 1930, reproduced in *The Best of Childhood*, pp. 29-30.
2. Sebastian Faulks, *Faulks on Fiction* (London: BBC Books, 2011), p. 4.

The Absent Father

At the beginning of the novel the Swallows are staying at their holiday home, Holly Howe, 'camping' by day, but sleeping in the farmhouse at night. Their ambition is to pitch their tents on the enticing tree-covered island which lies at the southern end of the lake. But their father is a Commander in the Royal Navy on passage to Hong Kong and, for all their mother's good sense, the social hierarchy of the time dictates that he alone can give permission: 'Mother could not take Vicky and the nurse to camp even on the best of uninhabited islands. Nor, without leave from daddy, could she let them go alone.'[1]

It is a commonly held myth that Ransome's children are left by adults wholly to their own devices: except in *We Didn't Mean to Go to Sea*, this is not the case. As he wrote in a draft of the opening of *Swallows & Co*:

> There is no getting away from it. Grown-ups are at the bottom of most things that happen in the holidays, even when it seems that they have been left out of it altogether.[2]

The Swallows may be given more than usual freedom by their forward-thinking parents, but they are never abandoned, and in the Lake District there is always a tight-knit community of friendly 'natives', as the children describe the adults, ready to come to the rescue. Mrs Walker not only frames the action of *Swallows and Amazons* as she bids her children farewell at the start and welcomes them home at the end, but she also intervenes at a number of crucial moments. On the first night on the island she is rowed across by Mr Jackson to deliver haybags as mattresses to make sure they are all right: they will collect their milk from Dixon's Farm every morning and she hopes they will call in occasionally at Holly Howe. She then joins her offspring for Vicky's birthday party (Vicky is the youngest of her children, who is not yet ready to go exploring) and a day later visits the island again, to find Titty on guard by herself. Against her better judgement, Mrs Walker leaves her there alone. On the last day of the expedition, after the storm, she arrives with a stream of 'natives' to help pack up the camp. It is worth noting how, in a remarkable sleight of hand, Ransome makes the Swallows old enough to go off on their own but still young enough to give themselves over to the make-believe of games (though two years later, in *Pigeon Post* and *Secret Water*, Nancy's game-playing begins to pall for the Swallows, especially for John and Susan).

---

1. Arthur Ransome, *Swallows and Amazons* (London: Jonathan Cape, 1930). Red Fox edition (London: Random House, 1991), p. 7.
2. Reproduced in *The Best of Childhood*, p. 300.

Then the telegram arrives from Commander Walker, with its famous answer, demonstrating the trust that he puts in his children – the sort of trust that Ransome craved from his own father, but never received:

BETTER DROWNED THAN DUFFERS IF NOT DUFFERS WONT DROWN.[1]

It is not until the seventh novel in the series, *We Didn't Mean to Go to Sea*, that Commander Walker appears in the sunburnt flesh, but from the first chapter of *Swallows and Amazons* he is a controlling presence. John in particular is determined to live up to his father's expectations: as 'Captain' of the *Swallow*, he becomes the patriarchal figure for his sisters and brother. The eldest of the Walker children, he is honest, determined, and practical; unlike the real-life Taqui, he takes himself too seriously and is rather lacking in humour, and he is sometimes dangerously over-confident. He is doubtless being brought up to follow his father into the Navy: the fact that in *Missee Lee* he knows everything about navigation but is bottom of the class in Latin may suggest that he attends a nautical college. In his need to impress his father, there is something of the young Ransome himself in John's make-up.

When they are loading stores for the island, John takes with him *The Seaman's Handybook*, and Part Three of *The Baltic Pilot*, both of which had belonged to his father and which he takes with him everywhere. As he snuggles down in his tent on the first night on the island, he is reminded of his father and the responsibility that has been placed on him:

> Then he remembered that the female native had done something in his tent just before she went away. He looked round to see what it was. Pinned to the tent wall near the head of his bed was a scrap of paper. On it was written, 'If not duffers, won't drown.'
> 'Daddy knows we aren't duffers,' said John to himself.[2]

But when, in one of his moments of hubris, John risks his boat and crew on an ill-advised night-time sail, he worries that he has betrayed his father's trust:

> He was the captain of the *Swallow* and must not wreck his ship. Daddy had trusted him not to be a duffer and, sailing in this blackness, he did not feel so sure of not being a duffer as he did by day.[3]

---

1. *SA*, p. 5.
2. *SA*, p. 62.
3. *SA*, p. 260.

Ransome's uneasy relationship with his own father and the guilt he felt after his father's death have already been highlighted, and these powerful emotions find expression in *Swallows and Amazons*. However, the theme of the father as an absent hero was nothing new. It was already a common theme in children's literature of the First World War and its aftermath. Indeed, it is not unreasonable to conjecture that Nancy and Peggy's absent father, Bob Blackett, was a late casualty of that war.

Fantasy and Colonial Adventure

It is tempting to say that Commander Walker's telegram begins a series of adventures for the Swallows, but in fact it is nearly a hundred pages before there is any notable action. Meanwhile, Ransome's intricate descriptions of sailing and camping, which prepare the Swallows for their ensuing adventure, are enough to engage patient readers. The often technical vocabulary becomes an initiation into the fictional world he creates, a secret language of sheets and halyards, of luffing and jibing, shared by the reader with both author and characters: we are all sailors now. The voyage to the desert island – which is later called Wild Cat Island – and the subsequent building of the camp is typical of Ransome's novels in two respects.

First, there is the way in which Ransome turns the lake into a new, imagined world. So, seen from the Swallows' perspective, the mile-long sail becomes a journey of discovery to distant lands:

> Above them was the peak from which they had first seen the island. The Peak itself seemed lower than it had. Everything had grown smaller except the lake, and that had never seemed so large before.[1]

Familiar places are transformed and become exotic:

> The little town is known in guide-books by another name, but the crew of the *Swallow* had long ago given it the name of Rio Grande.[2]

And a little later, when after a night under canvas John and Roger return to the mainland, Holly Howe is changed into somewhere 'foreign' and 'different', and the boys into 'explorers':

---

1. *SA*, p. 30.
2. *SA*, p. 33.

Since yesterday the field path and the gate into the wood on the way to Darien and the farm at Holly Howe had all turned into a foreign country. They were quite different places now that you came to them by water from an island of your own. They were not at all what they had been when you lived there and saw the island far away over the water. Coming back to them was almost the same thing as exploration. It was like exploring a place that you have seen in a dream, where everything is just where you expect it and yet everything is a surprise.[1]

However, the older children are always half-aware that they are playing a game and that reality is never far away. So when, at Titty's suggestion (Titty is always the romancer) they sing a rousing chorus from the traditional capstan shanty 'Spanish Ladies', the down-to-earth Susan remarks with just a trace of cynicism: 'Of course, really, we're going the other way . . . but it doesn't matter.' Such shifting between the game and real world is a recurring feature of the novel, providing much of its comedy and highlighting how the story sometimes exists only in the children's imagination as they transfigure mundane facts into pirate adventures. For example, during 'the parley':

'Thunder and lightning,' said Nancy Blackett, 'what a chance we missed. If we'd only known we'd have given you broadside for broadside till one of us sank, even if it had made us late for lunch.'[2]

And:

'Look here,' said Susan, 'hadn't we better have dinner before all the lemonade has gone?'
'Jamaica rum,' said Titty with reproach.[3]

Secondly, there is the way in which the Swallows are likened to British adventurers going out to colonise foreign countries; in a sense, they are enacting their father's warship voyage from the colony of Malta to the colony of Hong Kong. As colonial adventurers, they are lifted from the pages of one or more of the heroic, Protestant, imperial histories of the Victorian and Edwardian eras, and not least, it is fair to conjecture, Cyril Ransome's *A Short History of England* (1891). Ransome would also have been influenced, at least indirectly, by the now discredited historiography of the most influential Victorian historian of sixteenth-century England, J.A. Froude, who

1. *SA*, p. 69.
2. *SA*, p. 121.
3. *SA*, p. 134.

saw Henry VIII's breaking with the papacy as an identifiable break
with the medieval past – a process completed with the defeat of the
Spanish Armada in 1588, which gave England control of the seas and
symbolised the victory of the forces of modernity.[1] In *Our Colonies
and India* (1887), Cyril Ransome firmly echoes Froude's view that
British colonies gained much from being part of the Empire: 'The
union between the English who live in England and those who live in
the Colonies gives us all a better position in the world than we should
have as little independent States.'[2]

As her contribution to the 'ship's library' Titty takes with her a copy
of *Robinson Crusoe* which, she thinks, will tell them what to do on an
island, and on one level the adventures of the Swallows on Wild Cat
Island are a lightly comic parody of Defoe's novel. When, in Chapter
18, Titty is left to guard the island, she turns to *Robinson Crusoe* for both
advice and comfort. Mrs Walker, who visits the island unannounced
and is silently disturbed by Titty's being left by herself, plays the part
of Man Friday, and mother and daughter slip in and out of reality, in
and out of the story of *Robinson Crusoe*, and in and out of the pirate
adventure. For example:

> Robinson Crusoe and Man Friday . . . kissed each other as if they
> were pretending to be Titty and mother.[3]

And:

> 'Weren't you scalded?' said Robinson Crusoe.
> 'Badly,' said Man Friday, 'but I buttered the places that hurt most.'
> And then Man Friday forgot about being Man Friday, and
> became mother again, and told about her own childhood on a
> sheep station in Australia. . . .[4]

And (as Titty slips from one game to another):

> 'Mother,' she called.
> Mother stopped rowing.
> 'Want to come?' she called.
> But in that moment Titty remembered again that she was not
> merely Robinson Crusoe, who had a right to be rescued by a

1. J.A. Froude, *History of England from the Fall of Wolsey to the Defeat of the
    Spanish Armada* (1856-1870).
2. Cyril Ransome, *Our Colonies and India: How We Got Them and Why We Keep
    Them* (London: Cassell, 3rd edition 1887), p. 42.
3. *SA*, p. 218.
4. *SA*, p. 221.

passing ship, but was also Able-seaman Titty, who had to hoist the lantern on the big tree behind her, so that the others could find the island in the dark. . . .[1]

But Crusoe's attempts to civilise his island can no longer be read as a simple allegory of good overcoming evil and *Robinson Crusoe* is now recognised as a crucial text within postcolonial criticism.[2] Roxann Wheeler argues that 'Several colonial factors . . . give impetus to the plot: Crusoe's desire to improve his station in Britain and in the colonies; his fear of bodily harm from the Caribs; the necessity of eradicating the cannibals; and the desire to domesticate Friday'.[3] So on another level Titty's copy of *Robinson Crusoe* informs a significant layer of colonial imagery in *Swallows and Amazons* – highlighting the binaries of white and black, civilised and savage, master and servant. The 1930s were, after all, a time when schools still celebrated Empire Day and school children blacked up to play the part of savages in far-off colonies, although there was already a growing realisation that the Empire was a threatened anachronism.[4]

Having somewhere of one's own – a camp, a den, a secret place – is part of the experience of childhood, and for the Swallows the island at the southern end of the Lake is just waiting to be occupied: 'It was *the* island, waiting for them. It was their island';[5] and, after the telegram from Commander Walker, 'It was to be their island after all'.[6] But the repeated 'their' in the opening chapter of *Swallows and Amazons* is more than an expression of the children's excitement; it also suggests a sense of imperial entitlement – the island actually *belongs* to them as imperialist explorers.

---

1. *SA*, p. 223.
2. See, for example, Martin Green, *Dreams of Adventure, Deeds of Empire* (London: Routledge and Kegan Paul, 1980); Patrick Brantlinger, *Crusoe's Footprints: Cultural Studies in Britain and America* (New York: Routledge, 1990) and Michael Seidel, *Robinson Crusoe: Island Myths and the Novel* (Boston: Twayne, 1991).
3. Roxann Wheeler, '"My Savage", "My Man": Racial Multiplicity in *Robinson Crusoe*', in *ELH*, vol. 62, no. 4 (John Hopkins University Press, Winter 1995), p. 825.
4. Empire Day was first celebrated on 24 May 1902, and thereafter on the nearest Monday to that date. The idea was that children in every country of the British Empire would be reminded of the privileges and responsibilities of being part of such a glorious Empire. With imperial decline, it was renamed Commonwealth Day, but it is now largely forgotten.
5. *SA*, p. 7.
6. *SA*, p. 8.

Before the Swallows set sail they discuss the need for a map: '"We ought to have a chart of some kind," said John. "It'll probably be all wrong, and it won't have the right names. We'll make our own names, of course."'[1] The mapping of a country is a familiar metaphor for the way colonisers go about their business: it enables them to control territory and then exploit it. Naming has a particular force, either establishing ownership or (if there has been a previous name that is changed by colonisers) allowing a new beginning and the rewriting of history. The Swallows have already established ownership of some of the Lake by giving their own names to actual places. Titty christens the promontory overlooking the lake the 'Peak in Darien', taking the name from Keats's sonnet 'On First Looking into Chapman's Homer' which she has learnt at school, and we can assume (from the poem) that by extension the Lake is the Pacific Ocean. There is also a suggestion of Spanish imperialism, reinforced by the renaming of Bowness as 'Rio Grande'. Soon, and more prosaically, there will be Houseboat Bay and Cormorant Island as well.

In Chapter 10 ('The Parley') there is an awkward moment when the Swallows discover that the Amazons have not only already laid claim to 'their' island (and renew that claim by hoisting their flag in the Swallows' camp), but have also already named it:

> 'Look here,' said Nancy Blackett. 'What is the name of the island?'
> 'We haven't yet given it a name,' said John.
> 'It is called Wild Cat Island. Uncle Jim called it that, because it belonged to us. That shows you whose island it is.'
> 'But it's our island now,' said John. 'It was uninhabited when we came and we put our tents up here, and you can't turn us out.'[2]

Diplomatically, it is agreed that the Amazons' name of Wild Cat Island will remain if the Swallows' name for Bowness is also accepted, and while they parley they decide to fly both their flags together. As Phillips and Wojcik-Andrews comment:

> Effectively, in the interplay between the imagination of the children and the specific geography of Lake Coniston, the entire history of European expansion in America, Africa, and the Pacific becomes reduced to what might be called minutiae of mimicry.[3]

---

1. *SA*, p. 22.
2. *SA*, p. 120.
3. Jerry Phillips and Ian Wojcik-Andrews, 'History and the Politics of Play in T. S. Eliot's "The Burial of the Dead" and Arthur Ransome's *Swallows and*

When Mrs Walker insists on sailing with her children on their maiden voyage, she is likened by Titty to Queen Elizabeth: 'You can be Queen Elizabeth going aboard the ships at Greenwich that were sailing to the Indies.'[1] Entering into the spirit of Titty's game, she asks John: 'Can I come aboard, Captain Drake?'[2] John, her over-serious son who is sailing *Swallow* for the first time, has 'quite enough to think about without queens', but as they set off the children have become Elizabethan founders of British imperial greatness.

Having made their preparations, the Swallows begin their voyage of discovery:

> . . . the *Swallow* and her crew moved steadily southward over a desolate ocean sailed for the first time by white seamen.
>
> They were getting near the island.
>
> 'Keep a look-out for a good landing place,' said Captain John.
>
> 'And keep a look-out for savages,' said Titty. 'We don't know yet that it is uninhabited, and you can't be too careful.'[3]

Significantly, they are 'white' seamen. They look out for 'savages' (who, by implication, are black). Once they land on the island they discover an old fireplace, showing that they are not the first to be there and that they may not be alone. There may even be cannibals:

> 'The natives knew how to choose the right place,' said Susan, 'and it's a fine fireplace.'
>
> 'There are no natives on the island now,' said Roger.
>
> 'They may have been killed and eaten by other natives,' said Titty.[4]

As colonisers they set up an orderly camp, directed by Mate Susan who, though only eleven, is typical of a 1930s homemaker – tellingly, her choice for the ship's library is *Simple Cooking for Small Households*. They establish a safe landing-place (where they later build a pier), discover a secret harbour, cut paths through the jungle, and start making a map; and all the time, the absent Commander Walker, who is aboard ship in Malta and about to sail for Hong Kong, serves as a reminder of Britain's continuing role as an imperial power.

A useful comparison can be drawn here between *Swallows and Amazons* and William Golding's *Lord of the Flies*, which, as Stefan Hawlin

---

Amazons', in *The Lion and the Unicorn* 14, No. 1 (1990), p. 58.

1. *SA*, p. 15.
2. *SA*, p. 19.
3. *SA*, p. 34.
4. *SA*, p. 41.

argues, 'makes an attempt to restate the old Empire misrepresentations of white enlightenment and black savagery'. Hawlin suggests that Golding's marooned boys are:

> Oxford and Cambridge graduates newly arrived as administrators in a colony. The pervasive image is of whites bringing light, order and culture into 'the other world'. . . . The boys are determined, like all good colonisers before them, to maintain standards of Englishness and to distinguish themselves from the natives.[1]

There are clear parallels between Golding's colonisers and the Swallows, and in Chapter 2 of *Lord of the Flies* ('Fire on the Mountain') *Swallows and Amazons* is one of the island books (along with *Treasure Island* and *Coral Island*) which the marooned boys recall. Ralph, the son of a naval officer, becomes the natural leader, and the fact that 'the Queen has a big room of maps and all the islands in the world are drawn there' testifies to the extent of the fading British Empire.[2] However, Ransome has a less pessimistic view of human nature than Golding, and his explorers remain 'good colonisers' who, by adhering to their moral code, maintain their 'standards of Englishness' and their grasp on civilisation. Like *Lord of the Flies*, *Swallows and Amazons* can be seen as part of a tradition of 'island' literature, which is almost inevitably imperialist in tone: for example, Shakespeare's *The Tempest* (1610-11), Daniel Defoe's *Robinson Crusoe* (as discussed above), Jonathan Swift's *Gulliver's Travels* (1726), Johann Wyss's *Swiss Family Robinson* (1812), R.M. Ballantyne's *The Coral Island* (1857) and R.L. Stevenson's *Treasure Island* (1883). In a significant essay, Anna Bogen also shows the debt Ransome owes to J.M. Barrie's *Peter Pan* (1904) and *Peter and Wendy* (1911). She draws comparisons between Wild Cat Island and Neverland, pointing out how the fantasy games played out in both settings are always tied to the real world:

> Through the uneasy Edwardian compromises that make up Peter and Wendy's Neverland, the island adventure took a significant leap into the realm of the social world, ensuring that sophisticated children's adventure stories would be forever haunted by the need for real-world resolutions.[3]

1. Stefan Hawlin, 'The Savages in the Forest: Decolonising William Golding', in Harold Bloom, ed., *Lord of the Flies: William Golding*, Modern Critical Interpretations series, (London: Chelsea House, 2008), pp. 71-84.
2. William Golding, *Lord of the Flies* (London: Faber and Faber, 1958), p.33.
3. Anna Bogen: 'The Island Come True: Peter Pan, Wild Cat Island and the Lure of the Real', in M.S. Thompson and C. Keenan, eds, *Treasure Islands: Studies in Children's Literature* (Dublin: Four Courts Press, 2006), p. 53.

1. The Start of the Voyage

Having made their preparations, the Swallows begin their voyage of discovery:
'The Swallow and her crew moved steadily southward over a desolate ocean
sailed for the first time by white seamen'.

Further similarities are obvious – Peter and John as father figures, Wendy and Susan as mother figures, islands inhabited by pirates and savages – while Phillips and Wojcik-Andrews suggest that 'Ransome's text is an open and playful dialogue with the classic texts of imperialist adventure'.[1]

In the musical version of *Swallows and Amazons*, which premiered at the Bristol Old Vic in December 2010 and subsequently toured the UK and played in London's West End, the part of Titty was given to a young black actress. In a way, the casting was a masterstroke, countering the complaint that Ransome's novels are about white middle-class children and only appeal to a white middle-class audience; but in another way it was entirely wrong. If in *Swallows and Amazons* the Swallows are symbols of British imperialism – white colonial explorers who go out to subdue black savages – then using a black actress to play Titty misses a key element of the novel.

Captain Flint's Trunk

On the third morning of the expedition, Nancy and Peggy Blackett (the Amazon pirates, aged twelve and eleven respectively)[2] are sighted, flying the 'Skull and Crossbones' from the masthead of their dinghy, *Amazon*; and the man on the houseboat inexplicably shakes his fist at the Swallows as they sail past. These are the starting points for the two main strands of the plot for the remainder of the novel. Although the Swallows and Amazons become firm friends as well as rivals, they are very different characters. The Amazons are inhabitants of the area, 'born on the shores of the Amazon river'.[3] John is jealous of the way Nancy can handle a boat more skilfully than he can. As pirates (and sometimes savages) the Amazons are cut off from civilisation and outside the law, but they are story-book pirates with right on their side: romantic rebels standing up against tyranny and corruption. More than that, Captain Nancy is a tomboy, fighting the female stereotype: she is reckless, feckless, and endlessly endearing. But, like Titty, she is also imaginative, though her imagination is far bolder and shapes all the Lake District adventures, and behind her piratical cries there are a sensitivity and an ease with people outside her immediate group (though sometimes this can spill into over-familiarity and rudeness). Peggy is practical and competent, and chatters incessantly, but only in

---

1. Phillips and Wojcik-Andrews, p. 64.
2. See note 2 on p. 20.
3. *SA*, p. 120.

Winter Holiday is she able to escape from her sister's shadow and comic put-downs. The Amazons' escapades all tell of an abandon that the Swallows (or at least the serious-minded John and Susan) never enjoy.

In the first strand of the plot, the Swallow explorers and the Amazon pirates agree with Nancy's plan that whoever can capture the others' dinghy will take command, with their vessel as the flagship and their Captain as Commodore. In a risky night-time adventure, the Swallows become lost and the Amazons are outwitted. But Titty, who has been left behind on Wild Cat Island as a rather frightened guard, succeeds in capturing the enemy ship and rowing it offshore to await the return of the rest of her crew. In this symbolic story it is no surprise that the imperialist explorers should be the victors and that the male explorer John should become Commodore, though ironically in subsequent novels it is always Nancy, the pirate, who is in charge.

At the same time, in the other strand of the plot, the Swallows and Amazons unite against Captain Flint, the Blacketts' Uncle Jim (Turner), who is living on the 'gondola' houseboat with his parrot and with a cannon on deck. A 'retired pirate',[1] with his roots in Stevenson's *Treasure Island*, he is Ransome's more appealing adult alter ego: Moscow, Egypt, and China — Ransome's old stamping grounds — figure among the travel labels on his trunk.[2] Generous, caring, practical, quick-tempered, curmudgeonly and impulsive, Captain Flint, like Ransome, remains a child at heart; like Ransome, he is an obsessed and frustrated writer. His nieces are angry that he has stopped playing pirate games in order to work on his memoirs, *Mixed Moss* by 'A Rolling Stone'; they let off fireworks on his houseboat and take parrot feathers as trophies. But he mistakenly blames the attacks on the Swallows, and when John tries to make peace and pass on a warning from the charcoal-burners that there are actual burglars in the area, he brands him a 'liar'. Here the injustice of the real world collides with the simple but rigorous moral code instilled in the children and John is desperately upset. The old charcoal-burners, at once both kindly and a touch sinister, are a remnant of the rural past of Ransome's childhood. They live in the darkness of their wigwam, nurturing for luck an adder which hisses and darts like the damped down fire, mesmerising the children and symbolising a serpent in their innocent Eden.

When Captain Flint is away in London, it is inevitable that he has his comeuppance when burglars break into the houseboat and steal his trunk, burying it until they can retrieve it. It is these thieves whom Titty

---

1. *SA*, p. 33.
2. *SA*, pp. 366-67.

hears landing on Cormorant Island, and after further excitements and dogged persistence the trunk is discovered and returned to its grateful owner. Disappointingly, the treasure in the trunk is not the glittering hoard that Titty has imagined, but a typewriter, a pile of canvas-bound diaries and a large manuscript: months of work which are far more valuable to Captain Flint than any pirates' gold. On a metaphorical level, the treasure represents Ransome's creativity, locked away and stolen, and only now released by the children who inspired him. Says Captain Flint:

> 'If I'd lost this, as I thought I had, I'd have lost all the diaries of my pirate past, and I've put all the best of my life into this book. It would have gone for ever if it hadn't been for you.'[1]

A storm symbolises the end of summer. John and Nancy check their dinghies and Titty, always close to nature, slips away to watch the waves on the Lake as she faces the wind and the spray. Back in their tents, and playing another game, they imagine themselves as shipwrecked sailors and, foreshadowing *Peter Duck*, make up their own story within the story. Titty imagines, hopefully, that they will be marooned on the island for twenty years. Then the book and the holidays end, with the return of the Walkers to Holly Howe, the Blacketts sailing off to Beckfoot, and a reassuring restoration of order.

*

In *Swallows and Amazons*, Ransome creates a world of childhood freedom and adventure with an array of believable characters and a wonderfully evoked Lake District setting. It does not patronise and is largely unsentimental. But it has its weaknesses, too: the plot is thin; the villains are hardly convincing; there is a confusion between 'natives' (mainly adult and friendly, although the Amazons, as inhabitants of the Lake District, are also described as 'natives') and 'savages' (mainly children and dangerous); just occasionally the authorial voice intrudes; originally there were no illustrations. Unsurprisingly, the subsequent novels in the series are technically more assured. Although *Swallows and Amazons* was not an instant commercial success, it was taken up in America by the publisher Lippincott and promoted by the Junior Literary Guild. Fortunately for the future direction of children's literature, Jonathan Cape recognised that he had discovered something very special, and immediately commissioned a sequel.

1. *SA*, p. 370.

2.

Swallowdale:
'Things Will Go Onward the Same'

Swallowdale (1931) feels very different to its predecessor. Although it revisits many of the themes of *Swallows and Amazons*, it has even less in the way of plot and is largely shaped by a series of events and descriptions of places and people. What action there is slips from time to time into the realm of fairy tale, often through Titty's imagination. It is the summer after *Swallows and Amazons*, and the children wait impatiently for the Amazons' fearsome Great Aunt to go home so they are free to embark on a new adventure. Then, in a foolhardy moment, John wrecks *Swallow* on a rock and the Swallows' camp has to be shifted from Wild Cat Island to the mainland, where eventually they are all able to set out on a mountaineering expedition to climb Kanchenjunga. In some ways I think *Swallowdale* is more of an adult novel, full of nostalgia as it celebrates the continuity and renewal of rural life, though Ransome (somewhat disingenuously) balked at the distinction between writing for children and adults.[1]

I have already touched on the way in which the *Swallows and Amazons* novels fit into the context of twentieth-century children's literature, but there is another important context: that of literature about nature and the countryside. In his biography of Flora Thompson, *Dreams of the Good Life* (2014), Richard Mabey writes:

> The uneasy truth in Europe, the prolonged economic depression, the sense of an insidious cultural suburbanism, nurtured a widespread yearning for all things rural during the 1920s and 30s. . . . The countryside seemed a place where the fractured historical roots of a troubled nation might still be intact, or at least readily mended.[2]

---

1. Letter to Helen Ferris, 20 March 1931, reproduced in Roger Wardale et al., eds, *The Best of Childhood* (Kendal: Amazon Publications, 2004), p. 218.
2. Richard Mabey, *Dreams of the Good Life* (London: Allen Lane, 2014), pp. 135-6.

So it was that the uneasy years of the 1920s and 1930s, and the new horrors of the Second World War, saw the publication of such classics as H.V. Morton's *In Search of England* (1927); Flora Thompson's *Lark Rise* (1939), *Over to Candleford* (1941) and *Candleford Green* (1943); and L.T.C. Rolt's *Narrowboat* (1944). In 1942, Laurie Lee was writing articles on life in the Cotswolds as part of the war effort (this was the real England Britain was defending) – these were the genesis of *Cider with Rosie*, which would appear in 1959. At the same time in the United States, which was gripped by the Depression, Laura Ingalls Wilder was writing the *Little House on the Prairie* series (1932-1943). It is not unreasonable to see Ransome's Lake District and East Anglian novels, which celebrate the English countryside, and the 'camping and tramping' literature that followed, as part of this escape from a world in turmoil; or at least as a searching out of qualities and values that might outlast current events.

It is no coincidence that as Ransome embarked on *Swallowdale* he was also planning another book about nature and continuity, and the passing down of old traditions from one generation to another. In January 1931 he wrote to his American publisher, Ernestine Evans: 'I've a lovely book about an old schoolmaster and a fisherman and a boy and a river. This is going to be my very best book. But I want to keep it fermenting for a bit yet.'[1] In the event, and probably wisely from a commercial point of view, Ransome laid the project aside and the idea fermented for another eleven years before he finally began work on 'the gamekeeper book' late in 1942. But, for whatever reason, he gave up on the project altogether six months later, and we only have the fragments published under the title *The River Comes First* in *Coots in the North and Other Stories* to remind us again of how life is good in spite of great-aunts, and to give a tantalising glimpse of the book that might have been.[2]

It is also worth noting the influence of Richard Jefferies's *Bevis, the Story of a Boy* (1882) – originally aimed at an adult readership – both on Ransome and on *Swallowdale* in particular.[3] Jefferies and Ransome share a love of the countryside and a skill in describing it. Both authors use the rural landscape not just as a setting complete

1. Letter to Ernestine Evans, 12 January 1931, reproduced in *The Best of Childhood*, p. 51.
2. Arthur Ransome, *Coots in the North and Other Stories*, ed. Hugh Brogan (London: Jonathan Cape, 1988).
3. See in particular Janice Lingley, '*Bevis* and Arthur Ransome's *Swallowdale*', in *The Richard Jefferies Society Journal*, No. 23, 2012.

in itself, but also as somewhere that the children can transform, in their play, into an enchanted world of explorers and savages. So Bevis and his friend Mark imagine 'Longpond' to be the 'New Sea' and build an island camp on the 'New Formosa'. Their exploration of the 'New Sea' is mirrored later in the exploration of the Walton Backwaters in *Secret Water*, and as with the Swallows and Amazons their mapping and naming of their lake suggests conquest and control, with the same echoes of a colonial past. But whereas Bevis and Mark are described as 'savages', Ransome (as we've already seen) calls the Swallows 'explorers', largely reserving the term 'savages' for original and uncivilised inhabitants, whether it is the Amazons (who are more often pirates), the Eels, or the charcoal-burners. However, the real difference between *Bevis* and *Swallowdale* is the result of Ransome writing half a century later. Whereas Jefferies is describing a countryside still largely unaffected by the industrial revolution, Ransome is defending something that is already passing, and the charcoal-burners appear as people surviving from another age.

Peter Duck

Although *Swallowdale* is the second novel in the *Swallows and Amazons* series, in some ways it feels like the third. Its opening chapters are laced with references to *Peter Duck*, not to be published until 1932, and Peter Duck himself becomes Titty's make-believe friend throughout. So, for example, when in Chapter 4 Titty discovers the cave in Swallowdale, she declares: 'It's just the place for Peter Duck. . . . It's the most secret valley that ever there was in the world.'[1] And Ransome goes on to explain:

> [Peter Duck] had been the most important character in the story they had made up during those winter evenings in the cabin of the wherry with Nancy and Peggy and Captain Flint. . . . . [He] was the old sailor who had voyaged with them to the Caribbees in the story and, still in the story, had come back to Lowestoft with his pockets full of pirate gold.[2]

More explanation can be found in Ransome's letters. In August 1930, a month after *Swallows and Amazons* was published, he was already

---

1. Arthur Ransome, *Swallowdale* (London: Jonathan Cape, 1931). Red Fox edition (London: Random House, 2001), p. 55.
2. *SD*, pp. 55-56.

working on the plot of *Swallowdale*, but by November he had taken a different direction and began to draft the opening of *Peter Duck*. He was further encouraged in the pirate adventure when at the end of December the Altounyan children wrote to him suggesting his next book should be about 'treasure or something hidden somewhere – on an island of course so there will be something about boats in it'.[1]

Then Ransome's duodenal ulcer flared up and writing ground to a temporary halt. In the New Year of 1931 he was well enough to return to serious work. The focus was back on *Swallowdale*, which he now began enthusiastically. It seems that the decision to return to the Lake in the North for his setting was at least partly a commercial one, dictated by his readers and their demanding letters:

> My life won't be worth living over here unless the next book does what all the children I know assume it's going to, namely, tell what happened to the Swallows and Amazons when they met again next year. That is taken for granted and I'm told, in every tone of authority, what NOT TO LEAVE OUT.[2]

Ransome goes on to reveal that the new book will be an account of the Swallows' and Amazons' land adventures after 'a really jolly good shipwreck'. But *Peter Duck* remained very much in his plans, as he also confides to Miss Evans:

> After the direct sequel to *Swallows and Amazons*, on which I am now working, I have an indirect one (not so realistic) the tremendous tale invented by the Swallows and Amazons when they all spent Christmas in a houseboat that got frozen in so that they couldn't go sailing properly. . . . This is also begun.[3]

With two projects jostling together at the same time it is not surprising that they should have become a little tangled. It is perhaps more surprising that Ransome should have persevered with Peter Duck as an imaginary character in *Swallowdale* before we have been properly introduced to him in his own, subsequent novel, but already he had become an important part of Titty's imaginative make-up and too much might have been lost by his removal.

---

1. Letter from Mavis Altounyan, 28 December 1930, reproduced in *The Best of Childhood*, pp. 44–45.
2. Letter to Ernestine Evans, 12 January 1931, reproduced in *The Best of Childhood*, p. 50.
3. Letter to Ernestine Evans, 12 January 1931, reproduced in *The Best of Childhood*, pp. 50–51.

Return to the Lake

At the start of *Swallowdale*, the transition from the real world back to the playground of the Lake in the North is symbolised by the 'long railway journey from the south' which marks the start of the holiday.[1] The device of the railway journey to transport the characters from the world of school to the freedom of holidays is also used in *Peter Duck* (the Swallows have got off the train and are pushing their luggage to Lowestoft's North Quay), *Coot Club*, *Pigeon Post*, and *Picts and Martyrs* (just as Hogwarts School, the setting of J. K. Rowling's Harry Potter novels, is reached by train from Platform 9¾ of Kings Cross station). Once the Swallows are afloat, the reader is reminded of the children's sense of scale: for them, lakes become oceans, hills become mountains, pike become sharks, and the wash from a passing steamer makes them think that they are at sea. In contrast, the children are just tiny figures in this gigantic, almost fairy tale landscape: Ransome uses the word 'little' eleven times in the thirteen pages of the opening chapter. Indeed, the language of the chapter comes close to the language of fairy tale, almost elemental in its simplicity and its contrasts, disturbing, and hinting at a darker symbolism – the sort of language that Ransome used so effectively in *Old Peter's Russian Tales* (1916). The children's smallness is also emphasised in many of Ransome's illustrations, not completed until 1936 when Clifford Webb's drawings were finally replaced. For example, in 'The Camp in Swallowdale'[2] and 'On the March',[3] the miniscule characters are dwarfed by the rolling hills beyond.

Another emphasis in the first chapter of *Swallowdale* is on the reliving of the adventures of the previous summer. 'August had come again'; 'Everything would be just the same as it had been last year'; 'The thing they had been planning for a year was at last beginning'; 'To be on the lake and sailing again was enough for John'; 'Titty . . . was now once more the able-seaman'; 'Wild Cat Island, of which the whole ship's company had been dreaming ever since they sailed away from it last year'; 'the fireplace, left from last year'.[4] To an extent this is simply a matter of putting the new story into context, informing uninitiated readers of the adventures the children had enjoyed the year before. The first edition of *Swallowdale* actually begins with a short preface which

---

1. *SD*, p. 4.
2. *SD*, p. 202.
3. *SD*, p. 305.
4. *SD*, pp. 9–12.

summarises the action of *Swallows and Amazons*: this was dropped in subsequent editions and Ransome's later idea that the novels should only be sold in chronological order was swiftly rejected as impractical. But we also become aware of the theme of continuity that is central to *Swallowdale*. The children return easily to the game they were playing the year before, as if nothing has happened in between; nothing has changed, and even if they have grown a little older, they are now essentially what they were then.

There is also a sense of continuity for Ransome, who borrows from his own childhood holidays in the Lake District. In his *Autobiography* he tells how in future years, escaping from his own frustrations and miseries, he would rather theatrically 'dip my hand in the water, as a greeting to the beloved lake or as a proof to myself that I had indeed come home'.[1] In *Swallowdale*, when Titty lands on Wild Cat Island again, she too 'dipped her hands in the cool water of the harbour, just to show herself that she was really there'.[2]

Great Aunt Maria and Girlhood

But when the Swallows arrive on Wild Cat Island, eager for another adventure with the Amazons, they discover that there is 'real native trouble' and Nancy, Peggy and Captain Flint are confined to their home at Beckfoot by the selfish demands of their formidable Great Aunt Maria, who is seen as a sort of fairy tale stepmother or witch (Titty later describes her as a mythical 'Gorgon' who turns people to stone).[3] Long ago, in another of the novel's examples of continuity, the Great Aunt had looked after Mrs Blackett and Captain Flint when they were children. Now, overruling her liberal-minded niece, she demands that the Amazon pirates conform to a Victorian model of femininity and good manners, and restricts them to a 'native' world of prompt mealtimes, pretty dresses and afternoon carriage rides. As Nancy complains:

> 'We've only got to make a plan and it's scuppered at once. No camping. No gold-hunting. No piracy except just now and then between meals. And best frocks every evening and sometimes half the day. Native trouble? It simply couldn't be worse.'[4]

---

1. Arthur Ransome, *The Autobiography of Arthur Ransome*, ed. Rupert Hart-Davis (London: Century Publishing Co., 1985), p. 26.
2. *SD*, p. 22.
3. *SD*, p. 385.
4. *SD*, p. 41.

In fact, Great Aunt Maria is only glimpsed three times in *Swallowdale* – once when the Swallows see her in the pony cart with the primly dressed Amazons, once when John sees her in the bow of the Beckfoot launch as it passes Horseshoe Cove, and once when he sees her on the front lawn at Beckfoot – but she is still able to throw a cold blanket of disappointment over her great-nieces and their friends.

The first of these episodes is worth noting:

> A very prim elderly lady, holding a small black parasol overhead, was sitting stiffly beside Mrs Blackett. In front of them on the little narrow seat behind the driver, facing the grown-ups, were two girls in flounced frocks, with summer hats, their hands in gloves, clasped on their knees. It was a dreadful sight. As the carriage disappeared, the explorers looked at each other with shocked eyes.
>
> 'That's much worse than being shipwrecked,' said Titty at last.[1]

Titty's horror is not only a reaction to the capture of the pirates and their mother, so spoiling the holiday for all of them, but also a more serious comment on the nature of girlhood at a time when the emancipation of women was still a live debate. In playing up to the outdated expectations of their Great Aunt, the Amazons, looking back (in time as well as space) at their 'prim' and 'stiff' tormentor, mock the stereotype she would like them to be.

Like Nancy, the horrified Titty is endlessly imaginative, though she is more introverted and easy-going, and projects the books and poems she has read onto the world around her. It is Titty who was the unlikely hero of *Swallows and Amazons*, and now she and Roger are foregrounded in *Swallowdale*. It is they who discover Swallowdale and Peter Duck's cave. It is they who decide to follow the patteran trail back to the camp and get lost in the fog. It is Titty who effects Roger's rescue after he sprains his ankle. Titty sometimes appears a little distanced from the others, even lonely (perhaps this is why she needs Peter Duck as a companion); those who know Ransome's earlier work might wonder whether Lilian (described in one of 'Ten Little Papers' in *The Stone Lady*, 1905) is a precursor.[2]

But the characterisation of Susan offers another, contrasting perspective of girlhood. As the Swallows' substitute mother-figure, she is nothing less than a domestic goddess. She orders and looks

---

1. *SD*, p. 173.
2. Arthur Ransome, *The Stone Lady* (London: Brown Langham & Co Ltd, 1905).

after their camps, makes sure that they all wash and brush their teeth, supervises the stores, cooks wholesome food, insists on regular mealtimes no matter what crisis is occurring, and worries about bedtimes. Susan is thus at times an almost comic parody of a wife and mother of the period, leading the narrator to suggest wryly and rather apologetically that without her the adventures simply could not take place:

> Really, if it had not been for Susan, half the Swallows' adventures would have been impossible, but, with a mate as good as that, to see that everything went as it should, there was no need for any native to worry about what was happening.[1]

In adopting the role of substitute mother, Susan is following a convention in children's literature: Wendy Darling in Barrie's *Peter Pan*, Roberta in Nesbit's *The Railway Children*, and Mary Lennox in *The Secret Garden*, though perhaps the responsibilities and practical qualities demanded of Susan sit a little uneasily on one so young.

Swallowdale does not attempt to offer any conclusions about the nature of girlhood, but it opens up a debate which runs through the series.

Fairy Tale

In Chapter 4, after meeting up with the briefly escaped Amazons, Titty and Roger follow the stream which flows into Horseshoe Cove, in search of its source and to put it on their map. In Titty's imagination they again become explorers of a dangerous land:

> 'Boomerangs and arrows might come whizzing through the air. And even if we weren't killed at once the savages would tie us up and take us away, and then when the others came to look for us they would walk into the very same trap.'[2]

As they near the road a motor horn becomes 'the trumpet of savages' and the throbbing of a motorcycle engine becomes 'tom-toms'.[3] Once they have waded under the low-arched bridge, they are led on almost magically by the stream and the sound of a waterfall. On climbing up beside it, they reach the secret and magical valley that, as Swallowdale, is to be the focus of the novel. The description here is striking in its

---

1. *SD*, p. 361.
2. *SD*, p. 47.
3. *SD*, p. 47.

simplicity, though lightened by Roger's penchant for chocolate and so never tipping into sentimentality. There is again the suggestion of a fairy tale in the language:

> It was a little valley in the moorland, shut in by another waterfall at the head of it, not a hundred yards away, and by the slopes of rock and heather that rose so steeply that when the explorers looked up they could see nothing but the sky above them. In there it was as if the blue mountains did not exist. The valley might have been hung in the air. . . .[1]

Then, continuing the fairy tale, a tortoiseshell butterfly with 'brown and blue and orange and black wings' takes them to another secret, a cave hidden by a clump of heather.[2] But they are already late for tea so, leaving Peter Duck on guard, they head back to Horseshoe Cove where no one seems interested in what they have found.

Later in the novel Nancy's revelation of the depths to which the Great Aunt has sunk – 'Last night she made mother cry'[3] – is too much for Titty. In spite of Susan's protestation that it is 'a bad sort of magic' she determines to make an effigy of their enemy into which she will stick pins – not to kill her, of course, as Titty is too good-natured – but just enough to make her uncomfortable and leave Beckfoot.[4] We are back in the world of fairy tale (or, more precisely, folk tale), but now in more sinister mood: in the African and Jamaican stories of witches and their spells told by Mrs Walker. In the gloom of Peter Duck's cave, Titty heats the candle-grease and turns it into a grotesque doll. Now a witch herself, she holds the doll in front of her, walking three times round the cave and talking to the image as she walks: '*Be* the great-aunt! *Be* the great-aunt! *Be* the great-aunt!'[5] Then, darkly developing the ritual, she remembers that native wizards let their wax images melt over a fire until they are drained of strength and die: if she melts the Great Aunt just a little, the Great Aunt won't feel quite herself and will go away. But the fire is too hot, and the doll slips from her hands and dissolves in the flames. Titty believes she has killed her: 'I wish I'd never thought of it. But I didn't mean to kill her. I didn't. All I wanted was for her to want to go to the seaside.'[6]

1. *SD*, p. 55.
2. *SD*, p. 58.
3. *SD*, p. 243.
4. *SD*, p. 244.
5. *SD*, p. 258.
6. *SD*, p. 262.

Titty, her vivid imagination racing, weeps. 'Pretty Polly. Pretty Polly,' says the parrot, with immaculate comic timing. 'Go and wash your face,' says Susan, with no imagination but with her usual common sense.[1] She may be right to scoff at the powers of Titty's improvised black magic, but this powerful and uncomfortable scene, always controlled by humour and good sense, speaks of the power of symbols, of superstitions and evil forces, and the terror as well as the delight that can result from childhood fancy.

Shipwreck

But some things are real enough and in Chapter 5 the wrecking of *Swallow* is heavily signposted: John's frustration at the delay in leaving the island camp as the wind strengthens; his difficulty in controlling *Swallow* and his ignoring of the obvious need for a reef until it is too late. Pike Rock, so harmless the day before, is now menacing, and his sudden doubt is not quite disguised: '"We ought to be able to do it," he said aloud, and really because he began to be not quite sure.'[2] Then there is 'the last furious gust' and disaster strikes. Too late, John regrets his over-confidence: just as in the night-time sail in *Swallows and Amazons*, when he risked the safety of his ship and crew, he knows that he has been a 'duffer' and has again let his father down. His mind churns and his guilt is caught in a wonderfully appropriate and dark simile: 'And then a new flock of black, wretched thoughts came crowding in like cormorants coming home to roost.'[3] The holiday is doubly ruined. The summer had been 'the cargo of the little ship' and has sunk with her.[4] Without a dinghy, the longed-for camp on Wild Cat Island will have to be abandoned, even when the Great Aunt leaves.

It is Captain Flint, still trying to make amends for his behaviour in *Swallows and Amazons*, who comes to the rescue, arranging the repair of *Swallow*, persuading Mrs Walker to let her children camp in Swallowdale, and acting as porter to carry tents and stores up the steep path from the shore. So the valley becomes the new centre of play and at the same time allows the shifting of setting from water to land. The middle of the novel is full of longeurs, as the Swallows construct their camp and explore the countryside while waiting impatiently for a pirate attack by the Amazons and to be freed from the Great Aunt's clutches.

1. *SD*, p. 267.
2. *SD*, p. 69.
3. *SD*, p. 74.
4. *SD*, p. 75.

2. Candle-Grease Aunt

The fire is too hot, and the doll slips from Titty's hands and dissolves in the flames.
She believes she has killed her: 'I wish I'd never thought of it. But I didn't mean to
kill her. I didn't. All I wanted was for her to want to go to the seaside.'

In the new camp in Swallowdale a further symbol of continuity and
renewal is found in Peter Duck's secret cave, which turns out not to be
a secret to Captain Flint:

> 'Hasn't it got a cave in it, on the left as you go up?'
> Titty's face fell. Had all the discoveries in the world been made
> already?
> 'It's Peter Duck's cave,' she said.
> 'Thirty years ago I used to call it Ben Gunn's.'[1]

So the children are, in their turn, re-enacting the childhood adventures
of Captain Flint. (Ben Gunn is the marooned 'savage' from Stevenson's
Treasure Island, one of the parent texts, with *Robinson Crusoe*, which lies
behind *Swallows and Amazons*, *Swallowdale*, and *Peter Duck*: when at the
end of *Swallowdale* Roger hobbles home with the crutch that Young
Billy has made for him, he plays the part of Long John Silver.) Later
Captain Flint discovers the graffiti that as a child he had carved in the
cave thirty years before:

> 'We'll put Peter Duck's name there too,' said Titty.
> 'Ben Gunn'll be glad to meet him,' said Captain Flint.[2]

There is the same sense of continuity in the survival of the traditions
of the past which we witness in the ballads sung by old Mr Swainson,
in the vivid description of the hound-trails in Chapter 17 ('Later and
Later and Later'), and in Nancy's almost poetic tales of the guides races,
the pole vaulting and the sheep-dog trials.

Kanchenjunga

The Swallows keep themselves busy enough in Swallowdale, but it is
not until Chapter 25 (of 36) that the Great Aunt departs and a real
adventure can begin at last: the mountaineering expedition that Nancy
has planned – the climbing of Kanchenjunga. This again is a re-enacting
of the sort of colonial adventure which had captured public imagination
across Europe during Ransome's childhood, with the young explorers
turned into mountaineers: by the end of the nineteenth century
mountaineering had become more than an amateur sport, and races
to the summit were as much a matter of national pride as of personal
achievement. Although there had been an unsuccessful British attempt
to conquer the real Kanchenjunga in 1905, the episode in *Swallowdale*

---

1. *SD*, p. 178.
2. *SD*, p. 192.

would more probably have been inspired by the German attempts on the mountain between 1929 and 1931 which were making headlines at the time (Ransome had read Frank Smythe's *The Kanchenjunga Adventure*). Thirty years previously, the Blackett parents (before they were married) and Uncle Jim had called the same hill the Matterhorn, whose North Face route was first climbed in the summer of 1931 when Ransome would have been working on the final revisions of *Swallowdale*.

Crucially, in Chapter 27, there is the scene at the summit of Kanchenjunga. John and Roger look out to sea and imagine a voyage all round the world, which in the future they will make themselves, following in their father's footsteps and playing their own part in the Empire: 'We will some day,' says John. 'Daddy's done it.'[1] However, the most stunning moment, beautifully controlled by Ransome, is when the children open the small round brass box which Roger finds under a loose stone at the foot of the cairn and read the message from the past. This is not only another example of one generation enjoying again the adventures of another, but also a sad refrain of the theme of the absent father:

> Roger let Nancy unfold it. She opened it, began reading aloud, and then stopped. Peggy took it and read it aloud, while the others looked at it over her shoulder. It was written in black pencil that had scored deeply into the paper:

> 'August the 2nd 1901
> We climbed the Matterhorn.
> Molly Turner.
> J. Turner.
> Bob Blackett.'

> 'That's mother and Uncle Jim,' said Peggy in a queer voice.
> 'Who is Bob Blackett?' asked Susan.
> 'He was father,' said Nancy.
> Nobody said anything for a minute, and then Titty, looking at the paper, said, 'So that was what they called it. Well, it's Kanchenjunga now. It's no good changing it now we've climbed it.'
> 'That was thirty years ago,' said John.
> 'I wonder how mother and Uncle Jim escaped from the great-aunt to come up here,' said Peggy. 'She was looking after them, you know.'
> 'Probably father rescued them,' said Nancy.[2]

1. *SD*, p. 373.
2. *SD*, p. 376.

After they have written their own message and put everything back in the box, Nancy returns to the theme of continuity and renewal: "'You found it,' she said [to Roger]. "You put it back, and then perhaps in another thirty years. . . ." She broke off, but presently laughed. "Shiver my timbers. . . .""[1] Unlike Commander Walker, Bob Blackett is not even a memory here, though the message in the box shows how his daughters are reliving the childhood experiences of their parents. It is worth noting that beneath her pirate act, Nancy is frequently more emotionally aware and more farsighted than her companions. Here she is wondering if one day her own children will scale Kanchenjunga as well. I think it is episodes such as this (and John's guilt at the wrecking of *Swallow*, and Titty's despair when she melts the candle-grease effigy), when there is a pause in the action and time for an unobtrusive exploration of character, that set Ransome apart from almost every other writer for children.

The Charcoal-Burners

Only thin smoke without flame
From the heaps of couch grass;
Yet this will go onward the same
Though Dynasties pass.

(Thomas Hardy)

After the conquering of Kanchenjunga, the Swallows and Amazons head back to Swallowdale. The Amazons, with John and Susan, sail back down the lake in *Amazon*, while Titty and Roger decide to retrace their patteran trail over land. But almost without warning they are enveloped in fog and become disorientated. When Roger injures his ankle, Titty has to seek help and luckily the friendly charcoal-burners, whom we met in *Swallows and Amazons*, are working nearby. I think it is more than coincidence that Ransome, like Hardy, chooses the image of charcoal-burners to highlight how, in spite of all disaster, things 'go onward the same'. Hardy wrote 'In Time of "The Breaking of Nations"' in 1915, when the horror of the First World War suggested apocalypse rather than hope. But for all his famous gloom, Hardy always found a stoic reassurance in nature and the rural life of Dorset. In the same way, Ransome, another lover of nature, finds in Young Billy and the unseen Old Billy (created out of the charcoal-burners whom he met in Nibthwaite on his childhood holidays) a metaphor for the endurance

---

1. *SD*, p. 377.

of traditional skills and ways of life in the face of so-called progress. It is no surprise that Titty is not sure whether she is talking to Young Billy or Old Billy, or that Old Billy should in fact be away at Bigland (a nearby hamlet) watching the wrestling at which he had once been a champion, as had Young Billy after him. Roger, lying in the charcoal burners' wigwam, is enchanted by the magic of the past:

> The words went over his head like great poetry, only leaving him feeling that the old man who was talking was very much stirred up by something or other that had happened a very long time ago.[1]

The next day everything is brighter. The not too badly injured Roger is carried back to Swallowdale on a makeshift litter, the repaired *Swallow* is collected from the boatbuilder at Rio, the camp is moved back to Wild Cat Island, and the planned holiday can begin at last.

The Optimism of *Swallowdale*

Swallowdale is full of things that go wrong. The Great Aunt threatens to wreck the children's holiday; the over-confident John, so very nearly a 'duffer', wrecks *Swallow* so the camp on the island has to be left; Titty and Roger get lost in the fog; Roger sprains his ankle. Yet in this gentle, humorous book there is always the sense that everything will be all right. And it is.

A sense of optimism runs through all the *Swallows and Amazons* novels, each of which has a comfortable, closed ending until, surprisingly, *Great Northern?*. In *Swallows and Amazons*, for example, the villains are discovered by Titty and Captain Flint's trunk is recovered; in *Peter Duck*, a water spout conveniently puts paid to Black Jake and his crew; in *We Didn't Mean to Go to Sea*, the Swallows survive the North Sea storm and their father, another *deus ex machina*, makes a pier-head leap and sails back with them for a family reunion at Pin Mill; in *The Big Six*, the bully George Owdon gets his comeuppance and the Death and Glories are exonerated. Perhaps it is only in the underrated *Secret Water* that the underlying mood is bleaker as the children grow apart, friendships begin to crumble, and the final cheerful farewells are unconvincing. It is the sense of optimism that is one of the reasons for the success of the *Swallows and Amazons* books: for children still living in the shadow of the First World War, with a depressed economy and stirrings in Hitler's Germany, or living through the Second World War and its aftermath, the escapism of camping and sailing in an untroubled world was irresistible.

---

1. *SD*, p. 422.

But *Swallowdale* offers something more. It is not just that its mood and ending are optimistic, but that its whole structure and imagery are about continuity and renewal, as the past is relived and the old is made new. The most powerful symbol of this is the wrecking and rebuilding of *Swallow* herself. Victor Watson (*Reading Series Fiction*) suggests that 'she reappears in the end to become an image of healing, a simple metaphor for the values implicit in the story, and at the same time a focus for a complex patterning of words of *new* and *old*, of *youth* and *renewal*'.[1] In Chapter 5, as a result of John's bravado, *Swallow* founders within seconds. But almost immediately the revival begins, with John's emptying the dinghy of her ballast, the hauling ashore, and the careening to empty her of the lake water. There follows the patching of the hull, the voyage under jury rig to Rio, and the confirmation from the cheery boat-builder that *Swallow* will be at least as good as new:

> 'And will she really be all right again?' asked John.
> 'Better than a new ship,' said the boat-builder.[2]

So it is that, at the end of the novel, *Swallow* is 'a new ship, better than new, for she had renewed her youth and kept her memories and was still at heart the same old *Swallow*', and proves her return to health by the winning of the race with *Amazon* back to Beckfoot.[3] But although *Swallow* is taken out of the action for almost all the novel, her mast remains as another image of renewal. The breaking of the mast suggests John's emasculation as a result of his dufferish misjudgement and, as an of act of reparation, he busies himself for the remainder of the novel with the creation of a new spar out of the Norwegian spruce that Captain Flint brings. First, he shapes the pole with a plane (using calipers to ensure accurate measurements); then he smooths it lovingly with sandpaper before finishing it with liberal coats of oil. So when the repaired *Swallow* is discovered on the beach below Swallowdale, 'The new mast had already been stepped in her, pale gold with sandpapering and linseed oil, and hung with new buff lanyards for sail and flag.'[4] John, as well as *Swallow*, has been restored. He is a captain again.

As *Swallowdale* draws to a close, John re-establishes his authority by helming the repaired *Swallow* to victory in the race over Nancy and Peggy in *Amazon* – but, tellingly, this is only achieved by the taking of another chance: the risky crossing of the shallows. It is the same sort of exploit

---

1. Victor Watson, *Reading Series Fiction* (London: Routledge Falmer, 2000), p. 19.
2. *SD*, p. 111.
3. *SD*, p. 472.
4. *SD*, p. 472.

that sank *Swallow* in the squall, but this time there is no danger. Moreover, in another example of continuity and renewal, it is a re-enacting of one of his father's triumphs: "'John did what you told us father did in that race when he slipped over the shoals on his beam ends," said Susan.'[1] After a celebratory feast at Beckfoot (where we eavesdrop briefly on an approving exchange about the liberal upbringing of the Blackett girls), the Swallows take their mother home. As they sail past the boatsheds at Rio, it is now Mrs Walker who is reminded of another time and place. John is speaking:

> 'Yes, you can smell it. Tarred rope. Just sniff for a minute, mother.'
> And mother sniffed and remembered that same smell drifting from the open doors of the little shops along the water front, and from the sailing ships in Australian harbours long ago.[2]

This is not only a reliving of Mrs Walker's own nautical childhood in Australia, prompted by the smells that drift from the boat-builders and chandlers of Rio, but an allusion to Ransome's mother, Edith, who was also of Australian descent (the daughter of the landscape painter, Edward Boulton). Thus, as so often in the *Swallows and Amazons* novels, Ransome's life and those of his characters and settings are intermingled, and his own family is renewed in his fiction.

*

As a child, *Swallowdale* was one of my least favourite of the *Swallows and Amazons* series. This was chiefly because I was a sailor and was not so enthused by land-based adventures (I had much the same reservations about *Pigeon Post* and *The Picts and the Martyrs*). But with hindsight I think it was also because nostalgia is largely an adult emotion, and the central aspect of continuity and renewal appeals especially to the adult reader, who is more in tune with the past and more patiently accepts the lack of a strong narrative thread. All this notwithstanding, the writing in *Swallowdale* has become more confident than before, the characters are developed more fully, and the often lyrical descriptions of Swallowdale, the wrecking of *Swallow*, the candle-grease effigy, the summit of Kanchenjunga, the disorientating fog, and Roger's night in the wigwam remain among the finest episodes in the series. So, whatever my youthful reservations, I can see that Taqui was probably right to declare that '*Swallowdale* is EVEN BETTER than *Swallows and Amazons*'.[3]

---

1. *SD*, pp. 490-91.
2. *SD*, p. 499.
3. Letter from Taqui Altounyan, 15 November 1931, reproduced in *The Best of Childhood*, p. 61.

3.
Peter Duck:
Ransome and the Art of Metafiction

Peter Duck (1932) is very different from the two novels that precede it. *Swallows and Amazons* and *Swallowdale* recount gentle summer holidays and are notable for their surface realism. The children play games, but in those games they encounter small but real dangers. Within the games, they really get lost on the Lake at night; they really wreck their dinghy in the squall; they really become disorientated in the fog. *Peter Duck*, though, develops into a fantasy of another sort and into a sometimes frightening story, strongly influenced by R.L. Stevenson's *Treasure Island* (again) and E.F. Knight's *The Cruise of the Falcon* (1884) and *The Cruise of the Alerte* (1890). Ironically, since Ransome would not write another fantasy until *Missee Lee* nine years later, and even Titty would quickly forget her imaginary friend, it was *Peter Duck* that especially caught the imagination of young readers, quickly outselling its predecessors and at last firmly establishing his reputation as a children's writer. In this chapter I want to focus on Ransome's narrative technique and show how *Peter Duck* is a skilfully constructed metafiction, a novel which is aware of and utilises its own status as fiction; a teasing literary intrigue shared between author, characters and reader.

At the start of *Peter Duck* the action moves to Lowestoft in Suffolk, but the main cast of characters is the same as in *Swallows and Amazons* and *Swallowdale*. There are other important connections, too: Wild Cat Island, which in the first two novels is the centre of their imaginary world, is replaced by the schooner *Wild Cat*, and the freshly painted *Swallow* is hanging in the davits. Peter Duck, the aged and mysterious sailor who dreams of going to sea again before he is too old, is watching the Amazons help Captain Flint to prepare the ship for sea; but their adult crew cannot join them and it seems that the planned voyage will not happen. Then the comic procession of Swallows arrives from the railway station with a green parrot in a cage and a monkey on a lead. We have met Polly before, a fittingly exotic gift to Titty for finding Captain Flint's trunk at the end of *Swallows and Amazons* and prominent in the camp at *Swallowdale*. Gibber, who is to provide much of the comedy, is a new entrant, suggested by Jacko the monkey in *The Cruise of the Alerte* and who only figures again in Ransome's other fantasy, *Missee Lee*.[1] Here, on Lowestoft's workmanlike North Quay, they are both out of place and it is small wonder that Peter Duck should think that the children have taken a wrong turning. We learn that Polly has just caused trouble, screeching 'Pieces of Eight' at the local 'ne'er do well', Black Jake, whose black hair, gold earrings and preoccupation with treasure all hint at a pirate tale. So it straightaway becomes clear that this will be a different sort of adventure from the harmless games the children have played on the Lake in the North, watched over by the friendliest of natives. Captain Flint may be in command of *Wild Cat* and stand in again as a substitute father, but he is to prove too hot-headed and too set on a treasure hunt to be reliable: the contrast with Peter Duck makes it clear that he is another game-player and not a proper captain at all:

> 'And now,' said Captain Flint at breakfast, 'the first thing to do is to get across the island, find Mr Duck's tree, and bring the stuff aboard.'
>
> 'Begging your pardon, sir,' said Peter Duck, 'the first thing's the ship.'[2]

Mothers are now conveniently out of the way and things like school and homework, which intrude on and frame many of the other novels, are never mentioned.[3]

We have learned in *Swallowdale* that *Peter Duck* purports to be a story told by the Swallows and Amazons themselves while they are spending a winter holiday with Captain Flint aboard a wherry on the Norfolk Broads. But with the exception of a note on *Peter Duck*'s title page that it is 'based on information supplied by the Swallows and Amazons'

1. In Ransome's discarded opening for *Peter Duck* the monkey is actually called Jacko, but this was later diplomatically changed to Gibber.
2. *PD*, p. 252.
3. The dedication to *Peter Duck* is 'To Mrs Robert Blackett and Mrs E.H.R. Walker – A humble apology for the ungrateful brutality with which their children eliminated them from these adventures'.

there is no mention in either the first chapter or anywhere else that it is a made-up story and not a 'real' holiday. This is disorientating, both for those who have read *Swallowdale* and for those who are meeting the Swallows and Amazons for the first time.

The explanation is that before Ransome set to work on *Swallowdale* he drafted a fascinating but involved opening for *Peter Duck* which describes how the Swallows and Amazons set about telling a treasure-island tale to pass the time while their wherry is fog-bound. More than a year later, after *Swallowdale* was published, he returned his attention to *Peter Duck*, but discarded the first, rather slow, opening. Instead, he plunges straight into the scene at Lowestoft and, from the very beginning, lays the foundations for an unlikely account of greed and murderous intent.

The Discarded Opening
and Ransome's Narrative Technique

Ransome understood the art of writing. His *A History of Storytelling* (1909) is nothing of the sort. It is a study of the technique of writers in Britain and Europe from the authors of *The Romance of the Rose* to Flaubert and De Maupassant. Later Ransome was to write critical studies of Poe (1910), Wilde (1912) and Stevenson (recently discovered, and published in 2011).[1] He was so intrigued by the development of narrative form that we can assume the complex structure of *Peter Duck* is no accident.

Ransome's discarded opening to the novel is published in Christina Hardyment's *Arthur Ransome and Captain Flint's Trunk*.[2] On board the wherry *Polly Ann*, the Swallows and Amazons are discussing a book they've all read, called – *Swallows and Amazons*: 'It must be written by someone who knows us,' says Susan. 'You can tell that because he's got such a lot of the things that happened right.' This sums up Ransome's practice of taking characters from life as his raw material (in this case the Altounyan children, though he was later to deny it) and, as John says, making them 'a bit different from what we really are'. But Nancy is unimpressed by such pretended realism and by Ransome's habit, born of his journalism, of starting with descriptions or adaptations of real people and incidents and only afterwards linking them through an often tenuous plot:

1. Kirsty Nichol Findlay, ed., *Arthur Ransome's Long-Lost Study of Robert Louis Stevenson* (Martlesham: Boydell, 2011).

2. Christina Hardyment, *Arthur Ransome and Captain Flint's Trunk* (London: Frances Lincoln, 2006), pp. 162-75.

> 'That book [*Swallows and Amazons*] makes out it's a story but you've only got to read it to see that it's just telling the truth, or trying to anyhow. No, it's just someone has pieced together the things we did and put them in the book.'

A tale worth hearing, Nancy argues, is one 'with all sorts of things happening that couldn't happen on the lake at home'. Thus the crew decides to escape from authorial control and create its own pirate adventure: 'We could alter it as we went along,' says Titty, 'supposing we didn't like what was happening.' But who, they wonder, should be the narrator? Susan and John 'can't'; Roger is 'too young'; Titty would get much too excited; Peggy would 'chatter on'; and Nancy is a doer, not a teller. So, with no one better, Captain Flint is chosen to do the telling. 'He'll tell it quite well,' says Nancy, then adding characteristically, 'and anyhow we can make sure it's good by telling him what to put in.' Although it is only in two novels (*Peter Duck* and *Missee Lee*) that Ransome takes Nancy's advice to avoid 'just telling the truth, or trying to anyhow', this passage describes his technique throughout the series of using an omniscient narrator, but through the frequent use of dialogue turning the characters themselves into disguised (or dramatised) narrators and allowing the reader to see things from their own particular points of view.[1]

When Captain Flint comes aboard, Nancy returns to attacking the realism of *Swallows and Amazons*:

> 'That book only tries to tell just what happened. What's the good of that? It happened anyway, whether anyone tells about it or not. And it's silly being tied down like that. Why shouldn't we have a properly gorgeous story, much better than anything that could have happened to us on the lake with little boats like *Swallow* and *Amazon*.'

Notice Nancy's scathing use of 'little'. Ironically, of course, it is the fictional *Swallows and Amazons* (whatever its roots in the actual world) that features the fictional character of Nancy Blackett (and Captain

---

1. In *The Rhetoric of Fiction* (Chicago: Chicago University Press, 1961) Wayne Booth discusses the use of 'disguised narrators' in a chapter on 'Telling and Showing'. Similarly, the shifting between an 'authorial persona' and 'dramatised narrators' who 'focalise the action' is investigated by Gérard Genette in *Narrative Discourse* (Oxford: Blackwell, 1972). He describes as 'mimesis' the use of 'dramatised narrators', who operate through direct speech and thus give the reader the illusion of hearing and seeing things at first hand.

Flint, and everyone else), who is now, in another fiction, complaining about its realism, belittling the games she loves to organise. So, originally, *Peter Duck* was to be a fiction created by fictional characters. Drinking their cocoa, the children decide on the sort of ship they want to sail in the story. They settle on a rakish schooner (later to be called *Wild Cat*, tying their fantasy to the 'real' island that has been part of their exploits in *Swallows and Amazons* and *Swallowdale*) and the story-telling begins:

> 'You're going to tell it,' said Nancy Blackett, 'only it won't be interrupting if anyone has a good bit to put in.'
> 'I hope it'll all be good bits,' said Captain Flint. 'Then I shall be able to listen instead of telling.'
> 'We'll all listen and we'll all tell it,' said Nancy, 'Nobody can remember everything. Anyhow, don't let's waste time. We've started.'

It is uncertain whether there turned out to be so many 'good bits' that Captain Flint was happily redundant as a narrator or whether Ransome decided that reverting to the use of an omniscient narrator outside the story would be technically simpler and more effective. But the published version of *Peter Duck* opens in a mostly familiar vein and the children are at least allowed to start out in a setting grounded in the actual before travelling back in time and into a darker fantasy world.

The initial move from the actual world to the fantasy world, and the shifting between them throughout the novel, is central to Ransome's method and to the reader's deliberate disorientation. What is a 'properly gorgeous story' of eighteenth-century pirates doing in the present of 1932? Is it still something made up by the Swallows and Amazons, even if there is no internal evidence to support this? It is certainly the case that the reader is constantly teased and challenged by the differing perspectives of the main players. Even if they are not the explicit tellers of the tale as Ransome originally intended, they remain disguised narrators who help to convey a gripping adventure played out on the high seas.

The actual world, the harbour at Lowestoft, is described with Ransome's usual attention to detail, reinforced with an accurate sketch map:[1] the 'swing bridge', the 'Custom-House with the big crest over the doorway', the 'fishing vessels', the 'noise of men chipping rust and riveting' as they work on the steam trawler.[2] When Ransome returned from Syria in May 1932, where he had stayed with

---

1. *PD*, p. 31.
2. *PD*, pp. 17-18.

the Altounyans and written most of the first draft of *Peter Duck*, he immediately visited Lowestoft to 'get the background right for some important scenes in the first part of the book'.[1] Typically, there is also an accurate description of the *Wild Cat*, with an illustration which shows the names of the sails, a deck plan and another plan which shows the lay-out of the accommodation below deck.[2] *Wild Cat* had been a Baltic trading schooner and is modelled on the coastal schooners the Ransomes had encountered while sailing *Racundra* in the Baltic only ten years before.[3]

But already there are hints of the fantasy world of pirates and treasure. The railway porter comments on Polly's altercation with Black Jake: '"Pieces of eight!" your bird said. Well, there's many a boy of this town got a sore head for shouting that after Black Jake. You mustn't speak of treasure to Black Jake. No. Nor yet of crabs.'[4] In case we forget, Polly keeps up her screamed refrain of 'pieces of eight' at every opportunity. Nor are we allowed to forget the 'man with gold earrings'. There is another clue as to what's to come when we learn of the ship's stores: 'We've pemmican for a year at least and jam enough for ten,' says Peggy.[5] Captain Flint points proudly to the water tanks under the cabin floor: '"It isn't that he means to go very far," said Nancy, "but he just likes to feel he could."'[6] And when Peter Duck is signed up as replacement crew we suspect that, for him, sailing down channel isn't going to be excitement enough: 'It was blue water as I was thinking of,' he says.[7] So when the first chapter ends with the relief that with Peter Duck aboard they'll be able to go to sea after all, there still remains the 'black' threat from the other side of the dock:

> And away there on the black schooner at the other side of the harbour, Black Jake, that dark, scowling man with the black ringlets and the gold ear-rings, was watching all that was going on through his long telescope.[8]

Clearly, something else is going to happen.

---

1. Letter to Edith Ransome , 27 March 1932, in Hugh Brogan, ed., *Signalling to Mars: The Letters of Arthur Ransome* (London: Jonathan Cape, 1997).
2. *PD*, p. 12.
3. See Arthur Ransome, *Racundra's First Cruise* (London: George Allen & Unwin, 1923).
4. *PD*, p. 6.
5. *PD*, p. 14.
6. *PD*, p. 14.
7. *PD*, p. 19.
8. *PD*, p. 22.

The tension rises further in the following chapters, where Black Jake remains a scowling presence. Notice how Peter Duck regards him (in the fantasy world) as a black-hearted pirate, while Captain Flint (still playing games in the actual world) sees nothing to worry about:

> 'Why do they call him Black Jake?' Titty asked. 'Is it because of his hair?'
> 'Because of his heart,' said Peter Duck.
> 'Queer sort of cove,' said Captain Flint.[1]

Desperate to find out Peter Duck's real intentions, Black Jake rows across to *Wild Cat* under cover of darkness, climbs on the anchor and listens to the crew talking on deck. But something – Titty still believes 'that Black Jake's ear-rings jingled' – alerts Peter Duck and he lets go the anchor with the eavesdropping Black Jake clinging to it, smashing his dinghy and sending it to the bottom of the harbour.[2] It is a wonderful moment, not without a certain comedy, but what is it all about? Captain Flint, who until now has remained resolutely in the comfort and security of the actual world, is 'a little astonished' and demands answers.[3] Thus Peter Duck 'spins his yarn' and together with the Swallows and Amazons the reader is drawn inexorably into 'a story of wrecks and pirates and distant islands . . . a long way from the snug little deckhouse of the *Wild Cat* lying comfortably in Lowestoft inner harbour'.[4]

Peter Duck's Yarn

In *Swallowdale* Peter Duck is described as a fictional character, but to an extent this is misleading. To start with, he is no more fictional than the rest of the *Wild Cat*'s crew. He is inspired by the real Captain Sehmel, who a decade earlier had helped the Ransomes with the building and sailing of their yacht *Racundra* on the Baltic, and perhaps also by the real wherryman who had accompanied Ransome on fishing expeditions on the Norfolk Broads.[5] In the discarded opening, Peter Duck features as the paid crew of the *Polly Ann* – a retired seaman from the merchant clippers who now makes his living by carrying cargo in

---

1. *PD*, p. 27.
2. *PD*, p. 63.
3. *PD*, p. 64.
4. *PD*, p. 79.
5. Arthur Ransome, *The Autobiography of Arthur Ransome*, ed. Rupert Hart-Davis (London: Century Publishing, 1985), p. 306.

his own wherry, *Arrow of Norwich*. But as the novel develops he is
recreated as a sort of 'ancient mariner', recounting in Chapters 5 and
6 ('Peter Duck Spins His Yarn' and 'And Winds It Up') an experience
of shipwreck, crabs and buried treasure which has haunted him for
a lifetime and, as another disguised narrator, sucking the children
around him out of their already way-out tale and into his own. They
leave behind the safe world of the Lake of the North, and even the
snug deckhouse of *Wild Cat*, and become part of Peter Duck's fantasy,
which is the main plot of the novel. Thus *Peter Duck* is now not just a
fiction created by fictional characters, but a fiction created by a fictional
character who is himself created by fictional characters: a story within
a story within a story; a metafictional delight.

In his yarn, Peter Duck takes us back into the world of *Treasure
Island*. He was shipwrecked in his youth and washed up on an island
infested by giant crabs where he witnessed the burying of treasure by
two pirates – a more serious echo of Titty's witnessing the burial of
Captain Flint's trunk on Cormorant Island in *Swallows and Amazons* –
and later secreted the bearings of the island by sewing them into the
lining of his jacket.[1] Forty years later, having fetched up in Suffolk, he
was hounded for his secret by Black Jake, who managed to steal the
document. But Black Jake's ensuing voyage to the island was fruitless,
so now, frustrated and enraged, he is intent on forcing Peter Duck to
lead him personally to the treasure.

Nevertheless, when the *Wild Cat* sets sail the following morning, the
passage down Channel has none of the hallmarks of a fantasy, and if
there is any thought of setting course for Crab Island it is only in Captain
Flint's mind. However, being at sea is very different to playing on the Lake:
John finds steering a straight course difficult, and Nancy and Titty are
horribly sick. With Ransome relying on the *Channel Pilot*, the description
of *Wild Cat*'s voyage is accurate in every detail, with the same sort of
poetry as today's shipping forecast: 'the Shipwash lightship, with its ball at
the mast-head' and the 'Long Sand, with its diamond'; the Kentish Knock;
the Elbow buoy off the North Foreland; the Goodwin lightships; the blaze
of Deal and the South Foreland light; the Varne off Dover; the lighthouse
at Dungeness; and so on down the coast past Beachy Head, Shoreham,
Worthing, Littlehampton, Bognor.[2] Then they are cutting inside the
Isle of Wight, with Peter Duck pointing out Spithead and the forts,
bringing up for the night at Cowes. This is Ransome at his realistic best.

---

1. Crab Island is inspired by Trinidad Island in E.F. Knight's *The Cruise of the
   Alerte* (1890; reprinted London: Granada, 1984).
2. *PD*, pp. 105-30.

But all the way they are tracked by Black Jake in *Viper*, and the children half-know that things are altering, that this make-believe summer holiday is becoming extraordinary and that they themselves – already characters in a book who are telling a story – are somehow becoming characters in yet another 'story of the distant past' that is still going on:

> Peter Duck's yarn . . . had been a splendid story but it had been a story of the distant past. It had explained why Black Jake had been inquisitive. It was only today that they began to understand that perhaps the story was not over and that perhaps Black Jake and Peter Duck, the *Viper* and the *Wild Cat*, and even they themselves were at that very moment taking a part in it.[1]

Captain Flint, 'who is just bursting to go off somewhere and do something', is clearly intent on treasure: when they row ashore for ice cream he buys two toy spades from the seaside shop ('toy' still suggests a game).[2] John notices that the chart on the deckhouse table would take them to the Caribbees. It is, though, the *Viper*'s attempt to kidnap Peter Duck and the subsequent rescuing of Bill (the *Viper*'s cabin boy), set adrift by Black Jake in the fog, which finally changes everything. Captain Flint, the pretend retired pirate who wants one more shot at finding treasure, now has another motive for heading for the Caribbees: 'Why not spike his guns for good by lifting that treasure of yours, Mr Duck, and bringing it home?'[3] Peter Duck, who has vowed never to return to Crab Island, is tempted and sees the chance of blue water sailing again. Yet, surprisingly, it is cautious, sensible Susan who decides things. For her, the morality of the situation overrides everything else: '"I think we ought to go," said Susan. "Black Jake's almost a murderer. He oughtn't to be allowed to get it [the treasure] after this."[4] Almost without the reader noticing, everything is changed and the *Wild Cat* is not just going foreign but heading for a violent romance on the other side of the Atlantic.

Crab Island

Peter Duck is divided into two 'books', a structure which reinforces the tension between the real and the fantastic. The first describes the voyage down channel, Peter Duck's yarn, the decision to sail to the

1. *PD*, p. 128.
2. *PD*, p. 138.
3. *PD*, p. 183.
4. *PD*, p. 183.

Caribbean, and the continuing of the voyage to Madeira. The second book describes the fantasy played out on Crab Island and the return to the apparently real world.

To begin with Crab Island appears a magical place. The language sings. In the darkness the children are entranced by the fireflies:

> . . . suddenly millions of lights showed along the edge of the forest, moving all the time. It was as if millions of small bright sparks were dancing there in the dusk. . . .
> 'This is the real thing at last,' said Nancy.[1]

Next morning Titty wakes up to find:

> . . . colours even brighter than she had seen them in her mind, the burning sky, the bright green feathery plumes of the palm trees, the black rocks of the hill towering above them.[2]

She discovers that Duckhaven, which reminds of the harbour in the safe world of *Swallows and Amazons*, is 'a perfect boat-landing': protected by rocks from the Atlantic swell, it is 'quiet and smooth'. But danger still lurks. The children may find it easy to forget Black Jake, but Bill knows that he will not be far away. Captain Flint, plunging over the ship's side, is lucky not to be savaged by a shark. Peter Duck is reluctant to go ashore.

When Peter Duck finally lands, he finds that Crab Island is an anti-climax. He has only seen it before in his youth and through adult eyes it is different. The giant crabs aren't giant at all, and the place where he was shipwrecked has altered as well: 'I never would have thought it was such a little place. . . . Shrunk it has, like them crabs. They was a sight bigger when I was here and all alone with them.'[3] Worst of all, so many years have passed that it is impossible for him to locate the tree where the treasure is buried. 'The lot of them'll be growed,' he says.[4] This is all a comment on childhood perception and imagination. If in old age the Swallows and Amazons were to return to their Lake in the North, they would no doubt find Kanchenjunga, the Arctic, Rio and their own Wild Cat Island dreadfully shrunk as well.

The action on the Island is melodramatic, with one disaster following another. Perhaps it appeals more to the child reader than to the adult, whose suspension of disbelief may be tested too far. Captain

1. *PD*, p. 245.
2. *PD*, p. 247.
3. *PD*, p. 278.
4. *PD*, p. 279.

Flint and the Swallows and Amazons set up camp but after three days of fruitless digging the weather begins to change and Captain Flint sets off back across the island to help Peter Duck and Bill take *Wild Cat* away from the dangers of the shore. Left alone, the Swallows and Amazons have first to shelter in their sleeping bags from a suffocating red dust cloud; then they have to take refuge in the crab-infested shipwreck when the Island is hit by storm and earthquake, wrecking their camp, uprooting trees and shifting rocks. They awake to a new landscape and, by happy and incredible chance, Susan and Peggy discover the treasure chest in a hole where a tree once stood. When *Wild Cat* returns to her anchorage having ridden out the storm, they pile into *Swallow* with the treasure and re-join their ship. All this excitement is recounted with enthusiasm and relish, but it owes more to the uncontrolled imaginations of the Swallows and Amazons than to the skill of an accomplished story-teller.

When the Swallows and Amazons arrive on *Wild Cat*, they discover that Captain Flint has already left to find them on the Island, while Peter Duck and Bill have been nastily beaten up by the *Viper*'s crew, who have also gone ashore. John and Nancy return in *Swallow* to Duckhaven to rescue Captain Flint before the pirates can reach him: shot at by their pursuers, it doesn't seem like a game or a melodrama or a fantasy anymore. The actual violence of the pirates is too much, even for Nancy's 'lurid taste'.[1]

Homeward Bound

The ending of *Peter Duck* is full of ironies, complexities and challenges. Once Captain Flint, John and Nancy are back on board *Wild Cat*, they weigh anchor and make good their escape from the Island and – for a time at least – from Black Jake and his crew, who are no longer (it seems) make-believe figures but a ruthless and violent rout. As the 'pirate' captain Nancy reflects, 'It was all very well to be the Terror of the Seas, but real pirates, like Black Jake and his friends, were altogether different.'[2] Of course, the novel is playing another of its tricks on us. The real children (who are Ransome's fictional creations) have become characters in the pirate story (though it is still not clear whether it is their own story or Peter Duck's), while Black Jake and company, who have stepped out of the pages of a pirate story book, have become disconcertingly real.

---

1. *PD*, p. 418.
2. *PD*, p. 417.

3. The Vipers Come Aboard

*Black Jake and his crew are no longer make-believe figures but a ruthless and
violent rout. As the 'pirate' captain Nancy reflects, 'It was all very well to
be the Terror of the Seas, but real pirates, like Black Jake and
his friends, were altogether different'.*

This reality comes more sharply into focus when *Wild Cat* is becalmed and *Viper* closes on her in a final attempt to steal the treasure. For a while, after leaving Crab Island, the children are relieved that the adventure is over: 'there they were, all together again in the *Wild Cat*, homeward bound, with the treasure, whatever it was, safely aboard'.[1] But the faces of Captain Flint and Peter Duck tell something different. Though the storm has passed, the weather has remained eerily unsettled. Then everything happens at once. From the horizon, a waterspout bears down on them – its changing sounds and colours, its swaying and dancing, are almost hypnotic in their power:

> A wild, shrill, rustling noise swept over the sea. The grey waves were white with foam under this twirling, swaying, monstrous pillar that was coming nearer and nearer, dancing as it seemed across the troubled water.[2]

At the same time, two rifle shots ring out from the *Viper's* bow. The first shatters Bill's arm; the second severs the *Wild Cat's* peak halyard, wrecking her sails but ironically saving her from the full force of the wind. But it is *Viper*, carrying full sail in pursuit of her quarry, which lies in the path of the waterspout. She is dismasted, split in two, sucked up and dropped back into the sea. Captain Flint, with typical generosity of spirit, heads back to search the area, but there is no sign of life amidst the wreckage. As Peter Duck would have it, the Devil has taken his own, and Ransome is able to conclude a moral tale with the Swallows and Amazons as no more than onlookers.

As in the archetypal seafaring novel, the homeward voyage is uneventful. The treasure itself is a disappointment (though, at least for Roger, far more exciting than the old book which they recovered in *Swallows and Amazons*), and slowly but inexorably the *Wild Cat* and her crew return to their own world. Even the waterspout 'seemed now like a dream or something that had happened not to them but to somebody else'.[3] John thinks they've had 'a grand voyage'; Susan reckons that 'nothing's really gone wrong that can't be mended'; Titty even bemoans the fact that exciting things don't happen to them.[4] After their landfall at Dodman Point, their beat up channel is guided this time not by the *Channel Pilot* but by a traditional sea shanty:

---

1. *PD*, p. 439.
2. *PD*, p. 446.
3. *PD*, p. 469.
4. *PD*, p. 464.

> And the first land we made, it is called the Dodman
> Next Rame Head off Plymouth, Start, Portland and Wight. . . .[1]

When they enter harbour at Lowestoft they are waved into the empty
berth apparently left so long before. Thus the children 'hurry back
into ordinary life' and have 'to make up for lost time'.[2] But has it been
a real adventure, or a story, or a dream? And how much time have
they lost? Is the bullet which shattered the lantern still embedded in
Swallow's planking (it is not mentioned when we next come across
Swallow in *Missee Lee*)? The treasure seems solid and, though not
worth 'a tremendous lot', is enough for each of Peter Duck's daughters
to have a genuine pearl necklace and for his wherry to have a new coat
of paint.[3]

So how real is Peter Duck himself, now back on his wherry? Is he no
more than the hired crewman on the *Polly Ann* who in the Swallows' and
Amazons' 'own story' has been translated into the hired crewman on
the *Wild Cat*? Or, further than that, is he a fictional character, created by
the fictional Swallows and Amazons in whose yarn they have, for a time,
become fictional characters twice over? It is a testimony to Ransome's
skill that Peter Duck's story, within the Swallows' and Amazons' story,
within Ransome's story, sweeps us along on a remarkable treasure-
island adventure and leaves such questions tantalisingly unanswered.
And what of Bill, now living with one of Peter Duck's daughters
and, when time allows, sailing with Peter Duck? Are his teeth actually
missing and, if so, how did he lose them?

What is clear is that for Peter Duck and Black Jake the action is
literally deadly serious. Peter Duck knows that even before the treasure
was buried, it had cost lives, and this is confirmed by the certificates
which the novel foregrounds in the penultimate chapter. Throughout
his life he has tried to escape from its grasp, and he knows that Black
Jake will stop at nothing to recover it. The action is serious for Bill, too.
He is the victim of Black Jake's violence when he is cast adrift in the
fog, is badly beaten up, and has his arm broken by the ricocheting rifle
bullet when the *Wild Cat* is attacked.

But until the novel's climax, the Swallows and Amazons and, for the
most part, Captain Flint enjoy it all as a game in which they are as much
observers as participants. They are ashore when the pirates board the
Wild Cat and back on board when Black Jake and his crew are pursuing

---

1. *PD*, p. 471.
2. *PD*, p. 474.
3. *PD*, p. 474.

Captain Flint across Crab Island. It is true that they survive the storm and earthquake, but these are portrayed as little more than tiresome inconveniences: "'Oh, bother, bother!" said Susan. "The kettle's gone, and so has the saucepan."'[1] It is Bill, younger in years than Nancy, who gives us an important comparison, especially in Chapter 15, 'Bill Finds His Place'. Taken in at first by Captain Flint's assertion that there are three captains and two mates in the *Wild Cat*, he never sees them as such: 'Cap'ns and mates! Cap'ns and mates! Why Black Jake and his gang'd eat 'em.'[2] He chews tobacco (which makes Nancy and Titty sick when they try it); he teases them about their sea sickness; he knows 'that at some jobs not one of these children could touch him'.[3] But when later the Swallows and Amazons sail off with Captain Flint to Crab Island, he concedes, 'They're good 'uns, for children' – with the nicely placed comma throwing the emphasis on 'children'.[4] The irony is that, though more experienced, he is a child himself, the same age as John and Nancy: the Swallows may have a naval commander for a father, but Bill was born on the Dogger Bank and has been at sea all his life.

'Bad Drawings'

Peter Duck was the first novel that Ransome illustrated himself and ever since (he writes) 'my bad drawings have come to seem part of the books, as indeed they are'.[5] Ransome had rejected Steven Spurrier's illustrations for *Swallows and Amazons* and had never been wholly happy with Clifford Webb's illustrations for *Swallows and Amazons* and *Swallowdale* – he regarded their work as 'merely skilful exercises by accomplished technicians'.[6] But Hugh Brogan is probably right in suggesting that Ransome's real motive in becoming his own artist was to make the books 'feel more entirely his own', just as he came selfishly and almost irrationally to exclude the Altounyans: 'So he put an end to intruders, and invented reasons for doing so afterwards.'[7] After *Peter Duck*, Ransome was to illustrate the entire *Swallows and Amazons* series, replacing Webb's illustrations in *Swallows and Amazons* and *Swallowdale*

---

1. *PD*, p. 366.
2. *PD*, p. 199.
3. *PD*, p. 206.
4. *PD*, p. 299.
5. *Autobiography*, p. 344.
6. *Autobiography*, p. 344.
7. Hugh Brogan, *The Life of Arthur Ransome* (London: Hamish Hamilton, 1955), p. 344.

in 1938. Just as it was his original plan to have the children and Captain Flint narrate *Peter Duck*, so he decided to enlist the children to help him with the drawings; except for Roger's two contributions, they are joint efforts, though later it is Nancy alone who is his assistant for *Swallows and Amazons, Winter Holiday, Pigeon Post* and *The Picts and the Martyrs*. Almost always the characters are seen from a distance or from behind: Ransome's argument was that if they are not made too physically detailed, his readers can more easily empathise with and 'become' one of them; or at least they can create their own mind-pictures, rather as we do when we listen to a radio drama.

Ransome was no great artist – his own assessment of 'scratchy line and uncertain anatomy' is not far wide of the mark[1] – but it is unfair to suggest that his skill fell entirely short at drawing faces (though he admitted that avoiding them saved him time): his unused sketch of the *Wild Cat*'s crew listening to Peter Duck's yarn depicts the features of John, Susan and Captain Flint in particular.[2] Roger Wardale's *Ransome the Artist* shows that Ransome's initial pencil sketches are much more sophisticated and lively than the published pen and ink illustrations, which were necessarily simplified for the available printing process. It is also worth noting that the perspective as well as the pen-work of the illustrations in *Peter Duck* is that of the children: Ransome's careful plans of *Wild Cat* show a small schooner of about fifty feet in length, which would have been cramped for the eventual crew of nine (as well as a monkey and a parrot) but the drawings of, for example, 'Sums' and 'Morning Splashes' portray the cabin and foredeck of a vessel at least twice the size. This children's perspective is also reflected by Titty who describes the *Wild Cat*, which is in fact 'only a little schooner with pole masts and rather small sails',[3] as 'a regular house of a ship, with towering sails higher than lots of houses'.[4]

*

Readers and critics hold divided opinions of *Peter Duck*. Peter Hunt feels that there is a difficulty about 'what happens when cosy child fantasy and harsh adult fantasy meet'.[5] Victor Watson, on the other

---

1. *Autobiography*, p. 344.
2. Roger Wardale, *Ransome the Artist* (Kendal: Amazon Publications, 1998), p. 3.
3. *PD*, p. 210.
4. *PD*, p. 53.
5. Peter Hunt, *Approaching Arthur Ransome* (London: Jonathan Cape, 1992), p. 148.

hand, argues that *Peter Duck* 'is concerned with the conflicts between good and evil' and that the children's innocence 'is toughened and defined through intimate contact with violence'.[1] However, the novel is always careful to avoid the children coming face to face with evil and violence. When they're shot at, we never think that the bullets are going to hit; they are never hurt, unlike Bill and Peter Duck. When Black Jake and his crew are drowned, it is not because of anything the children do, but because of a force of nature, and so it doesn't upset them one bit. Above all, the metafictional structure of the novel means that the Swallows and Amazons know that everything that happens exists only in a story which is of their own making, and is distanced again in another story within their story. They are kept safely out of harm's way.

For me *Peter Duck* suffers from too many episodes of melodrama to be considered among Ransome's best work, but (as Nancy originally intended in 'Their Own Story') it shows up the Swallows' and Amazons' adventures on the Lake in the North as the games that they are. With a cleverly constructed pirate story as the vehicle, and with plenty of humour along the way, this is a more serious and ambitious book than its predecessors. Ransome may well have felt that with it he had taken the Swallows and Amazons, and Captain Flint, as far as he could go, and although by January 1933 he had started on another Lake District novel, he was to introduce Dick and Dorothea Callum to the cast and edge the Swallows and Amazons away from centre stage.

---

1. Victor Watson, *Reading Series Fiction* (London: Routledge Falmer, 2000), pp. 20-21.

4.
Winter Holiday:
Enter the Callums

After the pirate fantasy of *Peter Duck*, Ransome returned to the real world of holiday adventure and, in many ways, *Winter Holiday* (1933) is *Swallowdale* on ice. This time Nancy has planned a trek to the North Pole across the ice, though frustratingly the Lake in the North refuses to freeze.

From the outset, the *Swallows and Amazons* novels proved popular in the United States, where they were published by Lippincott and promoted by the Junior Literary Guild. After the publication of *Peter Duck*, Helen Ferris of the Guild thought it to be probably 'the best of the lot' but she was aware that readers can become resistant to sameness and suggested that Ransome 'do something entirely different with a new set of youngsters'.[1] In the event he largely ignored her advice and *Winter Holiday* is not only set again on the Lake in the North with the usual cast of characters, but also reworks the already sketchy plot of *Swallowdale* for a frosty season.

The colonial theme remains. In *Swallowdale* the expedition to climb Kanchenjunga is delayed by the steely presence of the Great Aunt until the last few chapters; in *Winter Holiday* the expedition to the North Pole is put on hold because the weather is too warm, and then Nancy goes down with mumps. It only gets properly under way in Chapter 24 (of 29). Nevertheless, for all its familiarity, *Winter Holiday* has its own considerable strengths. It has an engaging *joie de vivre* which is appropriate to a winter's tale, with a pumpkin-faced Nancy controlling operations from her sick bed and Peggy making a sterling effort to

---

1. Letter from Helen Ferris, 29 October 1932, reproduced in Roger Wardale et al., eds, *The Best of Childhood* (Kendal: Amazon Publications, 2004), p. 85.

step into Nancy's very large pirate boots. But most striking is the way Ransome brings to life the tensions and resentments as two new holiday-makers, Dorothea and Dick Callum, edge their way uneasily into the *Swallows and Amazons* world.

The setting of *Winter Holiday* was inspired in part by Ransome's memory of the one time he had been tolerably happy at his preparatory school, Windermere Old College, when in the great frost of 1895 Windermere froze over and lessons were cancelled for a number of weeks. In his *Autobiography* he recalls his joy in skating, 'an activity,' he writes, 'in which I was not markedly worse than any of the other boys':

> After breakfast, day after day, provisions were piled on the big toboggan and we ran it from the Old College to the steep hill down into Bowness when we tallied on to ropes astern of it to hold it back and prevent it crashing into the hotel at the bottom. During those happy weeks we spent the whole day on the ice, leaving the steely lake only at dusk when fires were already burning and torches lit and our elders carried lanterns as they skated and shot about like fireflies.[1]

Such description is almost Wordsworthian in tone and perhaps even a conscious evocation of the well-known skating episode in the opening book of *The Prelude* (1805 and 1840). As with Wordsworth, such early encounters with nature were to shape both Ransome's life and his writing. Later, in the hard winter of 1929, Windermere froze again and Ransome and Evgenia were able to see the excitement at Bowness and walk together on the ice.

But Ransome found difficulty in fleshing out the trivial storyline. His first notes (written on 15 January 1933) get as far as Nancy's illness, the planned expedition to the North Pole, a night on the *Fram*, and a sail for the sledge, but then they stop. At the end of the month he drafted an opening for the novel: although it was quickly discarded, it was crucial in introducing two new characters, Elizabeth (quickly changed to Dorothea) and Dick Callum, who would add a new interest to the series and go some way towards allaying Helen Ferris's fears. He also decided that in *Winter Holiday* he would leave the children far more to their own devices. Mrs Walker is visiting her husband who is still aboard ship in Malta, Mr and Mrs Callum are on an archaeological dig in Egypt, and Captain Flint is on his travels abroad as well. So there are only the tolerant Mrs Blackett and kind-hearted Mrs Dixon

---

1. Arthur Ransome, *The Autobiography of Arthur Ransome*, ed. Rupert Hart-Davis (London: Jonathan Cape, 1976) p. 46.

to keep an eye on what is happening: the former contents herself with making sure Nancy is kept in isolation when she falls ill, and it is enough for the latter to see that everyone is well-fed. Captain Flint returns unexpectedly from his travels in Chapter 21 ('Captain Flint Comes Home') and helps Nancy to organise the final push to the North Pole, but he plays little part in the story.

At the end of February, Ransome wrote another, fuller 'Argument' for the novel, but it is still undeveloped: the calendar for the expedition has several days when nothing happens and there is little sense as to how it will all end. 'There is something fundamentally wrong with this story,' he despaired in his diary. 'I doubt if Dorothea and Dick fit this strange tale.'[1] At the beginning of March he wrote to his mother that 'The new book is much more difficult than any of the others; it is going to be a tough job all the way through'.[2] This struggle to establish a plot (which was to become an almost annual affair) was made worse by Ransome breaking his ankle in a fall (he claimed to have been distracted by a conversation with Dorothea) and by his stomach ulcer flaring up. But by the end of August, *Winter Holiday* was complete, even though he continued to have considerable misgivings (especially about the ending) and the illustrations troubled him.

Enter the Callums

'One at least of the two new characters you won't be able to help liking,'[3] declared Ransome to his mother, though a day later he was worrying that 'everybody will curse me for not letting the Swallows and Amazons be the principal characters'.[4] In fact, the Callums, who are staying for the first time at Dixon's farm and are strangers to both the countryside and to sailing, are not children to whom one immediately warms. They have the difficult task of winning acceptance from the reader as well as from the Swallows and Amazons. Dorothea, aged about eleven in *Winter Holiday*, is an aspiring author while Dick, a year younger, is more practical: a scientist, astronomer, ornithologist and

1. Diary entry for 28 January 1933, reproduced in *The Best of Childhood*, p. 85.
2. Letter to Edith Ransome, 3 March 1933, reproduced in Hugh Brogan, ed., *Signalling from Mars: The Letters of Arthur Ransome* (London: Jonathan Cape, 1997) p. 216.
3. Letter to Edith Ransome, 2 March 1933, reproduced in *Signalling from Mars*, p. 214.
4. Letter to Edith Ransome, 3 March 1933, reproduced in *Signalling from Mars*, p. 216.

budding engineer. Brogan suggests that the two characters represent two parts of Ransome's own make-up (the Callums' father is an academic, like Ransome's own father): the creative mind on the one hand and the practical, scientific mind on the other.[1]

Dorothea is a sensitive child, liked by the adults with whom she comes into contact, appreciative and without an ounce of malice in her body, but she is endlessly questioning herself and trying to make sense of the world by fixing it in the pages of a string of books that rarely get written; while life is frightening for its uncertainties, the plot of a novel, however sad, keeps everything under control. In *Winter Holiday*, Dorothea's changing stories are one of the main sources of amusement, not least because of their parody of the sickliest kind of melodrama, and because Dick, without meaning to, always succeeds in deflating her extravagant imagination. For example, when she is inspired by the old brown rowing boat hauled out above the landing-place at Dixon's Farm:

> 'They launched their trusty vessel, put out their oars, and rowed towards the mysterious island. No human foot had ever trod. . . .'
> 'Well, look,' said Dick. 'There's somebody coming now.'[2]

In later novels, Dorothea is sometimes used more specifically as a playful element of metafiction, an author of stories within stories into which the other characters are drawn, but in *Winter Holiday* her main role is to support and protect her younger brother.

In contrast, ten-year-old Dick, bespectacled and serious, is concerned only with things as they are. On their very first morning at the farm, Mrs Dixon counts the stairs out loud as she brings hot water for washing. When Dick hurries down to breakfast he automatically checks: '"There are twelve steps," said Dick, "she was quite right."'[3] In the same way, when he is trying to identify stars from the 'observatory' and asking Dorothea to read out their descriptions from his star book, where astronomy is strangely complemented by Tennyson's verse, he tells her to 'Skip the poetry'.[4] When the snow arrives and Dorothea immediately recalls snow-filled poems and stories, Dick prefers to examine the crystals under his microscope. But in spite of the differences, the bond

1. Hugh Brogan, *The Life of Arthur Ransome* (London: Hamish Hamilton, 1985), p. 332.
2. Arthur Ransome, *Winter Holiday* (London: Jonathan Cape, 1933). Red Fox edition (London: Random House, 1993), p. 4.
3. *WH*, p. 2.
4. *WH*, p. 15.

between them is as strong as it is unobtrusive. While the Swallows are bound by a hierarchical code and Peggy is dominated by her overbearing elder sister, Dorothea and Dick enjoy an often unspoken empathy. When they row for the first time their pride in themselves and each other needs no more than a look: 'They looked at each other . . . smiled faintly, but said never a word.'[1]

Like the Walkers in *Swallows and Amazons*, the Callums drink in the newness of their surroundings, though they see the same space through different eyes and their delight is not compromised by imperial ambitions. Used only to the roar of London traffic, they wake up to noises of the farmyard which are 'strange' and 'different'. When they take the path down to the lake shore, 'everything was new to them';[2] and when they discover the hilltop barn, which will become Dick's observatory and their signalling station, 'for the first time they saw the great ring of hills above the head of the lake'.[3] On the fourth day, it is as if they are also seeing snow for the first time: for Dorothea, 'There was a new world'.[4] At any rate, snow on the fells has a different effect from snow in the town, clothing the countryside in a sparkling white blanket:

> At home, in the town, Dorothea had seen snow more than once, where it lay for a few hours in the streets, growing grimier from the smoke, until it was swept into dirty heaps along the gutters. She had never seen anything like this.[5]

Soon, Dick is to see buzzards that until now he has only seen in a book.

But in this new winter playground, Dorothea and Dick realise that six children are there already and this spoils things for them. For Dorothea, what was the excitement of discovery turns into a sense of being left out when they discover that other children are there already and she and Dick are not included in whatever game they are playing. Later, she remembers 'a lonely morning'.[6] She becomes sulky when Dick discovers the farmhouse where he thinks the children are staying, and although she tries to change the subject their presence eats away at her. 'Perhaps we wouldn't like them if we knew them,' she says.[7]

---

1. *WH*, p. 94.
2. *WH*, p. 3.
3. *WH*, p. 11.
4. *WH*, p. 69.
5. *WH*, p. 70.
6. *WH*, p. 174.
7. *WH*, p. 13.

Strangers

Thus it is that the opening chapter of *Winter Holiday* is entitled 'Strangers' and Dorothea begins writing *The Outcasts*, a story that 'nobody would be able to read without tears'.[1] But while Dorothea feels that the other children exist in 'a different world', the more down-to-earth Dick invents his own game that might just bring them all together. Even if they are on another planet, it is worth signalling to them to see if there is a response. It is like 'signalling to Mars', and after a time signals are sent back by the aliens; ironically, from the Callums' point of view, it is the other children, not themselves, who are the interlopers.

Signalling is to become an important device in the novel, with the setting up of a signalling system between Dick's observatory at Dixon's farm and Holly Howe where the Swallows are again staying. The system was inspired by the one set up between Ransome at Low Ludderburn and his friend Colonel Kelsall at Barkbooth on the other side of the valley so that, without the luxury of telephones, they could plan their fishing expeditions (without the fish knowing what awaited them). There are diagrams of the hoisted shapes, the 'private code', semaphore, and another page from Dick's pocket book which mixes chemical formulae, his mother's birthday, and identification of planets. It is the stuff of those Schoolboys' Pocket Books beloved by generations of preparatory school boys. From the outset, signalling allows the established explorers to communicate with their new acquaintances and (symbolically) brings them together. Later it becomes crucial to the plot when Nancy semaphores instructions from her bedroom window and sends a coded message to the *Fram*, and when, at the novel's climax, there is the crucial and mistaken message: 'Flag on Beckfoot – Start for Pole'.[2] Today's readers, brought up with mobile phones, will wonder what it is all about.

The morning after contact has been established, the Swallows and Amazons meet up and Dorothea and Dick are at least drawn onto the fringes of Nancy's polar expedition. They have, it seems, led a solitary existence up to now, depending on each other for company. The previous day they were 'alone as usual', but now they are swept up by this lively band of sailors and explorers – or nearly. Susan, it seems, has reservations about the newcomers. She mocks them for using a newspaper to light a fire, and while they chatter happily with Titty and Roger, Dorothea overhears the always generous Nancy arguing for their inclusion. It must be Susan who asks the catty question:

1.   *WH*, p. 9.
2.   *WH*, p. 66.

4. The Martians in Sight

*The morning after contact has been established the Swallows and Amazons
meet up and Dorothea and Dick are at least drawn onto the fringes
of Nancy's polar expedition.*

'But what's *she* going to do?'
'We'll soon know if they're any good.'[1]

The Swallows, of course, are visitors to the Lake themselves, and no doubt feel similar to Dorothea: the Lake, and the friendship with the Amazons, is their preserve, and now it is threatened. Indeed, it is arguable that the Callums have a more substantial link with the Lake than the Swallows in that Mrs Dixon had long ago been Mrs Callum's nurse ('The very spit of your mother', she says to Dorothea).[2] More seriously for the Swallows, Ransome not only appears intent on removing them as the focus of the novel, but also finds a more jealous and selfish side to their previously untarnished natures.

When the Callums are invited to the Igloo, the old hut that has become the base camp for the expedition, Nancy insists that it is 'visitors first', but Dorothea and Dick are 'pushed aside' by the others; and when they go to fetch water from the waterfall Dorothea is desperate to be of use. As they make their way home that evening, it is Nancy, confident in her leadership, who suggests that Dorothea and Dick leave their mugs in the Igloo, as they will be part of the 'all' who will return tomorrow. Instead of having to invent yet another story as a refuge from life itself, Dorothea realises that they are now actually living in a story (though, alerted by *Peter Duck*, she should perhaps be told that really she is living in a story within a story).

After Dorothea and Dick have left, Ransome returns to the complex business of negotiating friendships. The Swallows and Amazons hold a Council to decide if the Callums should in fact become part of the expedition; and in spite of their ignorance of adventuring, even Susan admits it would be unkind to leave them out. It is hardly a ringing endorsement.

However, it is the skating on the frozen tarn in Chapter 5 ('Skating and the Alphabet') that goes some way towards settling things. Nancy and Peggy can get along in a clumsy sort of way; John and Susan have done a little skating at school; for Titty and Roger it is the first time. But Dorothea and Dick, with little else to do, have spent every day of the holidays practising at the indoor rink at home and are naturals. Like Ransome at the Old College, they win some respect: how can a polar team do without them?

---

1. *WH*, p. 40.
2. *WH*, p. 162.

Snow

'Softly, at first, as if it hardly meant it, the snow began to fall': the delicacy of the sentence displays Ransome's ability to create atmosphere in the simplest of ways. 'Softly' evokes not only the quietness – even the secrecy – of falling snow, but also its softness as, later, it will lie on the ground, while 'as if it hardly meant it' describes those first flakes drifting inconsequentially and deceptively from the sky – but it does mean it, and soon the landscape will be altered. It is with the coming of the snow that everything begins to change: 'Dorothea could almost feel Nancy stirring things up and filling the air with adventure.'[1]

The Igloo, until now no more than a derelict stone hut with a corrugated roof, becomes a 'real igloo in which any Eskimo would be pleased to live'.[2] As they eat the hotpot that Susan and Peggy have made, Mrs Blackett, aware of the underlying tensions, arrives to invite Dorothea and Dick to the Eskimo settlement at Beckfoot on the following day. We have met her briefly in *Swallowdale* when her liberal parenting is so criticised by the Great Aunt that she is reduced to tears, leaving the more conventional Mrs Walker, who always defers to her husband, to observe that her carefree approach 'certainly works with yours'.[3] Here Mrs Blackett is a homely figure, short and plump and warm, and, apart from her clear voice, quite unlike her elder daughter. But, an explorer in her youth, she is still game enough, perching on the bench by the fire as the others tuck into their lunch and uttering an endearing 'squeak' when she is taken home on a sledge at the end of the day. However, as well as drawing Dorothea and Dick further into the team of explorers, the point of her appearance is to renew the theme of circularity. She remembers the climbing of the Matterhorn – now Kanchenjunga – celebrated in *Swallowdale*, and how as a child, in the same frozen landscape, she and her friends also had hotpot for lunch. But her hotpot, sent down from Beckfoot, had been left on the ice while they skated and, leaving a clean hole, had sunk to the bottom of the lake.

The snow means that the Lake is going to freeze, making possible a trip to the North Pole across the ice, but the school holidays are coming to an end and the explorers will all be gone before the expedition can set off. Dorothea wishes that it wasn't all going to end so soon. But

---

1. *WH*, p. 72.
2. *WH*, p. 73.
3. Arthur Ransome, *Swallowdale* (London: Jonathan Cape, 1931). Red Fox edition (London: Random House, 1993), p. 494.

the next day, when they arrive at Beckfoot, she senses that somehow
they are not wanted after all. Captain Nancy, leader of the expedition,
has gone down with the mumps. There is no point in going ahead with
anything now.

But far from being downcast, it is Nancy who realises that mumps
is the best thing that could have happened. Each one of them will be
in quarantine for at least a month and so will not be allowed to return
to school when term starts. Their extended holiday means that when
the lake freezes they will be together after all. Although Nancy is now
unable to join in the fun, she can still direct operations in spite of her
comically bandaged face, and, not surprisingly, she will embellish their
polar game with ever new ideas.

The Cragfast Sheep

Some days later, after the clandestine visit to Beckfoot when Nancy
is able to semaphore from her bedroom window, the explorers are on
their way back from a training run across 'Greenland' that Nancy has
ordered. Dick, looking for a buzzard's nest high on a rock face, spots
a cragfast sheep trapped on a ledge and too weak to move. While the
three older children – who are taking their turn as 'dogs' hauling
the supply sledge – battle on, unaware of what is happening behind
them, the four younger members of the party go off to help. As Susan
remembers, it is reminiscent of the episode in *Swallowdale* when Titty
and Roger choose to walk home by themselves and the fog closes in. It
is fraught with equal danger.

Dick, the most unlikely hero, takes the initiative: as Dorothea says,
when he comes out of his dreams he can be 'more practical than anyone
else'.[1] Telling the others to go along the top of the ridge so that they
can hold him on a safety rope, he edges along the icy ledge, reasoning
to himself (as few ten-year-olds would) that:

> It isn't really harder than sitting on a chair. Scientifically speaking.
> The only thing that matters is to keep your Centre of Gravity on
> the right side of the ledge. . . . It'll be perfectly easy.[2]

Ransome builds the tension over five pages as Dick moves precariously
towards the sheep. The climax comes when he has to transfer the
safety rope to the helpless animal so that it can be lowered into the
gully. None of the others can help him now: 'This was something to be

---

1. *WH*, p. 139.
2. *WH*, p. 140.

settled between him and himself.'[1] Realising that something is amiss, the sledge party returns and John is there to receive the lowered sheep. His acknowledgement of Dick's heroism is characteristically unspoken: 'John said nothing about Dick's knot, but simply untied it, and, when Peggy had taken the sheep, made a new bowline loop at the end of the rope.'[2] Almost without our noticing, Dorothea and Dick, the Callums, become the 'D.'s'. When they return to Dixon's farm, Mr Dixon, whose sheep it is, comments simply: 'there's not many lads would go along that ledge.'[3] That night Mr Dixon and Silas build Dorothea and Dick their own sledge as reward, with the subsequent visit to the blacksmith's forge to craft the sledge's runners allowing the novel the opportunity to celebrate another rural skill.

Not only does the rescuing of the cragfast sheep help to cement Dick's acceptance by the Swallows (except, perhaps by Susan), but it is also the beginning of the strong bond which builds between Dick, the middle-class town boy, and the hitherto silent Mr Dixon whose life is restricted to the farm and the Lake, but who is steeped in kindness and not without imagination. In his own way, Mr Dixon becomes as keen on the expedition to the North Pole as anyone. One day he provides Dick with goose grease for their boots; on another he gives them furs. When Dick decides that the sledge will need a sail to keep up with the others, Mr Dixon finds a larch pole for the mast. He pores over the sketches Dick has made of Nansen's sledge, and between them they plan how the mast will be fixed. Mrs Dixon has never seen her husband like this. The children may not be competing in a race to the 'Pole', but 'he didn't see why the explorers settled at Jackson's should do any better than those lodging with himself'.[4]

Nansen and the *Fram*

Nancy's most gorgeous idea comes when she learns that Captain Flint's houseboat is trapped in the ice and she sends the cabin key to the explorers with the single word 'Fram' attached. *Fram* was the ship in which Fridtjof Nansen, the Norwegian explorer, attempted unsuccessfully to reach the North Pole in 1893-1896 by using the East–West current to drift with the pack ice towards the Pole and then to Greenland and Spitzbergen (both feature in *Winter Holiday*, but as

1. *WH*, p. 146.
2. *WH*, p. 152.
3. *WH*, p. 158.
4. *WH*, p. 164.

training grounds). In his *Autobiography*, Ransome numbers Nansen as one of his heroes and tells of several conversations with him in Latvia in 1921. Nansen recounts his Arctic experiences in *The First Crossing of Greenland* (1890) and *Farthest North* (1898), which are conveniently nestling on the shelves of the houseboat. With Captain Flint away, it is Nancy's plan that the houseboat should become the *Fram* of their own polar expedition, and after some misgivings the explorers leave the Igloo behind and make the ship their base. As well as the further excitements which it affords, the foregrounding of the *Fram* serves as a metaphor to link the children's expedition with the colonial quests and conquests of the Victorian and Edwardian eras.

Days on the *Fram* pass quickly enough as ice encroaches further across the Lake. Dorothea is asked to tell stories, though she always gets it wrong when she tells stories of the sea and brings upon herself an uproar of corrections. Dressing up becomes part of the game: Mr Dixon lets Dorothea and Dick help themselves to sheepskins which are spread on the *Fram*'s bunks and floor to give a more Arctic effect and Silas, the farmhand, provides rabbit skins which are sewn into suitable hats and mittens. On one of the expeditions to the far North they leave a message in a bottle under a cairn of stones, just as in *Swallowdale* they left a message at Kanchenjunga's summit. In Nansen's books they discover pictures of sledges under sail; John finds the remainder of *Swallow*'s broken mast from *Swallowdale* and steps it on the Beckfoot sledge – with catastrophic results when they attempt to come about. Dick's briefest of dispatches to Nancy sums it all up; the *Fram* is ten thousand times better than the Igloo:

$$Fram : \text{Igloo} :: 10{,}000 : 1^{1}$$

Then, via the doctor who is engaged by his patient as an unwilling messenger, Nancy sends a cryptic picture. It takes the explorers some time to decode the back-to-front semaphore message – 'Who is sleeping in the *Fram*?' – and more time to understand that the question is in fact an instruction: the explorers should be spending their nights afloat as well as their days.[2] Three things happen as a result: first – and uncharacteristically for children who are so morally upright – John, Susan and Peggy agree that without telling the Jacksons, Titty, or Roger, they will decamp secretly from Holly Howe by night. But once on board, John and Susan have second thoughts. What would their mother say? How could they leave the younger ones alone? Without

---

1. *WH*, p. 202.
2. *WH*, p. 222.

even waiting for the kettle to boil, they start back to Holly Howe, only
to meet Titty and Roger who have discovered their absence. It is the
first time that we have seen John and Susan abandon their siblings;
perhaps the tight-knit family and the childhood idyll are coming to
an end.

Secondly, and not wanting to let Nancy down, Peggy suggests the
next morning that Dorothea and Dick should sleep on the *Fram* instead.
This, it seems, is real acceptance. 'You're part of the expedition. Nancy
said so,' says Peggy. Dorothea 'had never hoped for such an honour'.[1]
But John and Susan, somehow feeling usurped, are hardly enthusiastic
at the prospect. Susan says unkindly: 'Look here, Dorothea. . . . But
how are you going to manage about the Primus?'[2] And when Titty
and Roger ask to stay with the D.'s, her frustration and resentment is
clear: 'No, you can't. . . . It's because of you that we can't either.'[3] Nancy,
though, is astonished and delighted at the outcome. Dorothea and Dick
are not just townies to be let into the game out of politeness. There is
more to them after all:

> But those two town children from Dixon's Farm, sleeping in the
> houseboat by themselves. Good for the D.'s. She had not thought
> they had it in them. Well done, Dick and Dorothea![4]

Thirdly, and before Dorothea and Dick have had time to have tea by
themselves on the *Fram*, Captain Flint returns to his houseboat, lured
by the weather and the prospect of skating on the Lake. It leads to a
sparkling comic encounter with Dorothea and Dick who are settling
themselves in for their night aboard (Dorothea is convinced Captain
Flint is a Dutchman with a case full of tulip bulbs and she is already
planning a new story of *Skates and Tulips*). From here on Captain Flint
is in league with Nancy in planning the final assault on the 'North Pole',
leading some critics to complain that his 'native' interference detracts
from the child-centred game.

It is Nancy hoisting a flag at Beckfoot to announce the end of her
illness that begins one of the most dramatic episodes of all the *Swallows
and Amazons* novels. Dick's meticulous notes, made nearly a month before
and forgotten by Nancy, show that the flag is a signal to 'Start for Pole'.
Believing that they have somehow been left behind, Dorothea and Dick
hurriedly load up their sledge and skate off on their journey northwards.

1. *WH*, p. 249.
2. *WH*, p. 251.
3. *WH*, p. 251.
4. *WH*, p. 262.

They hardly notice the blizzard rushing up behind them, hardly notice the crowds of merrymakers turning and leaving the ice. Or if they do notice, they do not understand the danger that awaits. In fact, Dick is delighted that there will now be a wind and hoists sail on the sledge; they scramble aboard and race towards their goal. There are moments here that prefigure the storm in *We Didn't Mean to Go to Sea*: 'Dick clung on, blind but happy.' Dorothea 'knew that she was afraid' and, as Susan will do that summer in *Goblin*, shakes Dick's shoulder: "'Let's stop!" she cried. "Now! At once!"'[1] But Dick is adamant: 'We can't go back. . . . We can't help coming somewhere if we go on.'[2] Then the sledge capsizes and the mast breaks. Roping himself to Dorothea and the sledge, Dick disappears into the storm to search for civilisation and safety, and glimpses a house through the gloom. It turns out to be no more than a summer house shut up for the winter, but by happy chance they have managed to sail to the top of the Lake and this is the 'Pole' itself. Their relief is tempered by the realisation that the others haven't arrived. Dorothea wants even more to go back, but Dick knows it would make matters worse. Life, Dorothea realises, isn't as easy as fiction: 'It was not like one of her own stories, in which it was easy to twist things another way or go back a page or two and start again if anything had gone badly.'[3] It is a nice irony that life here is itself a fiction and Dorothea is in the safe hands of the author.

Meanwhile, the 'Council' has met as planned in the *Fram*, with no one understanding why the D.'s have set off a day early. But the perils are obvious and what is now the Relief Expedition sets off in pursuit. Susan, who underneath is still resentful of Dorothea and Dick and scornful of the urban life that they represent, cannot contain her anger:

'If only they had any sense,' said Susan. 'But they haven't got any, not that sort. People oughtn't to be allowed to be brought up in towns.'[4]

John, too, though sympathetic, fears for the lost D.'s:

He thought of Dorothea, a little town girl, not tough like themselves, out all day in that blinding storm. He thought of Dick, who was full of good ideas but was nearly always thinking of the wrong one.[5]

---

1. *WH*, p. 343.
2. *WH*, p. 344.
3. *WH*, p. 378.
4. *WH*, p. 362.
5. *WH*, p. 367.

Fortunately, Ransome, like Dorothea, knows that in fiction it is easy to put things right if anything is going badly, and one by one the cast gathers at the North Pole: Nancy, who has seen Dick's Morse code signalling with the lantern; the Relief Expedition, who at first silently blame Dorothea and Dick for all the trouble, and 'have very little to say to the D.'s',[1] but after Nancy explains and recounts their epic voyage through the blizzard seem finally to accept that 'Dick was more than a mere astronomer';[2] and Captain Flint, who, having picked up Nancy's scribbled North Pole message and raced round standing down the search parties he has sent out, has arrived with Mrs Blackett while the children are sunk in exhausted sleep. It is all 'dreadful but splendid', thinks Dorothea.[3] Then as she begins to turn the night's excitements into yet another gruesome story within a story, she is brought back to reality by Mrs Blackett reminding them of school and asking for two lumps of sugar in her tea. Everything has worked out after all.

Those who complain about Captain Flint's involvement with Nancy in these final chapters probably miss the point. It may be that he is not being wholly truthful when he claims to have been 'nothing but a beast of burden' organising the welcoming supplies at the North Pole, but if he has tried to curb Nancy's wilder ambitions, the Swallows, Amazons and D.'s have nevertheless contrived to escape from what might have been a dull 'native' game. Susan, already a 'native' in spite of her young age, worries that they may all be too tired to do things properly on the following day, but Nancy joyously puts her right:

> 'That's the best of it. Now you're here there's no need to do it again. We've done it. We've all of us done it. This is miles better than anything we planned. . . . Sailing to the Pole in a gale of wind and a snow-storm.'[4]

*

In spite of its tenuous plot, *Winter Holiday* is arguably the most accomplished of Ransome's Lake novels. After the pirate games of *Swallows and Amazons* and *Swallowdale*, and the darker pirate fantasy of *Peter Duck*, the polar expedition offers a welcome new direction. The crisp winter setting is evoked by the lightest of touches in a multitude of finely judged descriptions. There is a rich seam of humour mined

1. *WH*, p. 385.
2. *WH*, p. 386.
3. *WH*, p. 394.
4. *WH*, p. 386.

from Nancy's joyful manipulation of the whole proceedings, and from Peggy's not always successful attempts to shiver her timbers and barbecue billygoats when for the only time in the series she is allowed to step just a little out from the shadow of her irrepressible sister. The characters of Mr and Mrs Dixon are sketched in more firmly, while the Swallows – eighteen months older than when we first met them – do not quite enjoy the too-good-to-be-true cohesion that we have seen before. The introduction of Dorothea and Dick is skilfully handled: neither as wild as the Amazons, nor as upright and self-confident as the Swallows, they depend heavily on each other but are forced to look outwards and earn the respect and friendship of their peers and of the series reader. Susan in particular doesn't make it easy for them, and the tensions which the novel explores reveal all the members of the cast as rounder and more complex figures than we have seen before. For me, though, Dick and Dorothea's hurtling through the blizzard, scared and courageous, is one of the high points of the series, only surpassed by Titty's dowsing (in *Pigeon Post*) and the Swallows' unforgettable battle with the North Sea storm the following summer.

5.

Coot Club:
'In the Cider Press'

The first chapter of *Coot Club* (1934) sets the lightly comic mood for the rest of the novel. It is a few months after *Winter Holiday* and Dorothea and Dick Callum, the D.'s, are joining Mrs (Admiral) Barrable, a retired school teacher 'who painted pictures', for a holiday on her sailing yacht *Teasel* on the Norfolk Broads.[1] Their train reaches a terminus in Norwich, but the engine is changed and still it goes on, taking them even further from their urban life into this unspoilt corner of England. Tom Dudgeon, late for the already moving train and outrunning the pursuing porter, throws his paint and rope through the open carriage window and then flings himself in. There is a gently amusing touch when the 'proper' Dorothea and Dick shut the door: 'Dorothea pulled the door to. Dick said: "They always like it shut," and reached out and closed the handle.'[2] It is clear at once that Tom, the central character of the novel, is very different from the Swallows and Amazons: a carefree Norfolk native, he is a capable, self-effacing boy with a sense of mischief. He has spent his childhood on the river and enjoys it for its own sake; he is 'more of a sailor even than John or Nancy' and is reluctant to play games.[3] Both Dorothea and Dick notice his hands, 'that looked so capable and hard-worked that Dick, at the sight of them, wanted to hide his own'.[4]

Dorothea and Dick are amazed at the number of boats. At Thorpe they see 'a steamer going down from Norwich' and 'crowds of yachts and motor boats tied up under the gardens'.[5] At Wroxham:

---

1. Arthur Ransome, *Coot Club*, (London: Jonathan Cape, 1934). Red Fox edition (London: Random House, 2001), p. 8.
2. *CC*, p. 5.
3. *CC*, p. 4.
4. *CC*, p. 5.
5. *CC*, p. 6.

There were boats everywhere, and boats of all kinds, from the
big black wherry with her gaily painted mast, loading at the old
Granary by Wroxham bridge, and meant for nothing but hard
work, to the punts of the boatmen going to and fro, and the motor-
cruisers filling up with petrol, and the hundreds of big and little
sailing yachts tied to the quays, or moored in rows, two and three
deep, in the dykes and artificial harbours beside the main river.[1]

'And . . . and . . . and': this long, breathless, bustling sentence, in which
the working boats and pleasure craft jostle with each other, creates
all the excitement and brio of a village that, for better or worse, is
turning itself into a holiday destination.[2] But Mrs Barrable knows that
in summer Wroxham is fast becoming overrun by tourists and 'must be
like a fairground'.[3] Somewhere among this confusion the Hullabaloos, a
rowdy party of urban pleasure-seekers, are also starting their holiday
aboard the motor cruiser *Margoletta*.

Laying the Foundations

Coot Club, like *Swallowdale*, is a celebration of the English countryside,
though here it is more immediately under threat than it is on the Lake
in the North and the busyness and buzz that are evident in the opening
pages are very different from the laidback Cumbrian landscape. In this
chapter, I will focus on how the novel defends a rural way of life which
is endangered by so-called progress and encroaching urbanisation. I
will also consider further Ransome's narrative technique. He struggled
to find a plot for *Coot Club*, but the account of that struggle in his
letters and notes gives a further insight into his creative process.

Although it had been Ransome's intention to 'build up a regular row
of these books',[4] the pressure from Jonathan Cape to produce a novel
each year for the Christmas market began to take its toll. He had been
advised that his debilitating stomach complaints were caused largely

---

1. *CC*, p. 12.
2. Harry Blake published his first brochure for the hire of leisure craft in
   1908. By the 1930s tourism on the Norfolk Broads was growing strongly
   and the inhabitants of this unspoilt part of England were suspicious of
   the increasing number of seasonal visitors who were encroaching on their
   previously undisturbed way of life.
3. *CC*, p. 13.
4. Letter of 12 January 1931 to Ernestine Evans, reproduced in Hugh Brogan,
   ed., *Signalling from Mars: The Letters of Arthur Ransome* (London: Jonathan
   Cape, 1997), pp. 180-83.

by the pressure of newspaper deadlines, but now the pressure of publishing deadlines was affecting him in the same way. He had found it difficult to complete *Winter Holiday* on time and to the standard that he (and the always critical Evgenia) expected, but even before it was published, Cape's treadmill meant that he was having to formulate the plot for the following Christmas's book. In *Peter Duck* he had taken the Swallows and Amazons to sea because he felt he had exhausted the possibilities of the Lake in the North, and while he had returned there with *Winter Holiday*, it was to a changed frozen landscape and with the introduction of new characters in the D.'s. Now it was definitely time to leave the Lake and find a new setting and a new cast.

As a young man Ransome had enjoyed one or two fishing expeditions in Norfolk and as early as December 1933 he wrote to his mother that his next book would be set on the Broads and 'had been working up for 2 or 3 years now'.[1] The catalyst was a holiday in the spring of 1931 when he and Evgenia hired a 20-foot yacht, the *Welcome*, from Jack Powles of Wroxham (probably the model for Rodley's in *Coot Club*), and he loved the place. They made a further visit in April 1933 when they chartered a new *Fairway* yacht from Powles. That September, after completing the illustrations for *Winter Holiday*, Ransome embarked on a Norfolk fishing holiday with his close friend Charles Renold (this time hiring a motor cruiser from Herbert Woods of Potter Heigham), doubtless searching for further inspiration as he cast his line. However, the expedition was cut short when Ransome was struck down by acute appendicitis and only an emergency operation in Norwich saved his life. After two months' recuperation at the King's Head Hotel overlooking the river in Wroxham, he and Evgenia took rooms in the Old Watch House on the quay of the Cornish fishing village of St Mawes.

The main characters Ransome envisaged at this stage – a 'principal boy and main thread of tale', 'two small girls, twins', 'two other girls contrasting with the twins by being generally proper careful gentle creatures but quite all right inside', and an 'admirable old lady in houseboat' – were rather too female a collection for his established readership of mainly boys.[2] However, he still had no idea for a plot, and it is notable that in his letter of 8 December 1933 to Margaret Renold he dismisses her initial ideas for a story which involved a 'mysterious

---

1. Letter of 7 December 1933 to Edith Ransome, reproduced in Roger Wardale et al., eds, *The Best of Childhood* (Kendal: Amazon Publications, 2004), p. 127.
2. Letter of 3 December 1933 to Margaret Renold, reproduced in *The Best of Childhood*, pp. 126-27.

cruiser'. His starting point was a different one: 'the essential point of
a plot is the change of relationship between the characters. . . . The
story such as it is puts into the concrete one after another of a series
of different relationships'.[1]

A working note, written during the Ransomes' stay in St Mawes,
also shows that even without a plot he had begun to settle on incidents
for the novel:

> Boy in canoe approaches ?houseboat ?yacht? with someone on
> board (assuming that someone is known to him, as the owner is).
> Collars a heavy anchor weight, puts [it] in his canoe, sinks the
> canoe close by the moored yacht, and himself hides among the
> reeds on shore. Pursuing motor boat turns up, and inhabitant of
> yacht, willy nilly, makes accomplice.[2]

Further incidents, though still no plot, are revealed in a detailed letter
written on 28 December 1933 to the Renolds:

> I am still putting myself daily in a cider press and trying to
> squeeze out a plot. I have masses of things to happen . . . stranding
> on Breydon . . . voyage in a wherry . . . meeting with a Thames
> barge . . . shopping at Roys . . . night with an eel man. . . . But main
> thread still to find.[3]

A later working note, probably written at the beginning of January
1934, lists further incidents: 'the boy Proper (?Dick) goes overboard
quanting' (note how at least one of the 'Propers' has become a boy);
the 'education of Propers preparatory to Grandmother's plan of
sailing round to ?Beccles or Norwich'; and Tom's hiding under the sail
in *Titmouse* in order to escape from the Hullabaloos.[4] After working
on a few opening pages, Ransome set the book aside until the end of
February, when he drafted (among other things) part of the eventual
ending: the stranding of *Teasel* and *Titmouse* on Breydon Water, and
William's heroism in carrying a rope between them. These extracts
illustrate Nancy's complaint in the discarded opening of *Peter Duck*

---

1. Letter of 8 December 1933 to Margaret Renold, reproduced in *The Best of
   Childhood*, pp. 127-28.
2. Reproduced in *The Best of Childhood*, pp. 125-26.
3. Letter of 28 December 1933 to Charles and Margaret Renold, reproduced in
   The Best of Childhood, p. 129. 'Roys', a large department store in Wroxham,
   still exists, dominating the town and claiming to be 'the largest village store in
   the world'. The 'night with an eel man' was eventually saved for *The Big Six*.
4. Reproduced in *The Best of Childhood*, p. 132.

that it was often Ransome's practice to start by writing about incidents, in no particular order, and only afterwards to settle on the narrative thread that would bind them together.

The letter of 28 December to the Renolds also shows that by now Ransome has firmed up on the 'principal boy' who lives in Horning, on 'the pair of twins, girls, who sail with their father, on 'a most spirited old lady, widow, water-colour painter, living in ?boat or ?houseboat?', and on the two 'well-brought-ups' who need to be imbued with a 'livelier spirit' by the Norfolk natives. He considers whether these gentle urban children should be Dorothea and Dick from *Winter Holiday*, but at this stage decides against it.

As far as the plot is concerned, the same letter introduces the idea of the twins chasing the chief character throughout the Broads using other people's boats (so allowing him to describe the East Anglian countryside and the 'wherries, tugs, barges' which had caught his attention). However, he worries that this would make the twins the chief characters and would draw attention away 'from the PB and the Well-brought-ups'. So he needs:

> some major Triumph, Goal, Aim, Achievement . . . which will be shared by the whole party, and allow the PB a chance of coming out strong, so that the chase etc., while giving the Twins a fine chance of spreading themselves and capturing the reader, will be, as it were subservient to the whole . . . or even work as a fuse, delaying, and therefore piling up the interest of the main theme.

In the event, of course, it is the chasing of Tom by the Hullabaloos which provides the main plot and 'the happy ending that must almost to the end look as if it can't come off', with the parallel action of the twins' escapades working as a delaying 'fuse'.

We are also let into other 'secrets of the cider press': not to concentrate 'the whole interest in ONE character' but to have 'a combination of collective interest and a fair share of the game for all the individuals, girls and boys. Sordid grasp at as wide an audience as possible'; and the importance of having 'one or more characters definitely younger than the rest. . . . Shove in a brat, and the rest gain independence at once'. But perhaps the real insight is into how Ransome saw the construction of a novel to be akin to engineering and the necessity for 'the calculations of comparative weights, stresses, tensions, etc.'. His skill is that the carefully-built structure of his novels is rarely intrusive, although much later Evgenia was to accuse him of writing to a pattern. This will be one of the focuses of Chapter 11.

But the 'cider press' at last did its job and on 6 March Ransome was able to write a very full synopsis of *Coot Club*. By the end of the month, after a binge of creativity, he had completed 168 pages. His initial plan was to make *Coot Club* entirely independent of the Lake novels, but – somewhat reluctantly and taking Evgenia's advice – he eventually decided instead to exchange the 'Propers' for Dorothea and Dick. This was an important choice, both artistically and commercially, that was to bind the two Norfolk Broads novels into the *Swallows and Amazons* series (the Norfolk characters of Peter Duck and Bill were never to reappear). He also introduced the three young boat-builders' sons – Joe, Bill, and Pete – the balancing male characters who, as the piratical 'Death and Glories' patrol the nests, organise the unreliable network of spies whom they bribe to report on the progress of the *Margoletta*, and in the climax arrive just in time to tow the sinking cruiser to the comparative safety of shallow water; in doing so they decide to give up their game of pirates and become salvage merchants instead. In their old ship's boat with its stumpy mast and raggedy sail, and with their 'bright coloured handkerchiefs round their heads and middles as turbans and belts', not to mention Pete's enormous telescope, they echo the Amazon pirates of the North and Ransome takes a similar delight in them.[1] However, they are younger than Nancy and Peggy, and less self-conscious about the pirate game they are playing; certainly they have no thoughts of war. Ironically, in fact, they are on the side of law: they have been brought up with the strict morality of their social class and their task is to protect their river and its wildlife against the real 'pirates', the Hullabaloos. Although the Death and Glories are from boat-builders' families, they are treated as equals by Tom and the twins, allowing *Coot Club* to break free from the middle-class strait-jacket which, in spite of Ransome's protests to the contrary, is a potential weakness of much of the rest of the series. In the first half of the novel, on the Northern rivers, the Death and Glories provide much of the exuberance and humour.

During April 1934 the Ransomes spent three weeks on the Norfolk Broads, typically following the eventual voyage of the *Teasel* to check the factual details and to take photographs on which to base his illustrations. Unlike in the Lake District novels, where Ransome takes liberties with the landscape, the settings of *Coot Club* are entirely real (with the exception of the Dudgeons' house, which seems never to have existed). The novel was continued over the summer and the second draft was finished on 1 September. On 3 September 1934, a pessimistic

---

1. *CC*, p. 21.

Ransome (further depressed by Evgenia's usual damning judgement) declared that the whole thing was 'bilge' and wrote to Wren Howard at Cape's postponing publication; but persuasion, flattery, and common sense prevailed and to Wren Howard's relief the book was produced on schedule and in time for the Christmas market.

Hullabaloos

The Coot Club centres on six children from the Broads village of Horning – Tom Dudgeon, Port and Starboard, and the three 'Death and Glories'. It is April, and a coot's nest which they have been watching and protecting is threatened by the *Margoletta*, which has moored in front of it, preventing the return of the mother coot to her eggs. The Hullabaloos refuse to move, so to save the eggs Tom breaks the unwritten law that locals should not get mixed up with 'foreigners' and casts the *Margoletta* adrift. He escapes the Hullabaloos' anger by taking refuge aboard the *Teasel*, the yacht occupied by Admiral Barrable and her novice crew, Dorothea and Dick. But the enraged Hullabaloos are not to be denied revenge and *Coot Club* is largely the story of their pursuit of Tom and the *Teasel* along most of the Broads rivers.

The *Margoletta*, with its blaring gramophones and the constantly arguing Hullabaloos who have no care for the countryside or its inhabitants, represents all that Ransome despised in contemporary mores. Although the apparent thrust of *Coot Club* is about the danger to the Broadland community from tourists, this is a metaphor for the destruction of the idyll of rural England by an urban population insensitive to its traditional values. Without the Swallows there is none of the colonial imagery of *Swallows and Amazons, Swallowdale, Peter Duck*, and *Winter Holiday*, and the dangerous worlds of *Robinson Crusoe* and *Treasure Island* have been replaced by the safer surroundings of East Anglia; but the repeated description of holidaymakers as 'foreigners' suggests again the wider symbolism of England under threat from the gathering storm on the European continent.

Dorothea as Novelist

Like *Peter Duck, Coot Club* is divided into two 'books'. In the first, set on the northern rivers of the Broads, the main interest lies in the *Margoletta*'s pursuit of the *Teasel*; at the same time the twins, Port and Starboard, teach Dorothea and Dick to sail in readiness for a cruise to the southern Broads so the Admiral can revisit Beccles, the Suffolk

town where she was born. This is the start of the education that will
change the D.'s from 'proper' children to accomplished sailors who will
eventually earn the respect of their nautical friends on the Lake. The
plot squeezed out of the 'cider press' is essentially a tame one, even by
Ransome's standards, but Dorothea, the aspiring novelist 'whose mind
was always busy with scenes that might do for the books she meant to
write', focalises the action (in the way that Titty has mainly done in the
earlier Lake novels) and transforms the novel into a comic melodrama,
with Tom as the 'outlaw of the Broads'.[1] So in Chapter 9, 'The Making
of an Outlaw', when Tom first hides from the *Margoletta* in the reeds,
Dorothea says of the Broad at Ranworth: 'Anybody could be an outlaw
hidden in here for weeks and weeks while people were hunting for him
outside';[2] and that evening, 'far away, at the edge of the marshes . . . the
watchers saw the glimmer of the outlaw's lonely light'.[3] The nicely
down-to-earth Tom finds 'all this romance . . . rather puzzling':

> Somehow this Dorothea, and even Port and Starboard, who were
> Norfolk Coots and usually as practical as himself, were talking of
> his misfortune as if it were some kind of exciting story.[4]

The effect of using Dorothea as a disguised narrator is twofold. First,
through her exaggerations, it highlights the 'proper' Dorothea as a
comic character, setting her apart from the more practical Norfolk
Coots who silently despair of her. In a similar way, her bespectacled
brother, forever in another place as he watches birds and makes endless
notes about them, remains an unworldly professor – though in both
cases the comedy is sympathetic and there is none of the reserve of
the Swallows in *Winter Holiday*. Secondly, by reporting and rewriting
much of the action through the eyes of Dorothea, Ransome's implied
omniscient author is able to create credible excitement and suspense
out of inconsequential circumstance. For the most part, the omniscient
author adopts in his turn Dorothea's romantic viewpoint and language
– for example with the posting of the dramatic 'REWARD' notice
on the Horning staithe and the dawn escape from the *Margoletta* at
Potter Heigham – thus drawing the reader willingly into what is a most
unlikely adventure.

Much of the enjoyment of *Coot Club* comes through Dorothea's highlighting of the contrast between the world of childhood make-believe

---

1. *CC*, p. 3.
2. *CC*, p. 115.
3. *CC*, p. 117.
4. *CC*, p. 116.

5. On Horning Staithe

For the most part the omniscient author adopts Dorothea's romantic viewpoint and language – for example with the posting of the dramatic 'REWARD' notice on the Horning staithe.

and the real world in which the novel is rooted. It is the same contrast noted in the differing viewpoints of the romantic Titty and the down-to-earth Susan in *Swallows and Amazons*. And, as in *Winter Holiday*, it is Dorothea who is again aware of the collision of the different worlds:

> Dorothea was seeing picture after picture of failure or success. In some the twins were in time to warn the outlaw, and all three of them hid somewhere in the reeds and watched the enemy go by. In others they were too late and the Hullabaloos met Tom all unsuspecting and had him at their mercy. That was the worst of it. When things went well, it was the outlaw, the romantic figure of a tale, who escaped triumphantly; but when things went wrong it was just Tom himself who was captured, Tom, the skipper of the *Teasel* and the *Titmouse*. Tom, who was teaching them how to sail. And Tom's misfortunes were far harder to bear than those of any hero of a story.[1]

In looking at this example of Dorothea 'transfiguring fact' it is clear that although Ransome again creates a disguised narrator within the story, in this playful metafiction she is hardly disguised at all. When Tom slips out of his role as the hero of Dorothea's novel and becomes 'himself', he nevertheless remains Ransome's fictional hero and his down-to-earth reality is itself an illusion.

The collision between the make-believe and real worlds is also highlighted by the good sense and natural fear of Mrs Dudgeon. When Dorothea reports frantically that the Hullabaloos are about to discover Tom, Mrs Dudgeon, a little naïvely, does 'not seem at all disturbed': 'I don't think you need worry about those people. They'll have forgotten all about him by now'.[2] But later, when it seems to the Coots that Tom has actually been captured, she is alarmed not by the children's game, which is trivialised by Dorothea's overblown imagination, but by real danger:

> 'They've got him,' said Dorothea wretchedly. She was on the very edge of tears. 'They've got him. We were too late. I knew we would be. And now they've got him. . . .' She saw Tom a prisoner, in chains probably, locked up, anyhow . . . bread and water . . . the captive outlaw . . . Tom!
>
> But Mrs Dudgeon was seeing something far worse. There was Tom's boat, a halyard flapping loose about the mast, Tom's boat,

---

1. *CC*, p. 193.
2. *CC*, p. 141.

towed by the twins . . . towed. . . . But where was Tom? . . . Those dreadful squalls over the marshes. . . . Small boats do capsize so easily . . . He could swim. . . . Water-weeds. . . . Cramp. . . . No one could ever be sure.[1]

Here Mrs Dudgeon suffers the anxiety that the liberal parents of the *Swallows and Amazons* novels must face: their faith in their children not to be 'duffers' will always be tinged by the knowledge of what could happen when they are left to fend for themselves.

Parents

So we return to the exploration of the relationship between children and parents: fathers, mothers and substitutes, present and absent. In the opening chapters Tom benefits from the reassuring presence of Dr Dudgeon, the respected village doctor. When he returns home after casting the *Margoletta* adrift, he is relieved to see his father sitting smoking at the water's edge. The saving of the coot's eggs is seen in human terms as the male's duty to protect the family:

'Look here, dad, what would you do if the only way to get to our baby was up this dyke, and you and me were all on the other side of the river, and a huge motor-cruiser was fixed right across the opening of the dyke . . . and we knew that if we didn't get to him soon he'd go and die?'[2]

But there is never a real closeness between Tom and his father (who is a fisherman, not a sailor, highlighted by the golden bream on his weather-vane). Dr Dudgeon's main concern is that Tom should not get caught by the Hullabaloos, with the inevitable damage to his own reputation ('I'll be very much obliged to you if you can manage not to let those rowdies catch you.').[3] Thus, at the end of the novel, Tom's fear of capture is not for himself but for the shame it will bring on his father. It is a reminder both of John's determination in the Lake District novels not to let his father down and of Ransome's own sense that he had failed to meet his father's expectations:

With every yard they made down Breydon they were nearer to the moment when the Hullabaloos would have to know whose son it was that had cast off their moorings and sent them

1. *CC*, p. 157.
2. *CC*, p. 78.
3. *CC*, p. 79.

drifting down the river. His father had told him to keep out
of their way, and now there they were, all being towed down
Breydon together.[1]

The Dudgeon household also provides comic reference to Ransome's
recent medical problems. Dr Dudgeon's patients are happily described
as victims and 'he may have to run into Norwich about some man with
a stomach-ache who thinks appendicitis would sound better'.[2]

However, like John in *Swallows and Amazons*, Tom is growing up
and beginning to take responsibility: his infant brother is referred to
throughout as 'our baby', and aboard the *Teasel* the Admiral defers to his
experience and skill. In negotiating the bridges at Acle and Yarmouth,
and in his deft handling of the yacht in the storm on Oulton Broad,
he proves both his maturity and his seamanship. The one time that the
Admiral ignores his instruction, disaster ensues. So, like Captain Flint
(and, later, Jim Brading in *We Didn't Mean to Go to Sea*), she fails as a
substitute parent. It is arguable that the presence of 'the Admiral' on the
Teasel throughout the novel is a weakness, since the children never feel
independent of the adult world (as they do in the other Lake District
and East Anglian novels); indeed, Ransome's original title for the novel
was 'The Web-footed Grandmother'. But the fact that she relies on the
children (and when she ignores them is nearly the cause of disaster), rather
than the other way about, only shows how capable they are.

Mr Farland, father of Port and Starboard, and a widower, is another
respected local, but he plays little part here. In a reversal of parent/
child roles, Port and Starboard have made it their 'daily business to see
that he went off with tidy hat and gloves to spend the day as a solicitor'.[3]
Moreover, they display their total loyalty towards him (though he is
blind to it) by foregoing a holiday voyage in the *Teasel* so that they can
crew for him in the sailing club races. Not only is there a contrast here
between Mr Farland's tidy professional life and the more natural life of
his daughters on the river, but there is also an echo of Ransome's fierce
and protective loyalty to his mother after the death of his own father.

Parallel Narratives

After the dawn escape from Potter Heigham, and with the possibilities
of the Hullabaloos' hunt for Tom almost exhausted, 'Book 2' of *Coot
Club* focuses on the cruise of the *Teasel* to the southern Broads, giving

---

1. *CC*, p. 395.
2. *CC*, p. 29.
3. *CC*, p. 82.

it an almost linear structure: Peter Hunt observes that, 'The very shape of the Broads – slowly flowing, winding rivers – seems to involve people more than the static, wide reaches of the Lake District in the North'.[1] For Dorothea, this cruise becomes the story of the Admiral's return to her birthplace at Beccles, and she rather grandly borrows Thomas Hardy's title, *The Return of the Native*. But even she finds it difficult to inject much excitement and for the reader the main interest lies in the descriptions of the East Anglian wetlands and in the simultaneous attempt of Port and Starboard to re-join the *Teasel* after it is no longer necessary for them to crew for their father in the Horning sailing race. So there are two parallel narratives (interconnected by the characters' expression of their concern for each other) which alternate through Chapters 16 to 22. In the first narrative, describing the cruise of the *Teasel*, the highlights of the action are Tom's skilful navigation through the bridges at Acle and (more dangerously) Great Yarmouth, followed by the long evening cruise across Breydon Water and along the River Waveney. With the *Margoletta* temporarily forgotten, there is time to dwell more on the Norfolk surroundings, seen either through the eyes of Dick as another disguised narrator (who, like the Swallows in *Swallows and Amazons*, and Dorothea and him in *Winter Holiday*, is experiencing everything for the first time):

> 'I say,' cried Dick suddenly. 'Isn't that a spoonbill, there, with hunched-up shoulders, and another, dipping in the mud where that trickle is? . . . White, like storks.'[2]

Or through the omniscient author:

> The *Teasel* sailed on up the broad channel of Breydon Water. The rising tide was spreading farther and farther over the mudflats on either side. Herons were stalking about knee-deep far away by the embankment. One rested for a moment on the top of a red post and then, as the *Teasel* came nearer, floated away with steady flaps of its long wings and a sharp indignant squawk. There was a constant chatter of quarrelsome gulls, besides the warning calls of the nervous greenshanks, the long whistling cry of the curlew and the restless shrill of the sandpipers.[3]

1. Peter Hunt, *Approaching Arthur Ransome* (London: Jonathan Cape, 1992), p. 123.
2. *CC*, p. 276.
3. *CC*, p. 277.

Here, in simple prose, Ransome describes the Norfolk birds in minute detail, but without a hint of didacticism. There is a feeling of space ('spreading farther and farther'; 'rested'; 'floated away with steady flaps'), while the air is full of the complaining calls of winged inhabitants disturbed by human intruders ('indignant'; 'warning'; 'nervous'; 'restless'). This is the rural idyll, threatened by the Hullabaloos, for which the novel is fighting.

In the second narrative, Port and Starboard try to catch up with the *Teasel*. Their characters are only sketched lightly, lest they draw attention away from Tom as the novel's hero (their job done, they are despatched to school in Paris in Ransome's other Norfolk novel, *The Big Six*, and are absent throughout). Their down-to-earth practicality contrasts with the 'properness' of the D.'s, as does their independence, their untidiness and their outrageous comic mimicry of Ginty, the Scottish housekeeper. As we have seen, Ransome had these episodes in mind before he constructed the plot, and their exploits as they hitch passages first aboard the wherry *Sir Garnet*, then on the tug *Come Along*, and finally on the Thames barge *Welcome of Rochester*, add suspense and prevent the novel's central chapters becoming no more than a picturesque travelogue written from the *Teasel's* deck. The descriptions of the old trading vessels and of the skills of the unassuming people who crew them are Ransome's homage to a way of life that was already passing, and would be killed by the 1939-1945 war. Look, for example, at *Sir Garnet* preparing to shoot Acle bridge:

> Simon and Jim, without a word to each other, seemed not to be hurrying at all. There was a long rattle of the winch paying out the halyard. The huge sail was down.[1]

And at the comic pride Jack Whittle, the captain of the *Welcome*, takes in his new engine and in not using it:

> 'Jack's darling, I call it. The time 'e spends on that engine polishing and oiling, you wouldn't believe. Use it? Not 'im. 'Es bin in sail all 'is life, Jack 'as, and 'e makes it 'is pride to use no petrol what 'e can't 'elp. But polishing and oiling, 'e's at it morning, noon an' night.'[2]

The engine is valued as a gleaming artefact, as long as it does not interfere with the traditional ways of doing things.

---

1. *CC*, p. 266.
2. *CC*, pp. 292-93.

Shipwreck

When the *Teasel* arrives in Beccles Dorothea anticipates the climax of her own story, *The Return of the Native,* but in another clash between reality and romance the Admiral disappoints her and 'seemed hardly to realise that she was coming home at last':

> 'I expect I shall hardly know the little place again,' said Mrs Barrable. Dorothea looked at her hopefully, but romance died as Mrs Barrable went on, 'Better bring both shopping baskets, Dot. I don't know what your mother would say if she knew how badly I've been feeding you.'[1]

It is at Beccles that Port and Starboard are at last reunited with the *Teasel,* and the subsequent voyage home demonstrates Ransome's control of pace and his mastery of comic relief. After the leisurely voyage south, the storm over Oulton Broad builds excitement and allows the comparison between the capability of the *Teasel*'s crew and the Admiral's later irresponsibility when, with Tom ashore, she urges the twins to sail the yacht 'just a little further' down Breydon Water in search of her lost youth (another example of circularity). Indulgence turns to fear as the fog rolls in, and then to ignominy as both *Teasel* and the returning *Titmouse* run aground. Then the comedy of Chapter 23, 'William's Heroic Moment', relieves the tension before the novel builds again to its climax, with William (the pug dog) struggling through the mud in order to link the two stranded vessels with a line for the passing of supplies. The melodrama as the *Margoletta* bears down on the stranded craft is controlled by the understated humour of Port and Starboard:

> On came the *Margoletta*, sweeping up with the tide, and filling the quiet evening with a loud treacly voice:
>> *I want to be a darling, a doodle-um, a duckle-um,*
>> *I want to be a ducky, doodle darling, yes I do.*
> 'Indeed,' muttered Port, with a good deal of bitterness.
> 'Try next door,' said Starboard.[2]

Finally, when the *Margoletta* rams a navigation mark and the Death and Glories arrive just in time to rescue the sinking cruiser and its ungrateful crew, Dorothea's instincts as a novelist mean she is disappointed that in real life (which here means Ransome's novel) things turn out better than in fiction:

---

1. *CC*, p. 305.
2. *CC*, p. 305.

'Of course,' said Dorothea, 'in a story one or two of them ought to have been drowned. In a story you can't have everybody being a survivor.'[1]

*

If *Coot Club* is not in the end the most exciting of Ransome's novels, it demonstrates clearly his peculiar skill and technique as an author. It shows his willingness to move away from the established and reliable cast of *Swallows and Amazons* to give fresh impetus to his writing and new interest to his audience, and his ability (using Dorothea as a disguised second narrator) to transfigure an actual landscape and trivial incidents into an often gripping story. The 'Postscript', a device that Ransome uses for the first time in *Coot Club* to give the security of a closed ending, tells how the Farlands win their sailing race, how Dick and Dorothea go home with proper discharge certificates, and how Rodley's, the grateful owners of the *Margoletta*, refit the *Death and Glory* as a reward. But in spite of this tidiest and happiest of conclusions, and the novel's pervading comedy, Ransome's personal ghosts and his consciousness of the threats in the real world to the dying rural way of life are never far from the surface.

Those readers who, in Ransome's phrase, 'like to be quite sure about everything' may still want to know a little more.[2] Ransome was right to be worried by the commercialisation of the Norfolk Broads. By the 1980s there were 2,400 hire craft, as well as a large number of private boats. Since then the competition from affordable overseas holidays has led to the shrinking of the boat hire industry, but the Broads have been repackaged as 'Britain's Magical Waterland' and in the holiday season towns like Wroxham, with their amusement arcades, pound shops and take-away restaurants, have become at least in part a refuge in bad weather for East Coast caravan dwellers.

Yet many of the Broadland villages remain unspoilt and the Coots would recognise the staithe at Horning, and the Swan Inn, though many of the boatsheds have been replaced by housing developments. Beccles, too, has retained its charm, and on Oulton Broad you will still find the bath house beside the Yacht Station, and the Wherry Hotel nearby. The Halvergate marshes, below Stokesby, are a bleak and lonely place, with the windmills mostly ruined. The Breydon Arms remains isolated on the edge of Breydon Water, but the Breydon Pilot has gone.

---

1. *CC*, p. 388.
2. *CC*, p. 404.

The tides surge under the Great Yarmouth bridges, ready to catch out the thoughtless and the foolhardy; and salvage 'sharks' survive, waiting to profit from the misfortune of holiday-makers who have got their calculations wrong. Eighty years on, there are yachts like *Teasel* still afloat and the Yare and Bure one-designs like *Flash* race on summer evenings.[1] The Thames barge *Pudge of Rochester*, which becomes *Welcome* in *Coot Club*, is also actively afloat, but the *Lord Roberts*, the possible forerunner of the wherry *Sir Garnet*, is a rotting hulk in a creek near Wroxham. What has happened to *Titmouse*, *Dreadnought*, *Death and Glory*, and the *Come Along* I cannot say, if indeed they ever existed – but the point is that whatever stories Dorothea imagines, and whatever games the Death and Glories play, part of the considerable attraction of *Coot Club*, more even than in the Lake novels, is the apparent realism that derives from its grounding in the actual.

---

1. Those who are willing to eschew home comforts for a few days can still hire a yacht very much like the *Teasel* from Hunter's Yard at Ludham.

6.
Pigeon Post:
The Unlikely Mystery of Squashy Hat

Pigeon Post (1936), which won the first Carnegie Medal (awarded by the Library Association for the best children's book of the year), is in some ways Ransome's most ambitious novel and sees him entering and exploiting the world of the thriller. It also marks a slight darkening of the underlying mood, which would last until *Missee Lee*. The novel is skilfully constructed, enjoys a strong storyline (the competition between the Swallows and Amazons Mining Company and a mysterious stranger to find gold on the fells above the Lake), and contains some of Ransome's finest writing (for example, the accounts of Titty's mysterious water-divining, the collapse of the old mine workings, and the fell fire which is the climax of the story). It also explores further the tensions between the children that are evident in *Winter Holiday*: they are no longer the cohesive and untroubled group of that first summer together in *Swallows and Amazons*, and *Pigeon Post* in particular explodes the myth that Ransome's central characters are impossibly and unchangeably good. Much of the action is focalised by the younger members of the group – Titty, Roger and Dick – and the novel exploits to the full the device of the parallel narrative, which allows the reader to see the same events through different eyes. But after the opening chapters *Pigeon Post* takes a while to move forward while the Swallows, Amazons and D.'s are confined to Tyson's farm, and the fact that the reader knows there is no gold in the hills and may realise long before the children that the long-awaited Timothy is in fact the ever-present though self-effacing Squashy Hat means that there is a danger of the dramatic irony becoming patronising in tone.

Before embarking on *Winter Holiday*, Ransome had intended that the winter novel would be the last set on the Lake in the North and featuring the Swallows and Amazons. But after his brief excursion to the Norfolk Broads in *Coot Club* the temptation to return to the North proved too great and *Pigeon Post* brings the Swallows, Amazons and D.'s together again on the fells above the Lake. The plot for this land-based story was inspired by Oscar Gnosspelius's discovery of copper near Coniston in 1929. Gnosspelius was a mining engineer who had married Ransome's close friend Barbara Collingwood in 1925 and was therefore an uncle of the Altounyan children. He advised Ransome on the technical details of mining and introduced him to 'Willie' Shaw, the inspiration for the character of Slater Bob, an old miner who tells of a lost gold seam on the fells. Ransome started work on *Pigeon Post*, which was dedicated to Gnosspelius, in February 1935 and had completed a rough draft by the summer of that year. Then he was distracted. This was the time when the Ransomes moved to Suffolk, and Ransome was further preoccupied by the purchase of a sea-going yacht, which he named *Nancy Blackett*, and by arranging alterations and improvements to her. To the disappointment of his publisher and readers, there was no publication that Christmas. Ransome's dwindling enthusiasm for *Pigeon Post* is highlighted by the fact that he chose to work on new illustrations for *Swallowdale* over the winter and, inspired by his cruising in *Nancy Blackett*, started to plan *We Didn't Mean to Go to Sea*, even writing a number of pages of the 'sea book'. During the first half of 1936, the revising of *Pigeon Post* continued to be interrupted by the illustrations for *Swallowdale*, and over the summer Ransome took more time off to cruise in *Nancy Blackett*. The manuscript was finally sent off in August 1936 and the book appeared in November. It had been a long haul.

Return to the Lake

The opening of *Pigeon Post* is the most effective in the *Swallows and Amazons* series, with Chapter 1 signposting everything that will happen in the ensuing novel (when later, during an 'afternoon of literary criticism' Dorothea reads her long and still unfinished *The Outlaw of the Broads* to Titty, she goes back to her first chapter 'to remind Titty of the little bits that were going to be important later on').[1] This sense of a carefully planned and unified structure, lengthy running jokes and the tiniest of details and clues laid and picked up, continues throughout.

---

1. Arthur Ransome, *Pigeon Post* (London: Jonathan Cape, 1936). Red Fox edition (London: Random House, 2001), p. 187.

It is the start of the school summer holidays, six months after the Polar Expedition, and while Mrs Walker is at home with Bridget (the Vicky of *Swallows and Amazons*) who is recovering from whooping cough and still infectious, Titty and Roger are travelling by train to stay with the Amazons at Beckfoot. John and Susan have already travelled separately from their own schools and, unbeknown to them, Dorothea and Dick have arrived as well. When the train stops at Strickland Junction, ten miles before they reach their final destination, the porter calls for Roger to tell him that a homing pigeon has been left in a basket for him to release.[1] The 'skull and crossbones' on the label shows that Nancy is organising things already, and Mrs Newby, the kindly farmer's wife who gets onto the train at the Junction, knows of the Swallows' exploits in the previous Lake novels. It is as if they, and the reader, are coming home to friends.

A few minutes later Titty and Roger are met at the railway terminus by Nancy, immediately recognisable among the crowd of passengers by her knitted red cap and breathless enthusiasm. The short ride to the Lake at Rio in Mrs Blackett's ancient and dented motor car – the 'Rattletrap' – is a comic masterpiece: they narrowly avoid a collision with Colonel Jolys, who has been organising a brigade of volunteer firefighters and who will come to the rescue when, in the novel's climax, fire sweeps across the fells. And then they are looking out over the sparkling bay. Sophocles – the pigeon released at Strickland Junction – has carried news of their arrival to Beckfoot, and there, sailing down to meet them, are Peggy and the D.'s. Thus the importance of 'pigeon post' to the plot is established at the outset. As Titty looks out over the lake, she reflects ironically that 'Term time was gone as if it had been wiped out. Real life was beginning again'.[2]

The Unlikely Mystery of Squashy Hat

Predictably, 'real life' turns out to be another of Nancy's games and in Chapter 2 she reveals her plan for the first fortnight of the holiday. Until Mrs Walker arrives with Bridget and the Swallows are allowed to launch *Swallow*, Wild Cat Island will be out of reach, so they will all camp at Beckfoot. From there, they will go prospecting for gold on the fells and the Swallows, Amazons and D.'s Mining Company (S.A.D.M.C.) has been set up for the purpose, with Dick as its geologist.

---

1. Strickland Junction is based on Oxenholme station, from where the train goes on to Windermere, just up the hill from 'Rio' (Bowness).
2. *PP*, p. 20.

Captain Flint, normally an integral part of their holiday fun, is still on his way back from a failed quest for gold in Brazil, and if the Mining Company can find just a jot of gold at home Nancy believes he will be less inclined to desert them in future. Like the conquest of Wild Cat Island, the climbing of Kanchenjunga, and the expedition to the North Pole, the quest for gold – the plundering of another country's resources – is another metaphor for colonial activity. Meanwhile, Captain Flint has sent the mysterious Timothy on ahead of him and there are instructions that he is to be looked after and given the run of his study: after Dick has consulted the natural history books, the children have concluded that Timothy is a South American armadillo and have built an appropriate hutch, but as yet no animal has arrived.

There is only one complication: a shady character, whom the children nickname Squashy Hat, appears to be spying on them. Twice he has been seen peering into the Beckfoot garden, and when they climb the foothills of Kanchenjunga to consult Slater Bob in the slate mine deep beneath Ling Scar, a promontory of the mountain, Squashy Hat is heading there too. Slater Bob believes there is gold in the area, discovered by a 'government chap' before the First World War but who never returned. However, the gold is alleged to be on High Topps, and that is too far to be reached each day without the mining company shifting camp from Beckfoot.

From now on Squashy Hat becomes the enemy, though Dorothea is not sure whether Nancy has deliberately created a fiction around him to spice up her plan ('Is he really prospecting too, or is Nancy just thinking so, to make it more exciting?');[1] and as Mrs Blackett later remarks: 'Oh yes . . . Your hated rival. Some harmless visitor, I expect. I don't suppose he knows the part you've cast him for.'[2] His presence becomes central to both Nancy's mining game and to the novel; without a suitable villain, it would be a very dull fortnight of prospecting, crushing and panning, and a very dull story. The miners believe (not altogether wrongly) that they and Squashy Hat are both searching for the same thing, and for them it becomes a race to see who will find gold first. Slater Bob is instructed not to give away secrets to the enemy; Squashy Hat's lodgings at Atkinson's farm are kept under close surveillance and scouts are posted every day to track his movements. The mystery deepens when Squashy Hat begins to mark rocks with white paint for no obvious reason (Dick realises that the paint marks out a line up the fell, but does not understand why),

1. *PP*, p. 94.
2. *PP*, p. 198.

appears like a jack-in-the-box from old workings, and buys a blowpipe from the chemist's shop in Rio when Dick is buying the same. But with his loping gait, and making no attempt to conceal himself from his supposed adversaries, he does not seem to be in a race at all, or indeed to suspect that the children are rivals. For some reason he only wants to avoid them: "'Straordinary thing," he was saying. "Never would have thought it. . . . Whole place seething with children."'[1]

In the final chapter, it turns out that Squashy Hat is in fact the long-awaited Timothy, Captain Flint's mining partner, who, after their failure to find gold in Brazil, has come back to prospect more realistically for copper on the fells. Although the Swallows, Amazons and D.'s Mining Company has been searching for gold, and Dick believes that he has failed everyone, they have in fact succeeded in discovering what Squashy Hat has been looking for: a rich vein of copper. It is the novel's joke that with all the children around Timothy has been too shy to show himself at Beckfoot and so potential allies have become irritating enemies: 'My dear Jim, how could I? There were children popping up all over the place. It was like a school feast. . . . You wouldn't have gone in yourself.'[2]

But for many readers the joke stretches credulity too far. A hardened Prairie miner, briefed by Captain Flint, would at least make contact with Mrs Blackett; and there is a discrepancy between the man who is frightened off by children and the one who takes charge of them with quiet authority when it comes to fighting the fire on High Topps. Moreover this gentlest of figures, characterised by his 'squashy hat' and looking like an 'ostrich', cannot in the end be taken seriously as a villain. Even the children rather lose interest in him once they turn their attention to smelting the quartz: 'Who cares?' says Nancy when Titty and Dorothea report that he has been with Slater Bob all day.[3] Squashy Hat is an inconsistent character and one of the main reasons why suspense in *Pigeon Post* sometimes flags.

Atmosphere

Unlike the other Lake novels, *Pigeon Post* is not a reassuring book, even though everything nearly reaches a happy conclusion. Ransome is attempting something more complex than before, with further strains developing between the children. For the first time, the 'friendly natives' are largely missing: Mrs Walker is looking after the quarantined

---

1. *PP*, p. 127.
2. *PP*, p. 433.
3. *PP*, p. 341.

Bridget; Professor and Mrs Callum remain in London as always, with Professor Callum tied to his endless marking of examination scripts; Captain Flint is still on his way back from Brazil and does not appear until the final chapter; Mrs Jackson, who looked after the Swallows in *Winter Holiday*, has visitors for two weeks and does not feature at all. Mrs Tyson allows the Mining Company to camp in her orchard, but she is a reluctant and fussy hostess, trying to insist on prompt meal times, worrying that the children will set light to the fells, and never beginning to understand their determination to adventure without adult interference. It is left to Mrs Blackett to keep everyone safe, but good-hearted though she is, she is no match for her elder daughter's powers of persuasion and far too busy with the redecoration of Beckfoot to keep more than a cursory eye on the children's exploits: her 'whirlwinding' amidst the customary chaos at Beckfoot and her delightfully haphazard driving reflect her approach to parenting and to life. More than ever, the Swallows, Amazons and D.'s rely on Susan's good sense and culinary skills: 'You see how it is, Susan. It all comes to depending on you.'[1] But Susan, little more than a minor player in the story, is fractious, almost as if she is beginning to resent the responsibility thrust upon her. Without natives in nearby support, her role as mother is no longer play. And all the time the not always reliable pigeons fly to and fro carrying messages that are equally unreliable. Often 'All Well' means nothing of the sort.

Ransome is usually masterly in his control of pace, but after the strength of its opening *Pigeon Post* loses some of its momentum between Chapters 4 and 12. Mrs Blackett agrees reluctantly that the Mining Company may move its base to High Topps to be nearer the goldfields, on condition that it keeps in touch through 'pigeon post' and there's a fresh water supply close at hand. Dick's ingenious device, which causes a bell to ring whenever a pigeon arrives at Beckfoot, means that the first condition is satisfied. But the failure of the miners in this driest of summers to find water on the fells is a blow, and the ideal base which they discover, an old pitstead once occupied by Old Billy and Young Billy (the charcoal burners from *Swallowdale*), becomes a melancholy 'Camp Might Have Been'. Worse, it transpires that Squashy Hat has taken lodgings that give easy access to High Topps. It all results in the Swallows, Amazons and D.'s having to settle for a camp in Mrs Tyson's orchard, where their tents are in a neat row which matches the neat rows of fruit trees, and 'civilisation was jogging [their] elbows'.[2] The danger of fire means that they are no

---

1. *PP*, p. 49.
2. *PP*, p. 111.

longer allowed to cook for themselves, so breakfast is prepared by Mrs Tyson in the farmhouse kitchen and they have to return in time for supper each evening, echoing the regime of Great Aunt Maria. On the first morning at their new camp they have to wait for Mrs Tyson to make up their packed lunches when all the time Squashy Hat may be prospecting on the goldfields ahead of them. As Nancy says, it's like being at school, with 'supper in the parlour' and 'bed in the dormitory'.[1]

For a time the whole atmosphere is one of gloom. In the stifling summer heat the once lush landscape is 'all grey rock, and drab withered grass, and dusty bracken'.[2] Susan is edgy and John is strangely detached. Even the quest for gold becomes half-hearted: Dick is more interested in identifying caterpillars; Roger bats away flies and dozes. Susan, in native mode, is more worried about whether Squashy Hat will see them as rude – the worst of middle-class crimes; what would mother say? – than about his discovering gold before them. As the novel attempts the difficult task of conveying the frustration and boredom of the Mining Company, it comes close to alienating the reader. But at supper on the second evening at Tyson's, when they are late again, Dick suggests that the green reeds at 'Camp Might Have Been' may be a sign of water. He displays the scientist's scepticism of the 'dowser' who had visited his school and, using a forked hazel twig, had found water in the playground, but, typically, Nancy grabs at the idea and has no such doubts. After a too-protracted pause, the adventure is back on course.

Titty

In another well-tuned comic scene the children become dowsers themselves: if only they can find water on the fells they can move to High Topps after all. One by one they parade with a forked hazel twig around the farmyard pump. One by one they fail until, in Roger's hands, the twig at last wags up and down and he triumphantly discovers a jam-jar of water he has hidden in the orchard. When they have all but given up, it is Titty's turn. As in fairy tales (and as we more than half expect), it is the last attempt that brings success and, defying all logic, the hazel twig jerks in her hands and comes alive. This is more than her fertile imagination at work and the comic mood turns to something darker and more frightening, reminiscent of the candle-grease episode and black magic. Titty is taken over by the twig, cannot drop it, cannot free herself from it, however much she fights against it, until it twists

1. *PP*, p. 130.
2. *PP*, p. 115.

violently from her grasp and she runs scared and sobbing into the woods. Susan reassures her that 'It's over now' and John makes sure that Nancy won't ask her to do it again.[1] Dick, who seeks a rational explanation for everything, does not believe that the stick can have twisted by itself: 'She must have thought it did.'[2] But it is Nancy, more disappointed than anyone that Titty is too frightened to dowse, and perhaps even sensing more of what has happened (symbolically at least), who stops the conversation and takes a grateful Titty to wallow in one of the pools of the drying-up stream. Throughout the *Swallows and Amazons* series, and in spite of all her piratical bravado, Nancy often proves herself to be the most considerate and empathetic of the older children. It is something that we shall see again and more clearly in *The Picts and the Martyrs*.

The next day the Mining Company is even more despondent. Nobody talks about Titty's experience, but it is as if the possibility of finding water and shifting camp has been offered and snatched away. At 'Camp Might Have Been', Nancy is spotted by Dick and Titty as she secretly makes another unsuccessful attempt of her own to dowse. Titty in particular feels that she is letting the others down by not using her powers to search for water at the pitstead: 'Suppose the expedition had its own water diviner, and the water diviner, just at the moment of real need, was refusing to help them.'[3] So, after a supper of reluctant reminiscences, she slips away alone and heads for the clearing, half-fearful, but now also half-excited: 'She must try the thing again. . . . But not with anyone to see.'[4] She listens to the farmyard sounds of cows, sheepdog and hens rising from the valley below, and is reassured by an owl call, just like the one she had heard when (in *Swallows and Amazons*) she had been left alone to guard Wild Cat Island and everything had worked out. A hedgehog also in search of water snuffles out to meet her. In the dusky half-light she is seemingly at one with nature. She picks up the hazel twig that Nancy had been using in vain, but without anyone watching her everything feels different from the day before. There is a reassuring warmth in the way she nervously coaxes herself to start her search: 'Oh, come on. . . . You've got to. Better get it over'; 'Duffer'; 'Idiot'; 'It's all right. . . . Nothing to be afraid of anyway'; 'This is silly'; 'Well, it can't bite you'.[5] Now eager, she feels the hazel twig

---

1. *PP*, p. 151.
2. *PP*, p. 152.
3. *PP*, p. 163.
4. *PP*, p. 165.
5. *PP*, p. 168-69.

drawing her on; it is like a treasure hunt with someone shouting 'hot' or 'cold' and she is no longer afraid. After she finds signs of water she is 'suddenly very tired' but, as in *Swallows and Amazons* and *Swallowdale*, it is Titty who is able to save the day.[1]

The description in *Pigeon Post* of Titty's dowsing is another of the most powerful episodes in all the *Swallows and Amazons* novels. Titty is the most imaginative of the Swallows, Amazons and D.'s (Susan, as pragmatic as ever, wonders dismissively if the dowsing is not 'all Peter Duck'), and she always seems to be closest to the natural world.[2] But that is not enough to explain her initial fear and shame of something that takes her over and that she is unable to control; nor are her bravery and her desire not to let the others down sufficient to explain how she is drawn back to the dowsing, how she shares a secret between herself and the twig, and how, left by herself, she is exhilarated and exhausted by the whole experience. Ransome is often criticised for not allowing his characters to grow up but, in a passage that is loaded with Freudian symbolism, there is more than a hint of the beginnings of Titty's sexual awareness. Nancy is disappointed, and not just about dowsing: 'Giminy,' she says, 'I wish it had been me it had happened with';[3] Dorothea wonders if it was 'very horrible'.[4] Alan Kennedy offers a fuller and thought-provoking analysis of the dowsing in 'Titty and the Hazel Wand – Reflections on *Pigeon Post*'. He highlights how in folk tales the hazel branch is associated with fertility rituals and suggests that the episode may in part have been influenced by the fact that Ransome's daughter, Tabitha, whom he had left behind as an innocent child when escaping to Russia in 1913, had in September 1934 written as a grown woman to tell him of her marriage.[5]

After a well has been dug at the pitstead, and in spite of Mrs Tyson's protests, the camp is moved at last to 'Camp Can Be After All' and prospecting can resume in earnest. But it is unrewarding work and by lunchtime of the first day at the new camp, Roger, who in *Pigeon Post* is less biddable and more headstrong than before, has had enough. After worming through the heather and away from the others, he finds himself in one of the many abandoned workings which are spread across the fells. His desultory chipping of the rock dislodges a piece of quartz

---

1. *PP*, p. 173.
2. *PP*, p. 176.
3. *PP*, p. 152.
4. *PP*, p. 174.
5. Alan Kennedy, 'Titty and the Hazel Wand – Reflections on *Pigeon Post*' in *Mixed Moss 2016* (Kendal: The Arthur Ransome Society, 2016).

6. 'I Know What She's Doing'

*At 'Camp Might Have Been' Nancy is spotted by Dick and Titty
as in secret she makes another unsuccessful attempt of her own to dowse.*

which glints in the light of his torch. This, it appears, is what they have been looking for and from now on, directed by Dick, the Company's geologist, their days are filled with mining, crushing and panning. It is hard graft, and not much more engaging than prospecting.

Smoke Over High Topps

The oppressive weather and the threat of fire lie heavy on *Pigeon Post*. In contrast with the glistening snow-covered landscape of *Winter Holiday*, the view from the train window in the opening chapter is of withered grass and trackside fires. Mrs Newby's warning on the train – taken up later and more stridently by Mrs Tyson – always hovers in the background: 'It takes nobbut a spark to start a fire when all's bone dry for the kindling.'[1] At Rio, Titty and Roger notice that even the Lake has shrunk: the boat pier is strangely high above the surface and the water is no longer up to the road. At Beckfoot the beck that usually tumbles into the Amazon River is no more than a trickle, and the stream from High Topps is little more than a shingle path. On the fells the sun blazes down. The fields are 'brown and parched', the ground is cracking open, and what was once a waterfall is reduced to a stagnant pond.[2] The beck that would have been the water supply for Camp Might Have Been has all but disappeared and a dead sheep lies in it. Against the barn wall at Tyson's farm, fire-brooms stand ready. When Mrs Blackett is inspecting the pitstead camp, Dick sees smoke rising near the Dundale Road where a motor-car has stopped, and John and Nancy race down to stamp it out. It is a carefully planted warning of things to come.

After the 'gold' ore has been crushed and panned, it is time to smelt it into an ingot. This means making charcoal, like the Billies, which is then used to fuel a blast furnace powered by Mrs Blackett's bellows smuggled out of the living room at Beckfoot. The charcoal pudding, with the fire burning inside under clods of wet peat, is an effective image of fire waiting to break out on the fells. It has to be watched all the time, and damped down with more peat whenever flames lick out and fire threatens to escape. The blast furnace, which has to be fed by day and night if the crucible of panned gold is to reach a sufficiently high temperature, terrifies Mrs Tyson: 'You'll have the wood on fire for sure. And after all I tell you. With the smoke blowing I thought it was alight already.'[3] But Nancy ignores her and the pumping of the bellows

1. *PP*, p. 8.
2. *PP*, p. 86.
3. *PP*, p. 357.

continues: 'Wough . . . Wough . . . Wough.'[1] This is another chapter where the novel is at its most striking, with the miners black-faced and red-eyed, and food, sleep, and washing-up ceasing to matter as even Susan's native instincts weaken. A message is sent by 'pigeon post' to Beckfoot: 'TRIUMPH IN SIGHT. LOVE FROM ALL.'[2]

But triumph turns to catastrophe. After twelve hours of pumping – half-way through the planned time – the bellows give up, and the miners have to dismantle the furnace and hope they have done enough. The suspense builds as they remove the stones one by one, only to discover that the crucible has shattered and there is no trace of an ingot in the embers. There is no shying away from their misery: 'Two whole weeks had gone with the gold dust . . . the result of all their labours was a little heap of hot stones and smoking ash.'[3] So here hard work, which is one of the central tenets of Ransome's moral code, goes unrewarded.

It is Dick who feels the failure most, but he is immediately concerned with trying to understand why the crucible has shattered and the gold has disappeared. Although in many ways he dictates the action in the second half of the novel, and the other characters defer to his apparent expertise, he has little rapport with the other children and is never committed to the game itself. He builds the pigeon alarm, but as much for his own satisfaction as anything else; then, guided by a copy of *Phillips on Metals* from Captain Flint's study, he organises the business of turning the quartz into a gold ingot, but it is the process that inspires him and not the competition with Squashy Hat. When, for example, Roger asks him to help send the pigeon off, he is 'far too worried about the right methods of panning to think of anything else'.[4] To the others' horror, he wants to fraternise with Slater Bob, now in league with Squashy Hat, to find out how to make an ingot. He is clear-minded enough to lead Roger and Titty safely out of the collapsed tunnel, but he gets things wrong too. The blowpipe fails. The crucible breaks up in the furnace and leaves no trace of its contents:

He knew mistily that they were all miserable. He was miserable himself. They had counted on him and everything had gone wrong, but his mind was not on their misery nor on his own. Everything had gone wrong. But why? How had it gone wrong?[5]

1. *PP*, p. 355.
2. *PP*, p. 357.
3. *PP*, p. 371.
4. *PP*, p. 256.
5. *PP*, p. 370.

The only thing now is to follow Dick's suggestion: mine some more quartz and test for gold with the acids in Captain Flint's study. John, Susan, Nancy and Peggy head back to their mine and pan a pinch more 'gold'; Dick sets off with it to Beckfoot to conduct the experiment; and Titty, Roger and Dorothea are left to sleep at camp. While all this is going on, another carload of sightseers pause for a picnic.

Here *Pigeon Post* slips deftly into three parallel narratives as the picnickers – more urban hullabaloos – leave behind a careless spark, and the fire which has smouldered and flared throughout the action and imagery of the novel takes hold. In the camp Titty is woken by the frightened calls of grouse: the sun has been blotted out by smoke and a line of crackling flames is blown first towards them and then away. Sappho, the usually unreliable pigeon, is sent off with an S.O.S. while the youngsters try to keep the fire at bay with water from the spring – but the kettle, biscuit tin, sugar tin and pudding bowl, and the flailing fire-brooms all point to their helplessness. In the old working, the older children are too despondent and exhausted to carry on mining. They too fall asleep and are woken by the same smoke and crackling flame. They rouse Squashy Hat, who is lying nearby, and from a mortal enemy he turns into a calming presence. Together they shelter in the working as the fire roars past, then race back to rescue Titty, Roger and Dorothea. Meanwhile, Dick reaches Beckfoot and is inveigled into lunch, after which he tests the 'gold'. Captain Flint returns in time to explain to Dick that aqua regia dissolves everything, not just gold, and establishes that the ore is actually copper: Dick has got it all wrong. Then Sappho arrives with the S.O.S., Colonel Jolys's firefighters are summoned, and Captain Flint, Mrs Blackett and Dick pile into the 'Rattletrap' and head off to Tyson's farm and the camp.

The suspense increases further as the three narratives come together and rival prospectors, farmers and firefighters battle with the flames, bit by bit bringing them under control. Later, Mrs Tyson, who has unjustly blamed the children for starting the fire, apologises and goes back to milk the cows. Around the camp fire the loose ends are tied up; failure turns out to be success and Nancy plans a pirate battle. Best of all, Titty slips off into the dusk to discover that the hedgehog has survived the blaze and, along with a weasel, has crept back to drink from her well.

*

Critics disagree more than is usual about *Pigeon Post*. Ransome always worried about his writing, usually unnecessarily, but his diary entries for June and July 1935 are especially damning about the first draft: 'AWFUL. . . . No grip anywhere. . . . No tension. . . . No drama – and worse, a development of the undramatic bits.'[1] Evgenia, however, was more upbeat than usual: 'It is not very much worse than the worst of the others.'[2]

Young scientists may think differently, but I sympathise with Roger in finding the whole business of prospecting and panning less exciting than the earlier adventures, having to shift camp twice becomes a bore, and Squashy Hat is just too implausible to be taken seriously. Perhaps Ransome regretted his unscheduled return to the Lake District setting and Nancy's games, and was not rigorous enough in his revision of the manuscript to develop 'the undramatic bits' sufficiently.

But, for all that, *Pigeon Post* has sustained passages of powerful writing which show a writer at the summit of his craft. It captures vividly the uncomfortable atmosphere of a long hot summer, even if until 'The End' it is at the expense of the usual feeling of warmth and security that is a hallmark of the *Swallows and Amazons* series. In doing so, it reflects the uncertainty of the real world of 1935-36 when, as in the charcoal pudding, there was a sense that conflagration might break out at any time. It also suggests that John and Susan, who are always on the fringes of the action and play no part in the reconciliations of the final chapter, are growing up and are simply losing interest in Nancy's intrigues (something that will become more obvious when the Swallows and Amazons are reunited in *Secret Water* later that summer). These themes are explored further in *We Didn't Mean to Go to Sea*, which was already grabbing Ransome's attention: with fewer games to play and an almost Aristotelian unity, this would turn out to be his masterpiece.

---

1. Diary entry for 30 June 1935, reproduced in Roger Wardale et al., eds, *The Best of Childhood* (Kendal: Amazon Publications, 2004), p. 156.
2. Letter from Arthur Ransome to Edith Ransome, 4 August 1936, reproduced in Hugh Brogan, ed., *Signalling from Mars: The Letters of Arthur Ransome* (London: Jonathan Cape, 1997), pp. 237-39.

7.
We Didn't Mean to Go to Sea:
Confronting Reality

In *We Didn't Mean to Go to Sea* (1937), it is through the confronting and overcoming of a storm at sea in the sailing yacht *Goblin* that the Swallows grow up – inconveniently for the subsequent development of the *Swallows and Amazons* series. This is one of the main themes of the novel, reaching its conclusion in its immediate sequel, *Secret Water*. Another main theme (again) is that of the absent father: young Jim Brading, the skipper of the *Goblin* who is about to go up to university, acts as a substitute father like Captain Flint (and, like him, he fails). At the end of the novel, John at last wins the approval of his real father – something that Ransome himself, to his lasting regret, never had the chance to achieve. This chapter also sets out to show how Ransome creates suspense in the first part of the novel and to consider the confrontation between John and Susan, who until now have enjoyed the calmest of relationships, and how it is resolved.

In September 1935 the Ransomes bought the yacht which they christened *Nancy Blackett* and which was the inspiration for *Goblin* in the Suffolk novels; in October they moved to Levington in Suffolk, just across the River Orwell from Pin Mill, the starting point for both *We Didn't Mean to Go to Sea* and *Secret Water*. On 11 January 1936 Ransome wrote in his diary, 'Planned "We Did Not Mean to Go to Sea"', but there is no mention of *Pigeon Post*, the new Lake District novel with which he was struggling.[1] On 16 January he wrote to Wren Howard at Jonathan Cape about the proposed book:

---

1. Roger Wardale et al., eds, *The Best of Childhood* (Kendal: Amazon Publications, 2004), p. 161.

During the last four days I have seen, grabbed, clutched and pinioned a really gorgeous idea for another book. . . . Swallows only. . . . No Nancy or Peggy or Captain Flint. . . . But a GORGEOUS idea with a first class climax inevitable and handed out on a plate . . . lovely new angle of technical approach and everything else I could wish. . . . So I breathe again.[1]

It seems that Ransome toyed for a little with *Pigeon Post*, but on 13 February wrote eight pages of what he called 'seabook' before ploughing on with the Lake District novel in March and April. However, on 1 June he set sail in *Nancy Blackett* with a friend, Herbert Smith, researching in his usual meticulous way the voyage of the *Goblin* in *We Didn't Mean to Go to Sea*. Unfortunately, Smith suffered from seasickness and spent the passage below deck, while Ransome sailed single-handed; Smith returned to Harwich by steamer, leaving Ransome to hire a young Dutch crewman for the return crossing.[2]

After *Pigeon Post* was published (in November 1936) Ransome immediately returned to writing *We Didn't Mean to Go to Sea*, borrowing the main events of the story from Maurice Griffiths's *The Magic of the Swatchways* (1932). Griffiths describes what should have been a 'jolly cruise across to Holland and back' in his wife's yacht *Juanita* during the summer of 1931.[3] In the event, the crossing from Harwich was made in thick fog, and on the return passage the *Juanita* was caught in a storm. Just as when John tries to turn *Goblin* into the teeth of the gale, the motion on board *Juanita* was unbearable and the Griffiths both succumbed to the same seasickness that afflicts Susan and Titty. Ransome also draws on his own experience of sailing in the Baltic: in *Racundra's First Cruise* he describes a stormy voyage ('Pakerort to Reval') and fog at sea ('Reval to Helsingfors'). Again, *We Didn't Mean to Go to Sea* illustrates Ransome's method of using real experience as the basis of his fiction.

The first draft of *We Didn't Mean to Go to Sea* was finished in June 1937. Evgenia's verdict, reported in Ransome's diary entry for 11 June, was, as usual, cruel: 'flat, not interesting, not amusing, no dialogue, skeleton only.'[4] In a letter to Wren Howard of 25 June, Ransome pronounced gloomily:

---

1. Letter to George Wren Howard, 16 January 1936, reproduced in *The Best of Childhood*, pp. 161-62.
2. The log of the voyage can be found in Roger Wardale, *Ransome at Sea, Notes from the Chart Table* (Kendal: Amazon Publications, 1995).
3. Maurice Griffiths, *The Magic of the Swatchways* (London: Adlard Coles, 1977), p. 187.
4. Letter to George Wren Howard, 11 June 1937, reproduced in *The Best of Childhood*, p. 192.

WDMTGS has gone dead on my hands. Now trying to get a little oxygen into it. Blood transfusion or monkey gland is what is really needed. It is as flat as ditchwater.[1]

But a revised draft was sent to Wren Howard on 4 September, together with the suggestions that the opening chapter should be shortened, and a chapter in the middle of the book, which reveals to the reader at an early stage what has happened to Brading, should be removed altogether. Wren Howard responded positively, agreeing with Ransome's suggestions. The final draft was sent to the printer on 15 September and the novel was published on 12 November 1937. Wren Howard wrote to Ransome: 'I think in many ways it is the best of the lot.'[2]

Wren Howard was right and one of Ransome's typically downbeat letters (to Helen Ferris of the American Junior Literary Guild) goes a long way towards explaining its success:

It's a dreadfully seasick book, and the formula is not that of the others. The trouble is that one single incident fills the book, that the incident is all concentrated in about 48 hours, that reality presses so hard on the children that there is no room or need for romantic transfiguration of fact, and so on.[3]

The 'formula' of the previous novels is the binding together of a series of incidents and descriptions through an often inconsequential plot. Here, according to Ransome, a 'single incident' is the plot, and *We Didn't Mean to Go to Sea* benefits from the resulting focus and compression. In fact, there remain a number of incidents, but, rather than their controlling the plot, they are all subordinate to the central idea of the Swallows having to sail by themselves across the North Sea in a howling gale. The carefully constructed novel divides into four sections: the opening, in which the Swallows are invited to crew the *Goblin* with Jim Brading, lose the anchor overboard while Brading is ashore buying petrol in Harwich, and drift out to sea in a fog; centrally, the storm itself, where survival means running before the wind and so crossing the North Sea rather than returning to Harwich; landfall and making harbour in Holland; and, having fortuitously met their father, sailing home for a reunion with Mrs Walker and Brading.

---

1. Letter to George Wren Howard, 25 June 1937, reproduced in *The Best of Childhood*, p. 194.
2. Letter from George Wren Howard, 6 December 1937, reproduced in *The Best of Childhood*, p. 205.
3. Letter to Helen Ferris, 18 March 1937, reproduced in *The Best of Childhood*, p. 184.

Moreover, the fact that there is 'no room or need for romantic transfiguration of fact' – at least, in the tense central section – gives the novel the clarity and directness that is sometimes missing from the rest of the series (and from *Pigeon Post* in particular). In the storm, the Swallows are no longer playing a game. The Amazons and the pirate adventures they bring to the stories are missing (and would be redundant). Titty, seasick and frightened, never romanticises for an instant the dangers that they all confront. Life is really threatened. Adults, who largely control the other stories, or at the very least keep watch on them from a distance, are out of reach. While Commander Walker, the previously absent father, appears in the final chapter to sail home with his children, by then they have come through the storm by themselves and his role is a very different one.

The Absent Father

Jim Brading, skipper of the *Goblin*, is eighteen. Symbolically he stands between John, the child, and Commander Walker, the achieved male. He has just left Rugby School (Ransome's *alma mater*) and has won a scholarship to Oxford. His uncle has given him *Goblin* as a reward. Brading is apparently an experienced sailor and has completed a single-handed night passage from Dover, though, significantly, he fails to pick up the mooring buoy at Pin Mill. He meets the Walker children when they help him to moor, and it is not long before he is inviting them to spend a couple of days on board. Mrs Walker nervously gathers local opinion before entrusting her children to his care:

> Everybody here seems to think a lot of him. Miss Powell says he's the best-heartedest young man she ever knew. Frank, the boatman, says, 'What he don't know about handling that boat of his won't help anyone.' The boatbuilder says he'd trust him anywhere, and that old man scraping spars says, 'They don't fare to come to no harm along of Jim Brading.'[1]

Such effusive testimonials not only create misgiving in the reader, but they also hardly reassure Mrs Walker whose decision to let her children sail with him is taken reluctantly in the absence of her husband, who is travelling home on leave: "'It almost looks as if I shall have to [let you go]," said Mother. "But I wish I could ask Daddy."'[2]

---

1. Arthur Ransome, *We Didn't Mean to Go to Sea* (London: Jonathan Cape, 1937). Red Fox edition (London: Random House, 2001), p. 26.
2. *WDMTGTS*, p. 27.

In terms of the family romance, here is the central symbolic motif of the novel: the importance of the father figure is revealed through the anxiety about his absence. Without the father (the achieved male), Mrs Walker, the mother, goes wrong, entrusting her children to Brading (the immature male). She is right to be worried. For all his boyish enthusiasm, Brading makes mistakes: he fails to pick up the mooring buoy and is rescued by the Swallows; he fails to buy the bread; he fails to fill up with petrol, so *Goblin*'s engine stops at a crucial moment; and he rows ashore to find a garage, thus deserting the children. Commander Walker is to see this as his chief fault: 'Captain shouldn't leave his ship.'[1] In his hurry to buy the petrol, Brading runs in front of a bus and ends up in hospital, leaving the children to fend for themselves. At the end of the novel, when he rejoins *Goblin* on her return to Harwich, he appears a comic and emasculated figure, groggy and with his head swathed in bandages, making it clear that he never was the sufficient substitute father that he initially seemed to be. This is hinted at right from the start. For example, the fact that Brading is not yet properly a man is suggested in symbolic terms by his failure to keep his pipe alight:

> 'It must use an awful lot of matches,' said Susan, as yet another was thrown overboard to join the long trail of dead matches that was floating with the tide.
> 'Tobacco's a bit damp,' said Jim. 'Bother it. It's gone out again.'[2]

Later, in Chapter 24, we notice the contrast with Commander Walker, whose glowing cigar is an image of confident manhood:

> The match went out, but there was the cigar-end red hot in the darkness. Now and then, as Daddy took a puff at the cigar, that red-hot end glowed brightly enough to let John see Daddy's face behind it.[3]

It is a comforting Freudian, phallic moment – the symbolism is reminiscent of Conrad. It is Brading's failure as a substitute father which makes the appearance at last of the children's real father so much more effective, emphasising by comparison Commander Walker's genuine qualities of leadership and seamanship.

---

1. *WDMTGTS*, p. 376.
2. *WDMTGTS*, p. 29.
3. *WDMTGTS*, p. 339.

We've All Promised

The accidental voyage of the *Goblin* is heavily signposted from the moment Jim Brading shows Mrs Walker the chart of Harwich harbour:

> '. . . Those buoys . . . Beach End and Cliff Foot . . . show where the harbour ends and the sea begins.'
> 'And you won't go out beyond them?' said Mother.
> 'No,' said Jim.[1]

So when Mrs Walker makes them all promise not to go to sea (the chapter is entitled 'We've All Promised') perceptive readers will realise that their promises are certain to be broken, and it is these promises that come back to haunt Susan in particular:

> 'Now Susan,' she said, 'and you too, John. No night sailing. . . . No going outside the harbour. . . . And back the day after tomorrow. . . . Promise.'
> 'We promise. . . .'
> 'I promise too,' said Jim. 'It's high water at four on Friday. I'll have them here at Pin Mill in time for tea.'
> 'We've all promised,' said Susan.[2]

There is something homely and comforting in 'in time for tea' and as Mrs Walker rows away from the *Goblin*, 'she grew happier every moment as she saw how easily everything went'; but she has missed the irony of Titty's postcard drawing of *Goblin* sailing through huge waves.[3] For the reader the sense of foreboding increases as, back on the hard, she talks to Miss Powell:

> 'I do hope I've done right,' said Mother. 'It seemed a pity not to let them take a chance like that. I know their father would have wanted them to go.'
> 'They'll take no harm with Jim Brading,' said Miss Powell.
> 'Anyway, they're not going outside the harbour,' said Mrs Walker.[4]

But they will go outside the harbour; they will.

When the *Goblin* sails down the river, the children's excitement never quite masks the dangers that lie in store for them. Even Susan

---

1. *WDMTGTS*, p. 36.
2. *WDMTGTS*, p. 37.
3. *WDMTGTS*, p. 39.
4. *WDMTGTS*, pp. 41–42.

is distracted by the porpoises playing alongside, but as they swim into the distance the mood changes and she displays the edginess that we have seen in *Pigeon Post*:

> 'Lucky black pigs,' said Roger. 'Gosh! They'll be bobbing up to look at steamers in the middle of the night. . . . I wish we were.'
> 'What? Bobbing up from under water?' asked Jim.
> 'Going to sea,' said Roger.
> 'Well we aren't,' said Susan, almost impatiently. 'We've promised. Isn't this good enough for anybody?'[1]

Little does Roger know that they will in fact be 'off to sea' themselves and that their own encounter with a steamer in the middle of the night will be a terrifying experience. Susan's subsequent sight of the beached yacht ('She bit her lip pretty hard') is almost too much for her.[2] It is as if the others are willing *Goblin* out to sea, in spite of their promise: the sea is now clearly an image of the adulthood they yearn for and fear, each in different measure. At the same time, as the suspense builds, John acquires the skills that he will need when he is left in command of the *Goblin*. He learns about sails and how to reef them; about buoyage; about stocking the anchor; about avoiding the dangerous shoals that lie outside the harbour; about not letting rescuers aboard even if the ship is in difficulty, lest they make a claim for salvage. Roger discovers the properties of a 'Woolworth's plate' that will soon save their lives when the steamer bears down on them, and Titty conveniently finds out which signal flag is needed to request a pilot. Here Ransome manages to avoid being heavy-handed in his teaching and it is only in retrospect that we learn the importance of this lightly imparted knowledge.

Suspense increases further in Chapter 6. Its title – 'Nothing Can Possibly Happen' – is loaded further with irony. On board *Goblin* next morning, as they breakfast under way, there is the apparent security of Susan's ordered ship:

> But Susan had hardly slipped down the companion-steps, to get plates and spoons and cornflakes, before she remembered something else that ought to come before breakfast.
> 'Nobody's cleaned their teeth,' she said.[3]

And ashore it seems that all is right with the world:

---

1. *WDMTGTS*, p. 51.
2. *WDMTGTS*, p. 51.
3. *WDMTGTS*, p. 77.

> There was hardly a ripple on the water. A misty sun was climbing over Felixstowe. Smoke was rising from the chimneys of Harwich, where people ashore were cooking their breakfasts. The smoke climbed almost straight up and then drifted idly away. The movement of the tide shook the reflections of the anchored barges and of the ships in the harbour and of the grey jetties and houses of the town.[1]

It is a picture of contentment and calm ('ripple', 'misty', 'drifted', 'idly', 'reflections'), but Brading half-recognises that it is the calm before a storm and the foghorn is unsettling:

> 'I dare say there'll be wind later. Or fog. Or both. You never know what's coming with a day that starts like this.'
> As he spoke, a long wail sounded from out at sea.[2]

Titty, however, enjoys the moment. 'It doesn't look as if it could ever turn into waves,' she says, looking out over the 'oily water'.[3] Even the moment of unspoken apprehension, as the wind drops and the tide sweeps them towards the sea, is quickly forgotten when Brading starts the engine and they make their way back up river and 'further and further away from the danger of a broken promise'.[4] John and Brading work 'cheerfully' on deck; the stove breaks into 'a cheerful roar'; Brading 'grins'; breakfast continues, and, as the water in the saucepan bubbles merrily, the conversation turns to boiled eggs. Then the engine splutters and stops.

Into the Storm

Goblin is anchored just outside the channel and Brading rows off to Shotley to buy more petrol. 'I'll be back in half a jiffy,' he says. 'Nothing can possibly happen.'[5] Thus breakfast still goes on, with Brading's place in the cabin conspicuously empty. Titty, as the disguised narrator, imagines that they have just returned to home waters from an exotic voyage: 'To think that last time we anchored there were palm trees on the banks, and crocodiles.'[6] Hinting back to the fantasy of *Peter Duck*, they wish they had the ship's parrot and Gibber, the monkey,

---

1. *WDMTGTS*, pp. 77-78.
2. *WDMTGTS*, p.78.
3. *WDMTGTS*, p. 79.
4. *WDMTGTS*, p. 85.
5. *WDMTGTS*, p. 88.
6. *WDMTGTS*, p. 91.

with them. But when Jim does not return and the fog closes in, such 'transfiguration of fact' only heightens the sense of real danger. Even Roger's comic playing of his penny whistle and the banging of a frying pan are loaded with dramatic irony:

> Everybody felt happier. When you are lying anchored in a fog, even 'Home Sweet Home' on a penny whistle and the clatter of a spoon on a frying-pan make you feel that other boats will have less excuse for running into you.[1]

One of the novel's high points is the description of the disorientating effect of fog. It recalls the climax in *Swallowdale* when Titty and Roger become lost in the fog; and the episode in *Peter Duck* when the Swallows and Amazons play 'blind man's buff' with the pirate Black Jake and the fog presages a north-westerly gale. Here, in Harwich harbour, what had been a glorious panorama of the town becomes a 'grey wall', as 'the pierheads, dim and shadowy, were swallowed up'.[2] There is the 'taste' of fog, and new sounds, each from an unexpected direction: 'a sharp bark from the siren of a tug', 'a chorus of ship's bells', 'the long blast of a foghorn', the 'very slow drumming of a small engine'; and later the noises all seem to move around as the *Goblin* twirls in the tide.[3] Symbolically, the fog is a veil, starting to separate the children from 'home' and from childhood itself, and presaging the way they are going to be thrown into the big seas of adulthood.

As the tide sluices past and Titty, still 'transfiguring fact', imagines they are in the Atlantic, 'rushing along, keeping a look out for icebergs',[4] everything begins to go wrong. The barometer falls. The anchor drags, and, in trying to let out more chain, John loses both anchor and chain overboard. John and Susan lower the spare kedge anchor, but John fails to fasten the stock properly and it drags too. So they are swept past the clanging cage buoy: '"Oh, John," gasped Susan. "That was the Beach End buoy. We're out at sea."'[5] For Susan, the horror of 'The Beach End Buoy' is not so much the danger that they face, but the breaking of the promise they have all made to their mother.

The next six chapters, 9 to 15, form the core of the novel, the gale-lashed crossing of the North Sea. They are packed with

---

1. *WDMTGTS*, p. 99.
2. *WDMTGTS*, p. 98.
3. *WDMTGTS*, pp. 98–100.
4. *WDMTGTS*, p. 105.
5. *WDMTGTS*, p. 123.

action and are arguably the most tense that Ransome wrote. For
these night-time hours the imaginative games are forgotten as the
children encounter and overcome the sea at its worst. As readers
we are blown with them from one incident to the next: debilitating
seasickness; the rain squall; the almost fatal attempt to turn back
to Harwich; John's reefing of the sail and the slip which so nearly
takes him overboard; the encounter with the steamer when they
are saved by the 'Woolworth's plate'; John falling asleep at the
tiller. But I want to look further at the way Ransome explores the
complex relationships between his characters, focusing mainly on
the breaking of the promise and the resulting conflict between John
and Susan.

John and Susan

When John hoists sail to regain control of *Goblin*, and heads out to sea
and away from the shoals, Susan reflects on the promise they have all
made not to go outside the harbour:

> They had been allowed to sail with Jim Brading only because
> everybody had promised that they would not go outside the
> harbour. . . . And here they were outside the harbour, sailing faster
> every minute, in a thick, choking fog and rising wind. They could
> not have broken that promise into smaller bits.[1]

It is Susan's despair and inner turmoil at the breaking of the promise
more than the uncomfortable motion of the ship that makes her so
terribly sick. She refuses even to hear John's plan to sail away from land
and their mother, and from danger:

> It was as if he were talking from far away. Perhaps he had already
> been talking for some time. What was he saying? No. . . . No. . . . He
> couldn't mean it. . . .[2]

Nor can she physically see on the chart what he is proposing: 'She
stared at it, but it was as if she were looking at a blank sheet of paper.
Her eyes simply would not work.'[3] When John recalls Brading's
advice ('Get out to sea and stay there') and Susan argues against him
('But we promised not to go to sea at all'), it is Titty's common sense
that nearly persuades her: '"We can't keep a promise when it's already

1. *WDMTGTS*, p. 138.
2. *WDMTGTS*, p. 141.
3. *WDMTGTS*, p. 141.

broken," said Titty.'[1] She thinks of what their father would say, yet notice how the tension is tempered by her comic naïvety and the gentleness of 'bumped':

> 'Let's do what John says,' said Titty. 'Daddy'd say the same.... You know.... When it's Life and Death all rules go by the board. Of course, it isn't Life and Death yet, but it might easily be if we bumped on a shoal.'[2]

But still Susan is adamant. She cannot bring herself to hold *Goblin* on her new course; and when the turn is made, she cannot accept what they are doing: '"It's all wrong," she cried. "We must go back. We oughtn't to do it. I didn't want to, and I can't bear it."'[3] For her, obeying the moral code with which they have been brought up and which has become part of their existence is more important even than their safety. She leans her head against the cabin and sobs.

John's reaction to the situation is very different from Susan's. He has played the 'father figure' in their games on the Lake, and now he must become the substitute father where Brading has failed. Although still a boy, he is responsible for them all, and the real hazard of his predicament is brought home by the way in which his lack of experience has caused him to lose one anchor and fail with the other. It is for him to redeem the situation: safety is necessarily more important than promises and his decisions are practical rather than moral. In spite of Susan's protests, he sets a course, north-east by east, to take them away from the shore because that's what Daddy would do; and when they near the Cork lightship he alters course to 'south-east by east', out into the North Sea, 'because there's nothing for us to hit for miles' and 'This is what Daddy would do too'.[4] While Susan despairs, John is confident in his decision, 'in spite of the broken promise', and relieved that the immediate danger is over: 'John, in spite of his troubles, was for the moment almost happy.'[5] Later, Commander Walker says approvingly to John of his decision to head for the open sea: 'Quite right, though perhaps your mother wouldn't say so.'[6] His comment on a mother's perspective is understanding of difference and not derogatory.

---

1. *WDMTGTS*, pp. 142, 143.
2. *WDMTGTS*, p. 144.
3. *WDMTGTS*, p. 148.
4. *WDMTGTS*, p. 146.
5. *WDMTGTS*, p. 146.
6. *WDMTGTS*, p. 319.

It is often argued that the relationships between the Walker children (and between the children and their parents) are too benign to be credible. But this is not the case in *We Didn't Mean to Go to Sea*, nor in its sequel, *Secret Water*. When Susan suggests turning back, John reacts angrily. If John is now the substitute father and Susan, by implication, the mother, what is staged here is a ferocious argument between them as parental figures. Susan vents her frustration by turning on Roger when he sounds the foghorn ('Oh, shut up, Roger!').[1] When John suggests that Roger, rather than the seasick Susan, should look after Titty, she reacts 'furiously'. Neither Titty nor Roger can believe the behaviour of their normally placid sister and look at each other 'with horrified eyes'. Roger 'stares' at her: this is a Susan he has never seen before.[2] The climax comes when, with the rain squalls over, John agrees to turn back. As he steers the boat into the waves, *Goblin* is 'shaken almost to pieces' and risks being swamped; Susan 'can't bear it'.[3] Then John manages to bring *Goblin* back to her original course, and the return to a more bearable motion proves him to be right. Susan's acceptance of this marks the end of the conflict between them. 'We're going on,' says Roger to Titty. 'But it's Susan herself who wants to go on now.'[4] Although there is no sign of the storm abating, Titty and Roger set to work on clearing the water-logged cabin. They light the lamp, which gives warmth and security:

> The little lamp, swinging wildly in its gimbals, sent shadows chasing all ways about the cabin, but gave a feeling of triumph to both the able-seamen, who, for a moment, sat holding on by the table, watching it. Having that little lamp properly lit in the cabin was almost like snapping their fingers at the storm.[5]

Order has been restored.

Or nearly. On deck, John knows that he has to reef the sails. He ties a lifeline round his waist and bravely climbs out of the cockpit. Away from the security of its high coamings, he 'had never felt so lonely in his life'; and, again, 'Lonely? It was as if he was outside life altogether and wouldn't be alive again till he got back'.[6] John's leaving of the cockpit is a metaphor for his stepping out of the security of childhood: suddenly

---

1. *WDMTGTS*, p. 142.
2. *WDMTGTS*, pp. 148-49.
3. *WDMTGTS*, pp. 162, 163.
4. *WDMTGTS*, p. 165.
5. *WDMTGTS*, p. 167.
6. *WDMTGTS*, pp. 171, 173.

he is even more aware of danger and adult responsibility. Watching him, Susan is pale and scared. But this is what sailors do; this is what Daddy would have expected. Indeed, it is almost as if his father is guiding him:

> 'One hand for yourself and one for the ship.' His father had told him that years ago, when he was a little boy and had tumbled down in the bottom of a fishing boat while using both hands to pass his father a rope.[1]

And:

> What was it Daddy had said? 'Never be ashamed to reef in the dark.' And it was going to be dark almost at once.[2]

We are reminded of Ransome's own unfulfilled relationship with his father and here, in a straightforward way, the novel is symbolically moving. With the job done, John grasps the shrouds and halyards, and stands up in triumph, but he pays for another of his moments of boyish over-confidence and is all but swept overboard. Saved by his lifeline, he somehow manages to scramble back. In her relief, and all passion spent, Susan is cured of her seasickness. Titty senses the reconciliation:

> Titty, climbing out, looked from John to Susan and from Susan to John. She was just going to ask a question, but did not ask it. She felt that the ship was suddenly full of happiness. John was grinning to himself. Susan was smiling through tears that did not seem to matter.[3]

Susan resumes her customary domestic role, producing a meal of pork pie and 'grog', and later she finds the iodine and a clean handkerchief for John's cut wrist. As 'mother', she tucks Titty and Roger into their bunks and sleeps herself. As for John:

> He had done his very best. . . . If anybody could have seen his face in the faint glimmer from the compass window, he would have seen that there was a grin on it. John was alone in the dark with his ship, and everybody else was asleep. He, for that night, was the Master of the 'Goblin', and even the lurches of the cockpit beneath him as the 'Goblin' rushed through the dark filled him with a serious kind of joy.[4]

---

1. *WDMTGTS*, p. 174.
2. *WDMTGTS*, p. 176.
3. *WDMTGTS*, p. 180.
4. *WDMTGTS*, pp. 212-13.

7. 'All But O.B.'

*With the job done, John grasps the shrouds and halyards, and stands up
in triumph, but he pays for another of his moments of boyish
over-confidence and is all but swept overboard.*

Clearly, John's 'joy' is that of newfound adult confidence. But as the night at sea wears on, he still needs Susan (now re-established as his 'Mate') just as father needs mother, and husband needs wife. When he succumbs to exhaustion it is Susan who takes the helm and steers the ship through the night, and it is her maternal care for the others that speaks of both the restoration of order and the strength of the family.

Peter Hunt (*Approaching Arthur Ransome*) argues that Ransome is 'undeniably sexist' in *We Didn't Mean to Go to Sea* and that for him 'girls simply do not survive as well as boys', but while the novel centres on the patriarchal family, I think Hunt oversimplifies.[1] Susan may fight unreasonably against the breaking of the promises they have made, but, equally, Titty knows that it is right to sail on in spite of the promises. In other novels it is Nancy, not John, who largely controls the action (Chapter 10 will discuss how *Missee Lee* challenges the gender stereotypes of the period). This episode in the North Sea suggests on one level that the adult world is more complex than the child's. In the Lake District (and for the Coots on the Norfolk Broads), the moral code by which the children live is a simple one. But real life is not so simple: promises cannot always be kept and, when they are broken, trying to mend them can be disastrous. It is this conflict that John and Susan have to work out, and in doing so they lose much of their innocence. But the argument between them – especially the ferocity of Susan's opposition to what is clearly the right thing to do under the circumstances – also hints at something more. Victor Watson believes that there is something personal lying behind this explosive scene, 'a strong authorial need to "deal with" whatever Susan represents' though 'what she represented in Ransome's life can only be guessed at'.[2] Susan Altounyan's identification of Susan Walker with Evgenia Ransome may be an explanation, and it is possible that on another level Ransome is here confronting his stormy relationship with his second wife.[3]

When dawn breaks, the mood lightens further. John can't stop 'grinning'. Symbolically he looks at the glimmer of light ahead: 'He looked back into the darkness and then forward again at that faint, promising glimmer.' Susan is 'feeling like a ship's mate and keeping

1. Peter Hunt, *Approaching Arthur Ransome* (London: Jonathan Cape, 1992), p. 140.
2. Victor Watson, *Reading Series Fiction* (London: Routledge Falmer, 2000), p. 45.
3. See Christina Hardyment, *Arthur Ransome and Captain Flint's Trunk* (London: Frances Lincoln, 2006), p. 38.

the crew in order';[1] Titty and Roger are 'feeling more like themselves with hot cocoa inside them and all that tongue and bread and butter'.[2] They decide to sail on to find land – it will be safer than turning and reaching Harwich in the dark, and they will be able to send a reassuring telegram home before they are due to return to Pin Mill. This time Susan accepts John's assessment of the situation without argument: 'The thing had been decided. From that moment on not one of them looked astern, not even Susan.'[3]

We Didn't Mean to Go to Sea is in large part a *bildungsroman*, especially for John and Susan. There may even be a suggestion of sexual confusion and confrontation as they fight with each other. The storm brings home to them more sharply that the holidays enjoyed on the Lake in the North were always the games that they knew them to be. When in *Swallowdale* John's over-confidence results in the wrecking of *Swallow*, the dinghy can easily be mended; in *We Didn't Mean to Go to Sea*, his careless mistakes with the anchors put them all into danger and his triumphant gesture when he has reefed the mainsail nearly kills him.

The Real Father

After the tensions and trials of the night, the rescue of a shipwrecked kitten is a diversion for both the children and the reader: the kitten is a metaphor for their own helplessness, and its rescue is another sign that order has been restored. Then, as they reach the safety of land at last and sail into the Dutch port of Flushing, we enjoy the comic episode of the pilot, who in spite of his joviality also represents the threat of foreignness: Ransome's skill is now to maintain interest as the novel moves calmly towards its conclusion. It is almost too much of a coincidence that Commander Walker should catch sight of his children from the deck of the Harwich steamer; and the moment when he closes on *Goblin* in a motor-boat has all the delicious sentimentality of that famous reconciliation of Roberta and her father – 'Oh! My Daddy, my Daddy!' – at the end of Edith Nesbit's *The Railway Children*:

> The little motor-boat was circling round to come up alongside, and sitting in it, holding on his grey felt hat was . . .
> 'DADDY!' they all four shouted at once.[4]

---

1. *WDMTGTS*, pp. 226-27.
2. *WDMTGTS*, pp. 226-27, 233.
3. *WDMTGTS*, p. 236.
4. *WDMTGTS*, p. 301.

Here, though, the Dutch pilot is on hand to lighten the situation and prevent it from becoming mawkish. We are reminded too of Mrs Walker, back at Pin Mill and desperately worried about her children. She, as much as her husband, has turned them into the people they are:

> 'Nodings,' he shouted. 'Nodings. You haf dam fine children mynheer . . . give my congratulations to your wife.'[5]

This is the first time in the whole *Swallows and Amazons* series that we have met Commander Walker, although he has often been a controlling presence, consulted by Mrs Walker on matters concerning their children, and whose wisdom is always recalled in times of difficulty. He is, Titty recognizes, 'very unlike anybody else . . . even Captain Flint'.[6] Unlike John, Ransome had never felt easy in his own father's company, never felt able to please him, and here he lives out what might have been if his father had not died so young. Titty notices the strength of the unspoken bond between John and Daddy: 'Silent they both were, John and Daddy, but she knew by the way they looked at each other across the sail they were showing how glad they were to be together.'[7] And when they are on their way to send the telegram home, Commander Walker makes the gesture that means everything:

> 'A lot of things were lucky,' said Daddy, and suddenly, while they were walking along, brought his hand down on John's shoulder and gave it a bit of a squeeze. 'You'll be a seaman yet, my son.'
>
> And John, for one dreadful moment, felt that something was going wrong with his eyes. A sort of wetness, and hotness. . . . Partly salt. . . . Pleased though he was, he found himself biting his lower lip pretty hard, and looking the other way.[8]

John may miss his father's parodying of Kipling's 'If' (1895); if so he misses both the implying of his own heroism and another lightening comic touch. But the squeeze on his shoulder is enough to move him to tears of pride and joy.

After they send cryptic messages to reassure but not frighten Mrs Walker, 'the sun was brighter'. The irony is typically understated:

> Already those telegrams would be flashing along the wires to let Mother know that nothing had gone seriously wrong.[9]

5. *WDMTGTS*, p. 302.
6. *WDMTGTS*, p. 305.
7. *WDMTGTS*, p. 306.
8. *WDMTGTS*, pp. 320-21.
9. *WDMTGTS*, p. 323.

Fittingly, the return passage is made in calm seas. The children sleep; their father sings sea shanties. At Harwich they are met by the bandaged Brading, who has escaped from hospital: that he is now a clown makes clear his symbolic status as a false or failed substitute father, the adolescent yet to achieve maturity. Both his appearance and the comparison with Commander Walker show how superficial his confident and worldly manner was in the opening chapters: he demonstrates the failure that could have engulfed John had he not acted so well in the storm. When the British Customs officer shakes John's hand, 'all four of his children knew that he [Daddy] was somehow rather pleased'.[1] At Pin Mill, Mrs Walker, who still doesn't know what has really happened, wants to be angry, but isn't. The family is reunited and Ransome's most orderly of worlds has survived.

*

What distinguishes *We Didn't Mean to Go to Sea* from Ransome's other novels is the fact that, for a time, the children stop playing games and confront reality, learning about their real selves. However there is also a larger metaphor at work. An underlying theme in the early novels is, as we have seen, a celebration of imperial adventure, though in *Coot Club* there is an implicit sense that all this may be coming to an end. In *We Didn't Mean to Go to Sea*, the *Goblin* more obviously symbolises Britain as a colonial power adrift in a world which threatens to overwhelm it. In the year that Ransome began writing the novel, M.L. Jacks, the Headmaster of Mill Hill School, was warning that his pupils must 'be ready, if need be, to serve in our country's forces, when its extinction is threatened from without', though he realises that any struggle would be for 'the welfare of humanity, and not one which desires to paint more and more of humanity's world red'; and Douglas Miller, High Master of Manchester Grammar School, was reflecting that modern youth 'is asking itself whether the system of international relationships is right, whether it is reasonable to expect peace when nations hold and possess primarily for their own advantage'.[2] The relief and fragile optimism which followed the First World War had evaporated and these headmasters were reflecting a period of huge change, both in Europe and in the wider world, that

---

1. *WDMTGTS*, p. 372.
2. M.L. Jacks, 'Education for Tomorrow' in *The Headmaster Speaks* (London: Kegan Paul, Trench, Trubner & Co., 1936), p. 149, and Douglas Miller, 'The School and the Community' in *The Headmaster Speaks*, p. 132.

foreshadowed the end of Britain's Empire and its position as a world power. When *Goblin* is approached by the Dutch fishing fleet, Titty is still able to recall one of the great imperial myths (though of course it recounts a glorious defeat):

> 'We'd be like the *Revenge* in the middle of the Spanish fleet,' said Titty. 'We wouldn't have a chance.'
> 'And we haven't any guns,' said Roger.[1]

But Ransome knew, half with regret, that the world restored at the end of the novel was in fact on the brink of catastrophe and that neither Commander Walker, who represents the authority of empire, nor John, would be able to outface the growing storm of 1930s politics. By the time the sequel to *We Didn't Mean to Go to Sea*, *Secret Water*, was published the following year (starting again in Pin Mill in the same summer holiday and developing the same themes), Britain was at war again.

---

1. *WDMTGTS*, p. 254. The capture of the *Revenge* by the Spanish fleet is one of the most heroic episodes in the history of the English navy. In 1591, under the command of Sir Richard Grenville, the *Revenge* fought by itself against the entire Spanish fleet in the Azores. She held out for fifteen hours (only 16 of a crew of 250 were uninjured) before being overcome. Grenville ordered the sinking of his ship in preference to capture, but his officers refused. The *Revenge* sank with the loss of all hands (including the Spanish 'prize' crew) while being towed back to Spain. The Walker children, who learn much of their history from learning poems, would have known the story from Tennyson's 'The Revenge: A Ballad of the Fleet' (1878). Christopher Ricks lists J.A. Froude (see p. 26 above) as one of Tennyson's main sources for the poem – Christopher Ricks, ed., *Poems of Tennyson* (London: Longman, 1969).

8.
Secret Water:
Growing Up and Apart

Secret Water (1939) celebrates the Essex marshes, another of Britain's unspoiled areas and one of Ransome's favourite haunts; and, like the other *Swallows and Amazons* novels, it transfigures the actual landscape into an almost magical setting. *Secret Water* also develops the central themes of *We Didn't Mean to Go to Sea*. First, it shows how, after the experience of the storm, John and Susan move away from the childhood world they have previously inhabited and continue the process of growing up. Although they play another extended game, John's main concern is to rise to the challenge set by his father, while Susan, as the established mother figure, takes her responsibility for the welfare of her siblings even more seriously and is rarely more than a reluctant participant in the adventure. Both of them share an excess of practical common sense and propriety, as well as a striking lack of imagination. Secondly, written on the eve of the Second World War, at a time when the British Empire and civilisation itself were under increasing threat, *Secret Water* tells the symbolic story of empire-building – and in its climax describes how white civilisation (the Swallows) is overrun by savages (the Amazons and the Eels). It introduces more explicitly the whole panoply of imperial clichés about the dualism of white and black, explorers and savages, Israelites and Egyptians, all of which are deeply racist constructions. However, *Secret Water* is no simple allegory and the symbolism is ambivalent. The novel sides as much with the savages as with the explorers, whose superior attitude (apart from Titty) is a target of an almost satirical intent.

Following the triumph of *We Didn't Mean to Go to Sea*, Ransome struggled yet again to find a plot for his new novel. It was his usual habit to start writing in January and to submit his manuscript (late

and in a rush) by September, so a new title could be published in time
for the Christmas market. Although in January 1938 he suggested
to George Wren Howard that he was planning an Essex setting, he
made little progress. In the same month a letter to his close friend
Margaret Renold raised the possibility of his long-planned book about
'a story bringing in my respected ancestor, fishing, poaching etc.',
but he accepted Evgenia's advice that he should stick to stories in the
present.[1] He went on to expand on the plot that was to become *The
Big Six* and the following month he drafted a number of chapters of
The Big Six before laying them aside and returning to the possibilities
of Essex. Then he became engrossed in a final summer of cruising in
Nancy Blackett, and fitting out and launching his new yacht, *Selina King*.
There was no Christmas book in 1938.

It was on a brief sailing trip in the first week of September 1938
– one of his last in *Nancy Blackett* – that Ransome finally settled on
an Essex adventure. The plot was still vague, but he pondered it over
the winter months and in 1939, with war looming, he divided his time
between the writing of *Secret Water* and cramming in as much time
afloat as possible before hostilities began. The novel was completed in
September 1939 and published that November. 25,000 copies had been
printed by Christmas.

Secret Water is written in a minor key: after the terrors of the North
Sea, the tamer environment of the Walton backwaters is at first sight
something of an anti-climax. But the novel is an appropriate and
necessary sequel to *We Didn't Mean to Go to Sea*, recounting how the
Walker children, who have experienced real danger, begin to grow
away from their imaginative world and from the Amazons. If there
is a weakness, it is that *Secret Water* is seriously diminished if read in
isolation from its predecessor.

Mapping the Backwaters

The setting of *Secret Water* is the network of creeks, islands, and salt
marshes that lies inland of Walton-on-the-Naze, half a mile south of
Harwich harbour. Ransome tinkers with reality through his redrawing
of the real Bramble Island as 'Blackberry' coast, and his inventing
of the 'North West Passage' for the needs of the story. All the other
geographical details of the 'Secret Water' – for example 'Swallow Island'
(Horsey Island), 'The Wade' across the 'Red Sea', 'Flint Island' (Stone

---

1. Roger Wardale et al., eds, *The Best of Childhood* (Kendal: Amazon
Publications, 2004), p. 210.

Point), 'Amazon Creek' (Walton Channel), Witch's Quay and the boat-builder in the town – are reasonably exact, though the creeks and marshes themselves have shifted significantly since the book was written.

It is just after the perilous voyage across the North Sea and Commander Walker is enjoying a week's leave before taking up his posting at Shotley (then the home of the shore-based training establishment, H.M.S. *Ganges*). He is planning a family expedition in *Goblin*, lent to him by the still concussed Jim Brading, to chart the Walton Backwaters. Then a message from the Admiralty cancels his leave and it seems that the expedition is over even before it has started: 'We can't go. It's all off. The First Lord's chucked a spanner in the works.'[1] Although it is 1932 in the chronology of the series, the unsettled atmosphere in Chapter 1 reflects that of 1939 when *Secret Water* was written. These are Ransome's frustrations as well as the Swallows': the First Lord of the Admiralty was Winston Churchill, whom Ransome had never forgiven for his criticisms of Trotsky, and who was now proposing a war which Ransome believed was ill-advised. There is a letter from Mrs Blackett, from which we learn that the Amazons have secretly been invited to join the expedition, but now they too must be put off.

So the mood turns sour, and the world with it. As the children try to make the best of things, Commander Walker hatches another plan. The children are to be 'marooned' alone, make camp and take on the mapping by themselves, using a borrowed dinghy, *Wizard*, to explore the creeks and inlets. Thus Ransome engineers another situation in which the children have to fend for themselves, but here 'there'll be nobody coming along every day to see that you're all right'.[2] As in the other *Swallows and Amazons* novels, it is the imaginative Titty who romanticises the actual (the role played by Dorothea in *Coot Club* and *The Big Six*). So the farm on Commander Walker's map is christened the 'native kraal' and talk of marooning transports her back to Stevenson's *Treasure Island*; but the real – represented by going back to school – is never far away:

> 'Marooned?' said Roger.
> 'What happened to Ben Gunn,' said Titty. 'They gave him a gun and put him on an island and sailed away and never came back.'
> 'Oh,' said Roger.
> 'We'll come back for you all right some day,' said Daddy.
> 'When?' said Susan.

1. Arthur Ransome, *Secret Water* (London: Jonathan Cape, 1939). Red Fox edition (London: Random House, 2001), p. 2.
2. *SW*, p. 17.

'Don't say,' said Titty. 'Much better if we don't know. We'll grow old and grey watching for a distant sail. . . . '

'Not very old,' said Daddy. 'And you won't have time to get very grey before you have to stop being explorers and go back to school.'

'Don't spoil it,' said Titty.[1]

Goblin is loaded up as a supply ship and, with *Wizard* in tow, the expedition sets off. As they approach their destination – just a few minutes' cruise from the bustle of Harwich – Ransome creates the impression that they are entering a different and unknown country, almost as if they are stepping through the back of the wardrobe in C. S. Lewis's Narnia novels, though here the town and houses and boats are never far away:

> And, as they came nearer to that round buoy with the cross, they saw that a much wider channel was opening before them with a smooth shining water stretching to the west and low banks on either side.
>
> 'There you are,' said Daddy. 'That buoy marks the cross roads. Turn left, follow that creek in there, past those masts, and you'll come to a town.'
>
> 'I can see houses now,' said Roger, 'and lots more boats.'
>
> 'You can get right up to the town at high water in a dinghy. But if you go, don't wait there too long, or there won't be water to take you back.'
>
> 'But we're going to an island aren't we?' said Titty. 'Not a town.'
>
> 'We are,' said Daddy. 'We leave that buoy to port and carry straight on.'
>
> 'Crossroads buoy,' said Roger as they passed it.
>
> A minute or two later they had left the open bay and the *Goblin* was slipping easily along in the quiet water of an inland sea. A low spit of land with a dyke along it already hid the creek that led to the town, though they could still see the tops of distant masts. Far away, on the opposite side, was another low dyke. Standing on the deck and in the cockpit they could see bushes here and there. Ahead of them the inland sea seemed to stretch on for ever.
>
> 'What's it called?' asked Titty, from the foredeck.
>
> Daddy smiled. 'Do you want the name on Jim's chart? I thought you'd give it a name yourselves.'
>
> 'It's a very secret place,' said Roger. 'You don't see it until you're almost inside.'

---

1. *SW*, pp. 17-18.

'Secret Water,' said Titty. 'Let's call it that.'

'Why not?' said Daddy and Titty scrambled into the cockpit and pencilled in the first name on Daddy's blank map.[1]

I have quoted this passage at length for four reasons. First, because it demonstrates again the effortless simplicity of Ransome's prose as he leads us, with the Swallows, from one world into another. Notice the words he uses: 'smooth', 'shining', 'stretching', 'slipping easily', 'quiet', 'hid', 'distant', 'far away', 'seemed', 'for ever', 'secret'. Secondly, Ransome reminds us that this new world is part of another game of explorers and savages, chiefly played out in Titty's imagination, even if as the novel unfolds it is a game which her brothers and sisters are, to varying degrees, happy to play. But Commander Walker notes how close the town is (though Titty doesn't want to know); Roger points out the houses and boats; and the 'crossroads buoy' and Brading's chart (on which everything is already named) remind us that Titty's unexplored place – 'Unexplored,' says Titty, 'until we've explored it' – isn't unexplored at all.[2] Thirdly, the warning about tides introduces an element absent from the Lakes (though, as we have seen, the tides on Norfolk's southern rivers are crucial to the plot of *Coot Club*) which will dictate much of the ensuing action. Finally, the filling in of the blank map chapter by chapter – in particular the naming of islands, seas, and creeks, the gradual owning of the *terra incognita* – is not only the narrative thread that binds together the people and the incidents of the novel into a satisfying whole (reinforced by the sequence of illustrations of Titty's developing chart), but also another example of the colonial symbolism we have encountered in earlier novels. In *Secret Water* there is a polarity between John's imperialist preoccupation with map-making, and Titty's game, later hijacked by Nancy, in which childishness is equated with savagery, blackness, and irresponsibility.

Growing Up

Ransome's working notes suggest that once more his creative process started with the setting and the people, and continued with the imagining of events:

Muddy creeks ... tidal ... an island ... like Walton Backwaters ... a hut ... a house. ...

Town children come to stay? Callums

1. *SW*, pp. 30-31.
2. *SW*, p. 32.

Local children . . . watch

The visitors know they are being watched but cannot see anybody. The locals show themselves when visitors have got into the dickens of a mess and are doing their best, but failing to get out of it. . . . In the end, of course, it is the locals who are in a mess and the visitors somehow help them through.[1]

As usual, it was only later, and with a struggle, that Ransome would meld his ingredients into a story. In fact, in *Secret Water* the Callums never appear and, in spite of Ransome's imperial 'of course', it is the locals (who play only a small part in the novel) who help the visiting explorers rather than the other way about. A later and very full note shows how Ransome went on to dream up the 'Mastodon boy'; but his ideas for a hunt, and a storm, and a raft to escape from a swamped island, came to nothing.[2]

Chapter 4 ('The Expedition Goes Ashore') and Chapter 5 ('Marooned'), which describe the setting up of the camp, are formulaic, and recall similar episodes at the start of both *Swallows and Amazons* and *Swallowdale*. They are nevertheless typical of Ransome's attention to practical detail. This is exactly how things should be done and, without any patronising, readers are given lessons in selecting a campsite, pitching tents, taking care with fresh water, checking off supplies, collecting firewood from the high-water-mark, building a fire, making a sundial and calendar. Moreover, the image of explorers taking control of a previously undiscovered territory is an important one: notice how 'the "Swallow" flag on a bamboo flagstaff fluttering in the breeze' is a symbol of their conquest.[3] There is enough comic interest in Roger's familiar penchant for food, especially chocolate, and in Bridget's uncertainty at being away from her parents for the first time, to prevent this section from becoming dull (Bridget is the youngest Walker, whom we have met as Vicky in *Swallows and Amazons*). However, unlike in *We Didn't Mean to Go to Sea*, there is a note of amusement, of scorn even, in the narrative voice, as if to question whether this is an extended middle-class picnic rather than a real adventure:

Susan with pencil and paper was making a list as they dug into the three boxes that Daddy had sent down to Pin Mill from the Army and Navy Stores.[4]

---

1. Diary, August 1937. Reproduced in Christina Hardyment, *Arthur Ransome and Captain Flint's Trunk* (London: Frances Lincoln, 2006), p. 206.
2. *The Best of Childhood*, p. 214.
3. *SW*, p. 40.
4. *SW*, p. 46.

And:

> 'Mother's done the whole thing,' said Susan. She went to
> the store tent and came back with the basket with a label on it,
> 'Tonight's supper'. Out of it came a parcel of chops, ready cooked,
> a bag of tomatoes, two lettuces with a bit of paper on which was
> written 'The lettuces have been washed', and a bag of rock buns.
> At the bottom of the basket was another bit of paper with a
> message. 'Fill up with bananas.' [1]

In fact, Susan's role in *Secret Water* is a small one and, changed by
her experience on the North Sea, she stands aside from Titty's
games ('Susan, thinking more of the explorers' dinner than strange
hoofprints, had picked up Sinbad and was hurrying back to camp.').[2]
Her role as 'mother' is largely restricted to looking after the others:
for example, providing meals and producing the antiseptic iodine when
Swallows, Amazons and Eels, urged on by Nancy, literally become
'blood brothers'. In particular, she looks after Bridget, who for the only
time plays a major part in a *Swallows and Amazons* adventure and is at
the centre of the novel's comedy.

Like Susan, John takes life even more seriously than before – there
will be no broken promises this time: 'He, like Susan, had heard their
father was depending on them.'[3] When it comes to pitching camp, he
wants to impress his parents: 'Let's have it looking like a camp before
Daddy and Mother come back.'[4] For him the challenge of the expedition
is to complete the exploration and, by doing so, to prove himself again
to his father. When their parents have gone, John and Titty investigate
all the mapping paraphernalia that Commander Walker has provided:

> 'Daddy was going to do it really properly,' said Titty.
> 'So are we,' said John. 'He'd be awfully pleased if we manage to
> go everywhere and get the whole thing mapped.'[5]

As night falls, it is John, symbolically lighting the hurricane lamp, who
feels keenly that he is there to protect them all and it gives him a quiet
satisfaction. No longer a child, but not yet an adult, he savours the moment:

> John was last into his tent. . . . He half thought he ought to
> keep awake this first night. Just in case. . . . An hour later John
> woke. . . . He remembered that he was in charge, in charge of a

1. *SW*, p. 55.
2. *SW*, p. 81. Sinbad is the kitten rescued in *We Didn't Mean to Go to Sea*.
3. *SW*, p. 25.
4. *SW*, p. 40.
5. *SW*, p. 46.

party of explorers marooned on a strange and desert island. . . . He crawled back into his tent, wriggled into his sleeping bag, and, with the torch, looked at the blank map Daddy had made. . . .[1]

Growing Apart

The next day Titty spots the strange 'Mastodon' footprints on the shore (there is a clear echo of Robinson Crusoe discovering Man Friday's footprints); they are in fact made by a local farmer's son, Don, who wears 'splatchers', like giant snow-shoes, to walk across the mud. The Mastodon, as they come to know him, is camping in the fore-cabin of a derelict Thames barge. He is awaiting the arrival of other savage friends – the Children of the Eel – who visit each summer:

> 'We do it every summer holidays,' said the Mastodon. 'You know, a good big fire, and necklaces dangling from the totems, and tomtoms going, and a corroboree and everyone dancing like mad and the victim waiting to be sacrificed.'[2]

They become friends and the Mastodon acts as a 'native guide', using his local knowledge to help with the exploration. The imperialist metaphor is extended as Titty describes yachts at anchor as 'dhows':

> The Mastodon looked over his shoulder. 'Traders,' he said, 'Probably slavers. But they haven't caught any of us yet.'[3]

But the most telling sign of John's growing up is evident in his changing relationship with the Amazons. When the expedition is announced, John is sorry that they can't join in (though there are enough clues to the reader that they are going to appear): 'I was only thinking what a pity it is that Nancy and Peggy can't come too.'[4] So when the Swallows see a sailing dinghy, *Firefly*, approaching, with a skull and crossbones flag breaking out at the masthead, there is excitement all round:

> 'It's Nancy and Peggy,' said Titty. 'It's the Amazon pirates. Hey! Hey! Ahoy!'
> 'Three million cheers!' said John.[5]

Soon, however, it is obvious that things are different. Nancy looks at the beginnings of Titty's map, but she is enthused not by the idea of surveying but by the potential for a grand nautical war:

1. *SW*, pp. 57–58.
2. *SW*, p. 104.
3. *SW*, p. 113.
4. *SW*, p. 22.
5. *SW*, p. 129.

'It's a grand place for a war,' said Nancy. 'Better than Wild Cat and our river. Surprise attacks from all sides. And savages too.'

John and Titty looked at each other in horror. . . .

'What a place for war,' said Nancy again. 'Specially with savages. Think of an attack . . . war canoes coming through there . . . and savages creeping through the reeds. . . .'

'But there won't be time for any war,' said John.

'And the Mastodon's a friend,' said Titty.

For some time the Amazons watched in silence.

'You'll get a medal from the Royal Geographical Society,' said Nancy at last. . . . 'The Walker expedition.'

Both John and Titty noticed that she said 'you' instead of 'we'.

'You're in it too,' said John.[1]

Although the Swallows – and Titty in particular – are already playing a game of explorers and savages, they feel threatened by the arrival of their friends, who want to take the game in another warlike direction, even if it is the direction they have all enjoyed together in the Lakes. For John especially, there is the threat that a war will mean he won't complete the map for his father; and Ransome, who in 1939 agreed with the appeasers, knew that in the real world war would mean the end of the England he loved. For Titty, there is the knowledge that the Mastodon is a 'friend' – how far has the new friendship had the effect of excluding the Amazons? It is this thought that surely strikes Nancy as the Amazons watch 'in silence': suddenly, it seems, they are outsiders. Notice the mocking of the establishment in 'You'll get a medal from the Royal Geographical Society' and how it is the Walkers now, not the Swallows; 'you', not 'we'; them and us.

Nancy and the Mastodon strike up an immediate friendship, and Nancy, no longer content with being just a pirate, is determined to turn savage and join forces with him and his Eel tribe (the Eels spend their holidays here, like the Swallows on the Lake in the North, and engage in savage games). John recognises her unaccustomed silence at supper and 'began to fear that she was relapsing into thoughts of war'.[2] In Chapter 12, 'Blood and Iodine', the explorers and the Mastodon mix their blood, which means (argues Nancy ominously) that 'you could borrow one or two of us if you happened to be short of savages'.[3]

---

1. *SW*, pp. 138-39.
2. *SW*, p. 142.
3. *SW*, pp. 143-44.

Explorers and Savages

When the Eels arrive to set up camp on Flint Island, the Mastodon feels he has betrayed them by fraternising with the Swallows and Amazons – he has revealed their secrets and their password, and has become blood-brothers with white explorers. Nine chapters are devoted to loyalty and betrayal – another of the novel's key themes, linking back to the broken promise in *We Didn't Mean to Go to Sea* – as parallel narratives explore the different viewpoints of Explorers, Eels, and the dejected Mastodon. However, it is not long before the savage Eels raid the Swallows camp (Titty, who has been left on guard, is far too engrossed in her mapping to notice), steal back their totem, and take prisoner the comically all-too-willing Bridget. When the Swallows land on Flint Island to recapture their sister, they find the Eels 'all in black bathing things'; later one of the Eels, Daisy, is to describe the Swallows as 'Palefaces' and 'White Chiefs', defining the black/white conflict more sharply. For the moment, however, the Eel password is enough to defuse the situation – 'best mistake you've ever made,' says Daisy to the relieved Mastodon – and friendship is cemented in a tea party hosted by the 'missionaries' aboard *Lapwing*.[1]

The Eels throw themselves into the surveying, but John is conscious that Nancy's thoughts are elsewhere. The pirate in Nancy – or the savage, or the child – is more powerful than the explorer:

> 'Barbecued Billygoats. . . . I mean Great Congers. . . . It'll be the best ever.' That was Nancy's voice, urging something, and he [John] knew that the explorer in Nancy was only skin deep. That was the pirate coming through. Or had the pirate got somehow mixed up with the Eel? Oh well, it didn't matter, so long as the map got done.[2]

Chapter 24 of *Secret Water* is ironically entitled 'Civilisation'. On the last full day of the expedition, the Swallows head for the town of Walton to have *Wizard*'s rudder repaired by the local boat-builder. The Amazons stay behind at the camp, where Nancy prepares the savages (Amazons and Eels together) for war. The bustle of the town and its kiss-me-quick holiday atmosphere are reminiscent of the Hullabaloos in *Coot Club*, and contrast sharply with the savage world on Swallow Island. Notice the Swallows' arrogant distaste for the pavements 'crowded with people dressed for a seaside holiday', for people without 'a spot of mud'.

---

1. *SW*, p. 261.
2. *SW*, p. 286.

'What did these people know of the real thing, of islands unexplored, of savages who that very night would be dancing in 'corroboree'?'[1] And notice how their fantasy life on the Island, much of which exists in Titty's imagination, is described as 'the real thing'. Frustrated by the queues in the grocer's shop, the Swallows are conscious that they must get back to the Island before the tide turns and the tension begins to mount: 'John pointed to a clock hanging out over the street' and at the boat-builder's 'the man looked at an enormous watch'.[2]

Titty, Roger, and Bridget start back early, but are waylaid when they stop for a rest. John and Susan, following after, miss Titty's patteran and return to the camp without them. So when the younger Swallows reach the 'Wade', which links the mainland to Horsey Island, the tide is already rising fast. They become isolated on a raised section of track in the middle of the 'sea', with the water lapping ever nearer:

> Crossing the Wade in the morning Titty in imagination had been under water, looking up at the keels of boats passing overhead. And now they were not Israelites, crossing dryshod, but Egyptians. They were trapped there in the middle of the sea. They could go neither forward nor back and must wait there, watching the narrow island of the road shrink under their feet.[3]

Now the suspense rises as inexorably as the tide, and all the time Titty and Roger have to disguise their fear from Bridget. As the water laps over their knees, Roger climbs one of the navigation posts and waves his shirt as a distress signal. Then, just as they are about to attempt to swim to safety (though Bridget can't swim), they see the Mastodon rowing towards them. Contrary to Ransome's original plan, but in line with the sympathies of the novel, it is the native who saves the explorers from drowning and not the other way about.

Corroboree

So the novel moves to its climax and the 'corroboree': an aboriginal war dance.[4] Just as Titty, Roger, and Bridget begin to tell of their

1. *SW*, p. 309.
2. *SW*, pp. 309, 310.
3. *SW*, pp. 335-36.
4. The 'corroboree', derived from the aboriginal 'karabari' (a festive or war dance), may be explained by the Australian ancestry of Ransome's mother. Here it stands in opposition to civilisation. Baden-Powell had already introduced the corruption 'jamboree' to describe a celebratory

adventures in the Red Sea, the Swallows are ambushed by the savages. There are six of them, not four; significantly, Nancy and Peggy have joined forces with the Eels:

> Six of them, not four. And what savages! Feathers in their hair, bodies striped and splashed with mud for war-paint, faces patterned with mud, black bars on cheeks, rays of mud upwards from each eye, like the rays of the setting sun. . . . And as for the explorers, when that howling mob rushed the camp from all sides, they stood there dithering.[1]

This is the conclusion towards which the novel has been moving: Nancy's thirst for war rather than map-making; Amazons and Eels against Swallows; 'howling' black savages against dithering white explorers. There is a demeaning note in the way that the so upright and uptight John is captured: 'John, Captain John, the leader of the explorers, found himself hurled to the ground.'[2]

But this is the moment for which Bridget has longed. At last she is granted her comic wish to be a human offering. There is a sense of virginal sacrifice as 'Bridget, in her clean white frock, stood in the midst of a ring of jumping, whirling figures':[3]

> A huge splash of red paint on her white frock, and the red mark of the eel on her forehead made Bridget look indeed as if she were being slaughtered at the stake.[4]

However, as the savages jump and whirl around Bridget, her brothers and sisters, the explorers, are managing to extricate themselves from their bonds and are planning her rescue:

> 'All right, Bridget,' cried Susan. 'It's all right. We'll cut you free. You're going to be rescued.'
> 'Oh go AWAY,' shrieked Bridget. 'Go AWAY. They're just in the middle of it. I don't WANT to be rescued.'[5]

The comedy here is entrancing, though the point is a serious one. Bridget, the 'baby' of the group, is relishing the adventure, the unsuppressed emotions, and the escape from the tame world of grown-ups. To be

---

get-together of Boy Scouts – ironically, since the Aborigines had suffered appalling racial genocide at the hands of the colonisers.
1. *SW*, p. 358.
2. *SW*, p. 358.
3. *SW*, p. 361.
4. *SW*, p. 365.
5. *SW*, p. 365.

8. Signal of Distress

The suspense rises as inexorably as the tide, and all the time Titty and Roger have to disguise their fear from Bridget. As the water laps over their knees, Roger climbs one of the navigation posts and waves his shirt as a distress signal.

rescued would be, in fact, to be imprisoned. On one level we are always aware that this is a game, that the savages are only savages in a symbolic way, that Bridget isn't going to be sacrificed and that for the children everything is under control. Bridget is comforted by the fact that she recognizes the savages beneath their war paint. In the midst of the 'fiery' dance we never quite lose the feeling of homeliness and safety:

> That large, long-legged one must be Nancy. She knew the tear in the back of Nancy's bathing dress. She knew the Mastodon by his stiff mop of sandy hair. Those two who had set upon John in the first attack must be Dum and Dee. . . . And that skinny one, who danced more fierily than any of the rest, must be Daisy who would have been the human sacrifice if they had not found a better.[1]

But on another level the real incident in which the young children almost drown in the 'Red Sea' is matched immediately by this culmination of Nancy's game where civilisation (represented by the Swallow explorers) is overrun by savagery. The episode is reminiscent of other colonialist literature in which white explorers are confronted and conquered by black savages, and it foregrounds again the contemporary fears about the disintegrating British Empire.

As explorers and savages struggle with each other, it is the password – 'Karabadangbaraka' – which bound them together as savages that reunites them now, though it is noticeable that John and Susan opt out of the game and remain silent during the otherwise warm and warming feast that follows. The narrator comments: 'Explorers and savages, now all savages, stood breathless and panting, looking at each other.'[2] But the characters and the language take us in a different direction; the explorers aren't savages at all. The battle over, Roger, in a nicely humorous touch, apologizes in good preparatory school fashion: 'I say, I'm awfully sorry I winded you';[3] and when Susan finally learns of the near disaster in the Red Sea, she comes over all grown up: '"Jibbooms and bobstays," exclaimed Nancy. "Be an Eel, Susan. Nobody got drowned. They didn't even get wet. At least not very."'[4]

For John, the real disaster is that Nancy and Peggy have distracted the Swallows from their mapping: when his father returns on the

---

1. *SW*, p. 361.
2. *SW*, p. 366.
3. *SW*, p. 366.
4. *SW*, p. 373.

following morning they will have failed in their task and he will be responsible for letting him down. The symbolic importance in the novel of map-making – which stands for order, control, and empire – is implicitly confirmed, as is John's mind-set as a potential part of the imperial machine. For him, it is a catastrophe that Nancy's game (representing the disorganisation of savagery) should get in the way of the imperial project. Nancy, however, is alert to John's anger and disappointment (and no doubt feeling guilty for abandoning his project on the previous day). As dawn is breaking on the last morning of the holiday, while John and Susan are still asleep, she, Peggy, Titty (also feeling guilty about the near disaster on the 'Wade') and Roger steal from their tents and set sail to complete the survey. When John discovers that they are missing and that without their help the camp will not have been properly struck, he is beside himself with disappointment. He sees *Goblin* returning and despairs:

> 'Every single thing's gone wrong,' he said bitterly, 'we've failed with the map, and now Daddy's coming for us, and nothing's ready.'[1]

Then *Wizard* and *Firefly* race back, their job done; the finished map can be presented to Commander Walker after all. In this novel of divided loyalties, Nancy's organising of the last-minute surveying expedition is a lesson to John, who has barely concealed his resentment at the Amazons' presence on the island and even now almost forgets her contribution:

> He couldn't speak, but grabbed Titty's hand and shook it.
> 'What about us?' said Nancy. There was joyful handshaking all round.[2]

The Eels, now acting as slaves, row the camping gear out to *Goblin*, and Commander and Mrs Walker engage with them in excruciating and belittling pidgin English. For the moment, the order of Empire is restored, but there is a sense that it is no more secure than the conquest of Swallow Island and here Commander Walker exhibits its worst qualities.[3] As the tide turns, the explorers head back to civilisation and school. They wave goodbye to their Essex friends, but there is only a half-hearted suggestion that they will meet again. Swallows

1. *SW*, p. 387.
2. *SW*, p. 412.
3. There is a similar sense of unease at the end of Golding's *Lord of the Flies* when the boys are rescued by the naval officers.

and Amazons may have been reunited, but the sense that they are drifting apart remains. This is not only goodbye to Secret Water but to childhood as well. The end-piece of *Great Northern?* is often seen as a final farewell; but, in reality, the Swallows sign off as the *Goblin* heads past the crossroads buoy and out of the Walton backwaters, making passage for Pin Mill.

*

Chapters 7 and 8 have considered the symbolism of *We Didn't Mean to Go to Sea* and *Secret Water;* the former focuses especially on the theme of the absent father and the difficult relationship between John and Susan, while the latter looks ironically at the colonial world as it begins to fragment on the eve of war. Above all, though, these novels when taken together are about growing up. Ransome is often criticised for trapping his characters in a time warp; it is argued that they never develop. But this is simply not the case. In the two years (and six novels, if we exclude the fantasy *Peter Duck*) since they first headed for Wild Cat Island, John and Susan in particular have learned through their experiences and changed.

It may be that *Secret Water* is one of the least popular of Ransome's novels (aside from the fantasies of *Peter Duck* and *Missee Lee*) because it is the most ambivalent towards its characters. Titty and Roger retain their enthusiasm and their innocence; Bridget is brim-full of infant spontaneity, and it is a disappointment that we never meet her again. But Susan has retreated almost wholly into her domestic responsibilities, bottling up those emotions let loose in the North Sea storm, and John's new seriousness becomes an unattractive imperial single-mindedness that spills into arrogance. So we are left with the Mastodon and Nancy, who from their first meeting form an unspoken alliance. There is even a hint of an emotional attachment that in a later era might have been made more explicit. The Mastodon's easy-going charm is balanced by his fierce loyalty to the Eels. In his nautical skill and his deep knowledge of his environment, he is similar to Tom Dudgeon in *Coot Club*, though neither the Mastodon nor Tom ever become fully-rounded characters. As for Nancy, she begins to develop the depths that are hinted at in the earlier novels, and in *The Picts and the Martyrs, Missee Lee* and *Great Northern?* she will become the focus of attention.

9.
The Big Six:
In the Shadow of War

The Big Six (1940) is at once one of the most amusing and the darkest of the 'Swallows and Amazons' series. It is the first of three essentially comic novels and although it ends on a light-hearted note, its world has become an even more threatening place. This is hardly surprising, since it was written in the first year of the Second World War; the Ransomes' Suffolk home at Harkstead Hall was subject to air raids and Jonathan Cape's block-maker (for the novel's illustrations) was to suffer a direct hit that September, destroying some of the blocks. Cape's wanted the title to be 'The Death and Glories', but Ransome rejected it on the grounds of its 'warlike suggestion'.[1] Perhaps it is the unsettling atmosphere of *The Big Six* that leads Christina Hardyment to describe it as a more adult book (as well as her least favourite).[2] Although Joe, Bill and Pete are sketched in and differentiated more than in *Coot Club*, the chief interest in the novel lies in the way they encounter the injustices and prejudices of adults rather than in their individual characters.

Although written six years later, the action of *The Big Six* is set only a few months after the action of *Coot Club*. The *Death and Glory* has had its new coat of paint, the reward from Rodley's for saving the *Margoletta* from sinking on Breydon Water. Tom's earlier casting off of *Margoletta* is used (briefly) in an attempt to incriminate him, and Dorothea's romanticised Broads story continues as a running joke (by now she is writing volume five). But there is little else which binds the two Norfolk Broads novels together and the mood has changed.

---

1. Letter of 9 July 1940 to Edith Ransome, reproduced in Roger Wardale et al., eds, *The Best of Childhood* (Kendal: Amazon Publications, 2004), p.237.
2. Christina Hardyment, *The World of Arthur Ransome* (London: Frances Lincoln, 2013), p.123.

Mrs Barrable has come ashore, and although Dorothea and Dick are staying with her in a holiday bungalow, she plays little part in the action. Port and Starboard have been sent off to school in Paris (just as Dora and Barbara Collingwood had been). The goings on are largely confined to Horning, so we miss the sense of space of the Norfolk landscape; we miss the buzz of Wroxham and Beccles, and the excitements of Yarmouth and Lowestoft. We also miss the range of lively Norfolk characters who people the earlier novel: only Tedder, the local policeman (now even more of a caricature), and Jim Wooddall, the wherry skipper, play a meaningful part. Whereas in *Coot Club*, Dorothea and Dick often refer to their friends in the North, here there is no mention of the adventures of *Pigeon Post* that they have enjoyed only weeks before (and which become part of the plot in the next novel in the series, *The Picts and the Martyrs*). If the end of *Secret Water* seems to be a farewell to the Swallows and Amazons, it may be that Ransome was indeed pondering whether their time was done.

In October 1937, after the completion of *We Didn't Mean to Go to Sea*, Ransome and Evgenia had celebrated by enjoying another holiday on the Norfolk Broads, this time hiring a motor cruiser from Jack Powles of Wroxham, with the aim of fishing the River Thurne. Almost immediately the scene of the catching of the pike above Potter Heigham Bridge began to form in Ransome's mind. Unfortunately he fell ill again and the holiday had to be cut short: he underwent two operations in Norwich – the second after a near-fatal embolism – and it was January 1938 before he was well enough to return home. But already he was thinking of a Norfolk sequel to *Coot Club*. On 24 January 1938 he wrote to Margaret Renold (who had helped with the plot of *Coot Club*): 'I have a very gorgeous episode with a pike, and a fisherman and an innkeeper and the Death and Glories'; he also envisages a winter adventure and mentions the comic smoking of the eels and the flaming of a Christmas pudding with methylated spirits.[1] The letter goes on to propose a detective story, with George Owdon, the bully glimpsed in *Coot Club*, blaming an as yet unspecified crime on the Death and Glories and so making them fight to unmask the real villain in order to clear their names. It was important to him that the boys were defenders rather than accusers and that the crime was trivial: that way they more easily gain the reader's sympathy. The following month Ransome wrote drafts of what were to become Chapter 7 ('The World's Whopper'), Chapter 8 ('At the Roaring Donkey'), and Chapter 3 ('The Eel Sett at

---

1. Letter to Margaret Renold, 24 January 1938, reproduced in *The Best of Childhood*, p. 211.

Night', which was originally entitled 'Night Affair'). As we have seen, it is characteristic of Ransome's creative process that he would write episodes that inspired him before he decided on the plot that would link them together. Arguably it is these chapters of *The Big Six* that most light up the novel, but, although they are incorporated seamlessly, it is unsurprising that they remain a little peripheral to the action.

But Ransome had already proposed to Wren Howard the idea of a different novel set on the Walton Backwaters, and in March 1938 he turned his attention to *Secret Water*, the coda to *We Didn't Mean to Go to Sea* which had been published four months before. So it was not until the New Year of 1940, after *Secret Water* had been published, that he revisited the Norfolk Broads story. Once he had finally settled on the plot, he wrote *The Big Six* more quickly than any book since *Swallows and Amazons*. By 23 July 1940 the second draft was complete, and even Evgenia seemed to approve.[1]

In *The Big Six* Ransome's original notion of a winter story has been abandoned and it is set loosely towards the end of September 1932 (though it is a mystery how the school term can begin so late), six months after the *Coot Club* adventure and with *Pigeon Post*, *We Didn't Mean to Go to Sea* and *Secret Water* already squeezed into the same summer holiday. Detective fiction was a genre that Ransome had always enjoyed (Margaret Renold had 'swamped' him with detective stories to read while he was recuperating from his appendicitis operation in the autumn of 1936).[2] Its morality – the uncovering of wrongdoing and the bringing of criminals to justice, with the world moving on as a safer and better place – suited both the optimism of the series and a country at war that was looking for reassurance. It is no coincidence that the uncomfortable interwar years should have produced English literature's 'golden age' of detective fiction, in which good almost always triumphs over evil. In 1910 Ransome had written a monograph on Edgar Allan Poe, a master of detective fiction; and in 1939–1940, the period when *The Big Six* was gestating, he was an enthusiastic reviewer of detective novels for *The Observer* (under the pseudonym William Blunt). So it is understandable that he should want to experiment with the form himself. But Brogan's claim that it is 'perhaps Ransome's most ingenious contrivance, and the book ought certainly to figure in any

1. Letter to G. Wren Howard, 18 May 1940, reproduced in *The Best of Childhood*, p. 234.
2. From an unpublished draft of Arthur Ransome's *Autobiography*, reproduced in Paul Crisp et al., eds, *Ransome Broadside* (Kendal: Amazon Publications, 2005), p. 21.

list of classics of detective fiction' is exaggerated.[1] In fact, Ransome adapts the conventional detective form for his own purposes. This is no 'whodunnit?' but an exercise in dramatic irony: although the members of the Coot Club and the people of Horning both remain blind to the almost obvious until the end of the novel, the reader very quickly works out that it is George Owdon who is setting boats adrift across the Northern Rivers. The problem with dramatic irony is that it gives the reader a sense of superiority over the fictional characters, which is dangerous in writing for children where any sense of patronisation can be disastrous. In *The Big Six*, the danger is compounded by Dr Dudgeon's adult asides (Dorothea as Portia, for example) and Mr Farland's ponderous summing up in the final chapter.

Thus the suspense of *The Big Six* lies not in the reader working out the identity of the villain(s) but in whether the young detectives will be able to discover the truth before the Death and Glories have a misguided summons taken out against them. Moreover, the whole thrust of the novel is not about the unmasking of Owdon but about proving what the reader already knows: the innocence of the children whose every value is opposed to the wrongs of which they are accused. (We are reminded of John's outrage in *Swallows and Amazons* when he is falsely accused of lying and of the Swallows and Amazons being falsely accused of starting the fell fire in *Pigeon Post*.) In the final chapter, Owdon and his accomplice Ralph Strakey become irrelevant once they have been proved guilty: they leave the village the next day and nothing more is heard of them. Instead, the focus is shifted to the restoration of the reputation of the Death and Glories as the embarrassed Tedder goes off to spread the news that they have been accused quite wrongly, and they go out together 'into the sunshine that seemed extraordinarily friendly'.[2]

From the start of *The Big Six* the interest shifts away from Tom Dudgeon, the central character of *Coot Club*, and rests instead on the Death and Glories. Although as river pirates (and now a salvage company) they display the same romantic free spirit as Nancy and Peggy Blackett, the fact that their fathers work as boat-builders rather than doctors, or lawyers, or naval officers, means that they are easier victims for Owdon and are less likely to be believed; this social injustice is one of the novel's main themes.

---

1. Hugh Brogan, *The Life of Arthur Ransome* (London: Hamish Hamilton, 1985), p. 387.
2. Arthur Ransome, *The Big Six* (London: Jonathan Cape, 1940). Red Fox edition (London: Random House, 2001), p. 418.

The opening chapter discovers Joe, Bill and Pete aboard the *Death and Glory*. Since *Coot Club* they have built a cabin on her and are looking forward to a cruise away from Horning. Their pride in their ship as they sort out the final details of her cabin is punctuated by Pete's comic jiggling of his about-to-drop-out milk tooth. This so exasperates his friends that Tom thinks up a ruse for its extraction, involving Pete's naïvety, a length of fishing line, a brick, and an upstairs window at Jonnatt's boatshed. But just as the comedy reaches its climax with the dropping of the brick and the painless outing of the tooth, the brick is mysteriously thrown back through the window, shattering the glass and beginning the series of incidents for which the Death and Glories are blamed. That night a motor cruiser is set adrift from Horning staithe, and because of Tom's previous untying of the *Margoletta* (tolerated and even applauded by the locals at the time because she was crewed by 'foreign' hooligans), his friends the Death and Glories are now seen as the culprits. Tom himself has a Teflon middle-class coating which quickly exonerates him. Jonnatt, the boatbuilder, takes his word, but assumes 'If it wasn't you it must have been those young friends of yours';[1] and Jim Wooddall will be quick to apologise for thinking it was Tom who untied the *Sir Garnet* ('I 'pologise, Doctor. Ought to have knowed it weren't your son. But as for them three by the staithe. . . .').[2]

Rod and Line

However, the novel is in no hurry and in Chapter 3, 'The Eel Sett at Night', Tom and the Death and Glories pay a visit to Harry Bangate, the Norfolk eelman, in his old tarred hulk. This remarkable set piece celebrates a dying Norfolk tradition. First, there is the description of Bangate's cabin, with its Jack Tar stove, and big black kettle, and shelves crowded with fishing gear. The walls remind of the Empire, now threatened by outsiders:

> The walls were covered with pictures of Queen Victoria's Jubilee, pictures cut out of newspapers, brown and smoky with age, pictures of soldiers off to South Africa, and pictures of the Coronation of Edward the Seventh. The old man's interest in history seemed to have stopped about then, for there were no pictures of anything that happened later.[3]

1. *BS*, p. 19.
2. *BS*, p. 146.
3. *BS*, p. 37.

The ending of Bangate's interest in history, which highlights and echoes Ransome's own concerns, reflects the decline in the British Empire after the end of Victoria's reign, the realisation of the threat to Britain's colonies (especially in the Far East) after the end of the disastrous Boer War, and the so-called 'progress' of the Edwardian era. Ransome was always entranced by the womb-like warmth and security of cabins and interiors: in the charcoal-burners' wigwam; in *Teasel, Welcome* and the *Death and Glory*; in *Wild Cat, Goblin* and the Mastodon's barge; and later in the 'Dogs' Home' and Missee Lee's 'Cambridge' study. Secondly, there are Bangate's tales of the Norfolk Broads as they used to be, with no holiday bungalows at Potter Heigham, but only trading wherries and reed-boats. To the dismay of the bird-protecting Coots, he tells of the shooting of 'buttles',[1] of the stealing and selling of eggs (suggesting he is more a soulmate of Owdon than of the Coots), and of the equilibrium of nature before commercial exploitation, though Tom is subsequently wise enough to change the subject:

> 'In old days we shoot a plenty and there were a plenty for all to shoot.'
> 'But that's why they disappeared,' said Tom.
> 'Don't you believe it,' said the old man. 'They go what with reed cutting and all they pleasure boats. . . .'[2]

Lastly, there is the magical drawing of the eel setts, where 'the light of the lantern was reflected from the glistening bellies of the eels'.[3] But again the wonder and the beauty of the moment are followed by the almost callous 'scotching [of] the warmints', undertaken by the eelman 'as easily and quietly as if he were thinking of something else':

> Bang. He had stunned the eel with a blow on its tail. The next moment he had picked up his knife, jabbed it into the eel's backbone close behind its head and dropped it into a bucket.[4]

Ironically, the killing of the eels doesn't seem to faze the young bird protectors for a moment.

But while the boys are witnessing the lifting of the eels, elsewhere more boats are being untied. In spite of Bangate confirming that the Death and Glories spent the night with him (though later on even he seems reluctant to protect them), the aggrieved boat owners are happier

---

1. Norfolk dialect for bitterns.
2. *BS*, p. 39.
3. *BS*, p. 42.
4. *BS*, p. 48.

to believe Owdon's accusations: in an ugly scene on the staithe it seems as if the entire village (which in *Coot Club* had stood behind Tom in his quarrel with 'foreigners') is condemning the children. Tedder, the previously good-hearted policeman, is taken in by Owdon's account and looks no further than what he is being told: the caricature of incompetent police being shown up by amateur sleuths is another staple ingredient of detective stories – think of the conflicts between Conan Doyle's Sherlock Holmes and Inspector Lestrade, and between Christie's Hercule Poirot and Inspector Japp. However, the 'Darkening Clouds' of Chapter 5 are parted for a little by the comic smoking of the eels (the Death and Glories succeed more in smoking themselves, and the eels are inedible) and by the arrival of the fishing launch *Cachalot* and her good-natured skipper (Ransome in yet another disguise).[1] Exhausted by a day's fishing for bait, the Death and Glories gladly accept a tow from the *Cachalot* to the upper reaches of the River Thurne and away from trouble.

After the pleasure of spending a quiet night in a new place above Potter Heigham bridge and away from their accusers, the boys wake up to a typical Broads scene, with the cattle and horses feeding in fields below the level of the river. In contrast to the changing landscapes of *Coot Club*, this is one of the few moments in *The Big Six* when there is time to enjoy the Norfolk surroundings. It is here that the boys are left to look after the *Cachalot* and the fishing lines while her owner fetches milk from the local inn, The Roaring Donkey. Almost the whole of Chapter 7, 'The World's Whopper', is devoted to recounting how, in his absence, they battle with and catch a giant pike, but the tension never wavers. Most of the action is described through their dialogue, which draws the reader into the action and shares their excitement and apprehension. There are comic moments too: the Death and Glories, now natives, scouting along the river bank 'stooping low and muzzled by their knives'; Bill's breathless blowing of the *Cachalot's* horn to attract the attention of her skipper; and Pete's falling headlong in the shallows when he attempts to drive the pike from its holt.[2] When the skipper returns he insists that it is for Joe to land his fish. But as with the killing of the eels, the pike's death is violent: 'The fisherman lifted a seat in the cockpit, took a short weighted club from the locker beneath it and brought it down heavily, once, twice, on the pike's head. The great fish lay still.'[3] The

---

1. Ransome was doubtless thinking of Frank T. Bullen's classic *The Cruise of the Cachalot: Round the World after Sperm Whales* (1898).
2. *BS*, p. 95.
3. *BS*, p. 104.

fish turns out to weigh more than thirty pounds, winning a bet that the fisherman has had with the landlord of The Roaring Donkey; generously, he divides his considerable winnings between Joe, Bill and Pete, swearing them to secrecy.

But the boys' good fortune does not last. During their night at Potter Heigham boats are set adrift there as well. Worse, it transpires that shackles have been stolen from Sonning's Potter Heigham boatyard and Mr Farland (father of Port and Starboard, and a supposed ally of the Coots) has been tasked with issuing summons against the culprits. When the boys spend part of their windfall on lavish provisions, it is assumed that their unexplained wealth is the proceeds of crime.

'A Regular Gang of Boys'

Things get worse for the Death and Glories in Chapter 10, 'Breakfast at Doctor Dudgeon's'. The previous evening, Tedder brought news of the trouble at Potter Heigham. Now, at breakfast, Dr Dudgeon, who stood half-heartedly behind Tom in *Coot Club*, is still mainly interested in preserving his reputation in the village and doubts the innocence of his son's young friends. 'Keep an eye on those young Coots of yours'; '[They] were away before anybody could stop them'; 'You must admit it looks rather funny. One coincidence is enough. . . . But three!'; 'You just keep your eye on those lads and give them a hint that casting off boats isn't cricket as a general thing'.[1] There follows the comically pompous letter in the local paper which describes 'a regular gang of boys masquerading under other auspices'.[2] Then, worst of all, the wherry *Sir Garnet* drifts down the river and is only saved by Tom's quick thinking; but her skipper, Jim Wooddall, once their friend, is someone else who has been convinced by Owdon that the Death and Glories are the culprits. At the staithe the boys are again mobbed by the villagers. Without taking a breath, the usually taciturn Joe pours out the story with a stream of 'and . . . and . . . and'; one sentence is fifteen lines long, with only a handful of commas to break the flow.[3] They have to 'emigrate', but let slip that they are sailing to nearby Ranworth to keep out of trouble.

Ransome hints at the power of class prejudice in the way that Dr Dudgeon and Mr Farland are prepared to think the worst of the Death and Glories; in the same way, Hannams would sack Joe's

1. *BS*, pp. 136-38.
2. *BS*, p. 139.
3. *BS*, pp. 149-50.

father if he wasn't such a good workman. Even the Reverend Saxby is convinced of their guilt, though Bill's mother is quick to pick up on his hypocrisy. Of the grown-ups, it is only Mrs Dudgeon, the skipper of the *Cachalot*, and the boys' parents who believe in the innocence of the Death and Glories. Pete's father, in comparison with the mealy-mouthed middle-class fathers, trusts his son's word and suffers a black eye defending him.

'Two Ways of Looking at the Same Thing'

To the reader, Owdon's guilt is obvious almost from the first chapter, when there is a suggestion of his motive. He wants to steal the birds' eggs that the members of the Coot Club – 'Interfering young pups' – have set themselves up to protect, and if he can have the boys taken off the river his way will be clear.[1] Thus when he and Strakey walk along Horning staithe after the first of the boats has been set adrift, it is obvious who is spreading rumours about the Coots that are cleverly reminiscent of Tom's casting off of the *Margoletta* six months before: '"At their old tricks again," said George loudly. "Casting off boats."'[2] Later that afternoon there is another prominent clue when Owdon and Strakey warn a yacht owner about the Death and Glories: when the Death and Glories find the yacht adrift and tow her back to the staithe, it is inevitable that Owdon and Strakey are there to accuse them of untying her warps, and they give a catalogue of all the other boats that have been set loose. There are further equally laboured pointers. Owdon overhears the Death and Glories telling their mothers that they are going to Potter Heigham; after the wherry *Sir Garnet* becomes the most dramatic victim of the vandals, Owdon is there to stir up trouble; when the Death and Glories struggle to escape to Ranworth, Owdon encourages the villagers to let them go – and it is small wonder that boats are soon cast adrift there; Owdon and Strakey borrow the Tozers' dinghy and are conveniently out each night masquerading as river watchers. As Dorothea says perceptively, 'Someone *must* be doing it on purpose. . . . But everyone thinks it's the Coots so they aren't looking properly for anyone else.'[3]

Dick and Dorothea arrive in Chapter 9 and give the novel a fresh impetus. They have grown and changed since *Coot Club* only six months before, when they were the novice crew determined to learn how to

---

1. *BS*, p. 5.
2. *BS*, p. 22.
3. *BS*, p. 185.

sail in order to impress the Swallows and Amazons on their next Lake holiday; when Dick was the absent-minded bird-watcher, forever distracted from the task in hand, and Dorothea was wrapped up in her stories. But although in *The Big Six* Dick remains in his own scientific bubble, he has found acceptance in *Pigeon Post* (both for his design of the pigeon alarm and his masterminding of the smelting), and here his photographic skills will finally save the day. Meanwhile, Dorothea – incidentally, the only girl in the cast – takes charge, lightly shouldering Tom into the background as she sets out, *contra mundum*, to prove the innocence of the boys. For her, this is as much a thrilling game as anything else. The Death and Glories may be sceptical, and sometimes resentful, but they are swept along by her newfound confidence.

Thus, as in *Coot Club*, much of the novel is seen from Dorothea's point of view:

> 'Why shouldn't we find out ourselves?' she went on almost as if talking to herself alone. 'I've never tried writing a detective story.'[1]

It is she who transforms the shed in the Dudgeons' garden into 'Scotland Yard'; she who coins the name 'The Big Six';[2] she who develops another story within a story, another game, in which the miserable Death and Glories are understandably reluctant to play their part:

> 'Why shouldn't we be detectives too?' said Dorothea.
> 'We don't need to be detectives to know we ain't done it,' said Joe. 'We know that without.'
> 'We could use my camera,' said Dick. 'They always have one.'
> The Death and Glories looked doubtfully from face to face.
> 'All the world believed them guilty,' said Dorothea. 'Their fathers' and mothers' grey hairs went down in sorrow to their graves. . . . Were going down . . .' she corrected herself. 'The evidence was black on every side. . . . And I say . . .' She suddenly changed her tone. 'William'll make a splendid bloodhound.'
> 'But William ain't a bloodhound,' said Pete. 'Nothing like it.'[3]

---

1. *BS*, p. 186.
2. Based on 'the Big Five' at Scotland Yard. In his first novel, *Death under Sail* (London: Heinemann, 1926), also set on the Norfolk Broads, C. P. Snow refers to the 'Big Five', so Dorothea's invention is hardly original. Perhaps Enid Blyton had the 'Big Six' in mind when she introduced the 'Famous Five' in 1942, and the 'Secret Seven' in 1949?
3. *BS*, p. 186.

9. Scotland Yard

It is Dorothea who transforms the shed in the Dudgeons' garden into 'Scotland Yard'; she who coins the name 'The Big Six'; she who develops another story within a story, in which the miserable Death and Glories are understandably reluctant to play their part.

Dorothea's exaggerated prose is a playful parody of detective novels of the time; as in *Coot Club*, it is her turning of the mundane into melodrama that in the second half of *The Big Six* shapes the novel and sparks much of its humour.

So begins the gathering of evidence to unmask the real villains, though the operation is hindered as one by one the outlying members of the Coot Club desert. From Ranworth there is the tube from the bicycle pump and Dick's drawing of the tyre tracks; there are the moving of the chain ferry at Horning by night, the scrap of flannel, the handprint on the *Death and Glory's* freshly painted chimney, and the green paint on the shackles and the fence. Of course, none of these prove anything, and all the time the gullible Tedder is building his own misguided case which everyone is lulled into believing (so close are Owdon and Tedder that Pete's belief that Tedder is the villain is not wholly unreasonable). However, it is not long before Dick, ever the scientist, realises that what is important is the 'highest common factor' of Dorothea's lists detailing the circumstances of each crime: George Owdon. But the night the boats were cast off at Potter Heigham he was keeping watch on the moorings at Horning. The puzzle is finally solved by Joe who realises, and then proves by doggedly re-enacting the ride, that although Owdon couldn't have been in two villages at once, he could have cycled to Potter Heigham to cast off the boats and returned to Horning in time to be seen on the staithe. What is more, young Bob Curten is prepared to swear that he saw Owdon at Potter Heigham on the night in question. It all seems to fall into place.

Even so, there is still no proof, and it is Dorothea, as much a criminal psychologist as a writer, who thinks herself into the mind of the villain. She knows that whoever it is will be worried that 'Scotland Yard' has more evidence than it actually has and will be desperate to cast off more boats. So the trap is laid, with the convenient return of *Cachalot* as bait and Dick setting up a camera and flashlight to capture anyone meddling with her. (Mrs Barrable, being rather Great Auntish, does not allow Dorothea to take part – ambushes are all right for boys – and Dick has to be home by ten o'clock.)[1] It works out perfectly, with growing suspense as the detectives wait for their quarry, the night-time chase, and the assault on the *Death and Glory* as Owdon and Strakey try to retrieve the incriminating film. The suspense is maintained as Dick struggles to develop the photograph in time (and, typically, the novel describes in detail each slow process of the developing). As in the best detective stories, he turns up late to 'court' but reaches Mr Farland's house just in time to unmask the guilty and so spare the innocent.

---

1. *BS*, p. 353.

When the photograph is laid on the table, the truth is out. But Ransome, standing behind Farland, cannot resist explaining the workings of the detective novel, nicely drawing out the discomfiture of Owdon, Strakey and Tedder: "'The value of evidence,' he said, "fluctuates with its context. . . . It gives an entirely new value to a great deal of other evidence that, without it, I should have been justified in dismissing as unconvincing.'"[1] Clues that are in themselves trivial – and often missed – suddenly become clear when the truth is revealed. It may also be that Farland is trying to justify why he and most of the other adults in the novel have failed to see the apparently obvious: blinded by class prejudice, they have lacked the context that the reader has recognised all along. But there is still an acknowledgement that the 'Big Six' have discovered the truth where Tedder has so obviously failed: 'I'm ashamed to think that if you had left it to the law things might have gone badly with you,' says Mr Farland damningly, while neatly side-stepping his own credulity.[2] Or as Pete says angrily when Owdon and Strakey are unmasked: 'Might have been us. . . . Only we didn't do it.'[3] It just remains for Tedder, restored as a likeable comic figure, to spread the news of the Death and Glories' innocence around the village and for Dorothea to round off the story she has created: 'Everything worked out beautifully. . . . Scotland Yard's won in the end. I knew it would.'[4] In the Postscript, the focus returns to the pike, which has been stuffed in Norwich and is now displayed at The Roaring Donkey, with the names of Joe, Bill and Pete in gold letters. They are heroes, not villains, after all.

*

The Big Six is narrower in scope than *Coot Club*, lacking both its sense of adventure and the feeling of space engendered by the wider horizons of the East Anglian marshes. In comparison with its immediate predecessors it misses the sustained drama of *We Didn't Mean to Go to Sea* and the brooding adolescent uncertainties and conflicts of *Secret Water*. But it is a disconcerting novel, because on the one hand – and more than any of the other books in the *Swallows and Amazons* series – it never lets us forget that much of the action is a children's detective game, while on the other hand the Death and Glories have to contend

---

1. *BS*, pp. 413-14.
2. *BS*, p. 416.
3. *BS*, p. 416.
4. *BS*, p. 417.

with the desertion of their supposed friends and the real fickleness and spitefulness of their elders, and it is only their own efforts that save them from injustice. The confining of the *Death and Glory* to Horning and its immediate environs means that the atmosphere becomes suffocating and the attacks on its crew relentless. At the same time, it is brimming with comedy, even if the laughter is sometimes stifled by the uneasy relationship between the children and the adult world. The main strength of *The Big Six* lies in its central characters: spirited boat-builders' sons, at the bottom of the social pile, who come alive in their Norfolk dialect and who gain the reader's sympathy because their honesty is perpetually and unjustly doubted by those who should know better; and Dorothea and Dick, no longer helpless newcomers, who have the intelligence and resourcefulness to root out the truth and are afforded the genuine respect of the Coot Club.

In spite of Wren Howard's urging of Ransome to avoid mentioning the war at all costs, the 'Darkening Clouds' of Chapter 5 allude at least in part to the increasing threats in the real world of 1940. It is also the case that the unlikely triumph of the Death and Glories against all the forces ranged against them, but with right, determination, and ingenuity on their side, reflects Ransome's hope for Britain's eventual victory over the evils of Nazism. With Britain beleaguered and facing almost insuperable odds, this was exactly the message that the original readers of *The Big Six* would have wanted to hear.

10.
Missee Lee:
Nancy and the Twenty-Two
Gong Taicoon

In *Missee Lee* (1941), we are back on board the *Wild Cat,* the converted trading schooner which took the Swallows and Amazons on their fantastic voyage to the Caribbees in *Peter Duck* and which now takes them to a different and magical place. This time, without explanation or comment, the children are embarked on a round-the-world voyage with Captain Flint, as if it is nothing out of the ordinary. After the *Wild Cat* is lost in a fire off the Chinese coast they are captured by pirates operating from the Three Islands and become caught in a tug-of-war between the twenty-two gong Taicoon Miss Lee and the ten gong Taicoon Chang. Miss Lee wins the tug-of-war – not least because she hankers after an academic career and sees the Swallows and Amazons as potential Latin pupils – and they become her prisoners. After endless Latin lessons and a series of adventures their lives are threatened, but they escape with the surprising help of Miss Lee under the cover of a Dragon Festival. However, Miss Lee has a change of heart and her plan to return with them to England (and thus to her alma mater, Newnham College in Cambridge) is abandoned at the last moment.

On the title page we are told that the novel is 'based on information supplied by the Swallows and Amazons', the endpaper map of 'Miss Lee's Islands' and the copy of the map of the Three Islands found in the cabin of *Shining Moon*[1] are both annotated by Nancy Blackett, and Nancy also writes the note about laundry which records her disagreement with Susan over what they should include in the

---

1. Arthur Ransome, *Missee Lee* (London: Jonathan Cape, 1941). Red Fox edition (London: Random House, 2001), p. 198.

story.[1] Unlike the Lake and East Anglian novels, there is no framing of the action by school or holidays. These are the only overt clues that Ransome is playing another metafictional game, although in a letter to the Renolds, worrying about his inability to come up with a plot, he reveals that the children are again the imagined authors, or at least the source of the tale: 'DAMN IT, what CAN those young devils, Nancy and Co, devise as a main object to stretch their minds on this time?'[2]

Although *Missee Lee*, Ransome's tenth novel, was first published in 1941, the year after *The Big Six*, it is unclear where it sits in the chronology of the *Swallows and Amazons* series. There is a reference to the sinking of *Swallow* in *Swallowdale* and Roger has already been promoted from ship's boy to able-seaman, but there is no mention of the encounter with pirates in *Peter Duck*; nor when the Swallows are riding out the storm after abandoning *Wild Cat* do they recall their fight for survival in *We Didn't Mean to Go to Sea*. The Swallows' young sister, Bridget, is never mentioned, and the D.'s, who have taken centre stage in *Winter Holiday* and *Pigeon Post*, are quite forgotten. There is method in this. As we have seen in Chapter 6, *Pigeon Post* is a fractious book, in which there is a growing unease with Nancy's games. We have also seen how in *We Didn't Mean to Go to Sea*, the Swallows, and John and Susan in particular, are changed by their experience so that in *Secret Water* there is no longer the close relationship with the Amazons which is central to the early novels; I have also suggested that there is a sense that *Secret Water* may be the natural conclusion to the series. *Missee Lee* is careful to ignore this later context and takes us back (if it takes us anywhere in time) to a more innocent era, before any tensions have arisen between the characters and before the D.'s arrive on the scene. This not only allows a more manageable cast but also means that the rollicking plot, rather than the children, can become the centre of attention. Roger and Titty revert to their irrepressible younger selves, though John and Susan seem to have grown older and, after the shipwreck and landing on Tiger Island, remain very much on the fringes of the action. It is as if Ransome has lost interest in them, or sees no way of developing them further.

The fairy tale quality observed in *Swallowdale* and *Pigeon Post* is even more in evidence in *Missee Lee*, with the innocent children straying

---

1. *ML*, p. 271.

2. Letter to Margaret and Charles Renold, 13 February 1941, reproduced in Hugh Brogan, ed., *Signalling from Mars: the Letters of Arthur Ransome* (London: Jonathan Cape, 1997), pp. 280-82.

from their parents, being trapped and threatened by a wicked lady (here a she-pirate instead of a witch), and using their ingenuity and bravery to escape: as in a fairy tale, it is the plot and its symbolism which are important, and not the characters themselves. Victor Watson offers a full discussion of *Missee Lee* as fairy tale in *Reading Series Fiction*: 'it is a fairy-tale disguised as a sea-yarn, a climactic and concentrated expression of all the imaginings and pretendings of the previous narratives'.[1] But where *Missee Lee* is different from most fairy tales is in its rich vein of comedy, especially in the imitative antics of Gibber, the 'velly uncultured' Captain Flint perched in his bamboo cage, the riotous Chinese meal with Taicoon Chang and his sea captains, and Miss Lee's 'pidgin English' and 'pidgin Latin' (today we regard the imitation of Chinese speech as belittling and politically incorrect, but Ransome's humour is never intentionally unkind).[2] So, almost remarkably, in view of its subject matter, it is a comfortable and reassuring story rather than an unsettling and frightening one: even the repeated threats to 'cut off heads' are softened by laughter and hardly seem to upset the children. There is never a doubt that it will yet again be all right in the end: 'It always is,' says Nancy, and series readers have the reassurance of a familiar and trusted author and the comfortable, closed endings of earlier adventures.[3]

The relationship of *Missee Lee* to *Peter Duck*, the other novel in which the Swallows and Amazons meet 'real' pirates, is more problematic. *Peter Duck* recounts the first time that the Swallows and Amazons, in their own story, sail in *Wild Cat*, but in *Missee Lee* there is no mention of their encounter with Black Jake and *Viper*. We have to accept that although the ship and her crew are the same, and in each novel *Wild Cat* is the means by which the children are transported from the real to the fantasy world, there is no other link between them and such a link would have complicated and weakened both. It is also worth remarking that whereas *Peter Duck* deliberately draws on and parodies the traditions of travel writing and pirate literature, *Missee Lee* largely stands by itself and is more sure-footed: given its undoubted strengths it is surprising that over the years it has been one of the least popular of the *Swallows and Amazons* novels. Perhaps this is because to an extent it is a 'one-off', a little outside the rest of the series, and at times somewhat bewildering to those who come to it first.

---

1. Victor Watson, *Reading Series Fiction* (London: Routledge Falmer, 2000), p. 52.
2. *ML*, p. 187.
3. *ML*, p. 210.

Ransome in China

By 1941, life in Suffolk was proving increasingly difficult for the Ransomes. The German bombing raids were becoming more frequent and threatening, their friends were moving away, and there was the worry that their home at Harkstead Hall might be requisitioned at any time. So, in spite of Evgenia's reservations about the rain and the damp, they decided to move back to the greater peace and security of the Lake District. Forgetting his resolution to move on from the Lake in the North, Ransome was now eager to return. However, Wren Howard at Cape's felt that readers would prefer something more adventurous to take their minds off the war; something more 'Peter Ducky', in fact.[1] Although at first sight Ransome continues to follow Wren Howard's advice to 'steer clear of the war', consciously or subconsciously it still simmers beneath the surface of *Missee Lee* as it had done in *The Big Six*: explosion and shipwreck; the careful rationing of supplies; and the threat of an alliance between Tiger Island and Turtle Island against Miss Lee and Dragon Island that reflects the 1939 Molotov-Ribbentrop pact between Germany and the Soviet Socialist Republics.[2]

Ransome quickly latched on to Evgenia's suggestion that he should use China as the setting for the new fantasy. He had been sent to China by the *Manchester Guardian* in 1926-1927 to report on the turbulent political and military situation that was threatening British, European, American and Japanese interests in the area. The country was slipping into civil war. On one side Chinese nationalists wanted to bring together the vast country as a republic with a central government and economy, and end China's exploitation by foreign traders and resident foreign communities in the so-called 'treaty ports'. ('No good landing just anywhere,' says Captain Flint after the shipwreck. 'It's got to be a treaty port or nowhere.')[3] On the other side were the Chinese warlords (and pirates) and the foreign traders who, with understandable self-interest, wished to maintain the *status quo* that was affording them huge profits. Ransome's subsequent account of his time in China, *The Chinese Puzzle* (1927), attracted little attention, not least because the situation

---

1. Letter from Edith Ransome to Joyce Lupton, 4 November 1940, reproduced in Roger Wardale et al., eds, *The Best of Childhood* (Kendal: Amazon Publications, 2004), p. 250.
2. Letter to Charles Renold, 19 February 1941, reproduced in *The Best of Childhood*, p. 255.
3. *ML*, p. 26.

was changing quickly and a delay in publication meant that it was out of date when it finally appeared. But in *Missee Lee* his experiences and memories could be put to good use, and, as in his other novels, it is in real people, places and events that it has its beginnings.

The inspiration for Miss Lee, the mysterious she-pirate, is Madame Sun Yat-sen, as Ransome tells us in his *Autobiography*.[1] She was the young widow of Dr Sun Yat-sen, the father of the 1911 Chinese Revolution (she was thirty-four when Ransome met her in 1927). Educated at the Wesleyan College in Macon, Georgia, she returned to China and on the death of her husband was elected a member of the Central Executive of the Chinese Nationalist Party; later she was to become the first woman Vice-Chair of the People's Republic of China. Ransome had also read Aleko E. Lilius's *I Sailed with Chinese Pirates* (1930), which describes how the ruthless she-pirate Lai Choi San, having inherited a fleet of armed junks from her father, terrorises the coastal area between Macao and Hong Kong, not far from Miss Lee's fictional Three Islands. It is probable that Taicoon Chang owes much to General Zhang Zongchang (they are both described as giants among the Chinese) and to a Yangtze river skipper whose boat was loaded with caged birds; Ransome met both of them during his assignment.

The opening of *Missee Lee* is immediately captivating. We are in the cabin of the *Wild Cat*, preparing to put to sea after a brief stay in a deliberately unidentified harbour. Even by night the place is alive with movement, sound and light. Sailors are chipping the rust off a Japanese merchant steamship; a pile driver is at work; stevedores and dockhands chant shanties as they go about their business. Arc-lights blaze down and more lights twinkle on the shore and on ships riding at anchor; lighthouses and buoys flash their friendly warnings. The Swallows, Amazons and Captain Flint are taking their leave of the harbourmaster, an old acquaintance of Captain Flint from a previous voyage and a colonial 'type'. The conversation flows, setting the wider scene: 'our hundredth port;'[2] 'round the world';[3] 'going across to the China coast';[4] and then the harbourmaster's ominous warning: 'I'd be sorry if the next thing I hear of you is a finger in a matchbox and a hint of more to follow. . . . Don't go and fall foul of Missee Lee.'[5]

1. Arthur Ransome, *The Autobiography of Arthur Ransome*, ed. Rupert Hart-Davis (London: Jonathan Cape, 1976), p. 326.
2. *ML*, p. 1.
3. *ML*, p. 3.
4. *ML*, p. 2.
5. *ML*, p. 3.

Of course, the harbourmaster's wise advice is disregarded, as it would be in a fairy story. The novel's title is a sure sign that it will not be long before the *Wild Cat*'s crew encounter 'Missee Lee', who runs a lucrative protection racket inherited from her father. She controls three islands somewhere along the Chinese coast, but no-one is going to let on exactly where, least of all to foreign authorities: 'We'd have had gunboats after her long ago if we knew where she was.'[1] Later in the novel the Chinese fear of gunboats resurfaces. Miss Lee refuses to let the children send a message to their parents in case they 'bling gunboats';[2] Taicoon Wu, once a bo'sun on British and Chinese ships, warns Miss Lee that by using his sextant Captain Flint can give away their location – 'Moa betta chop you head'[3] – and John's revelation that his father is a captain in the British navy brings the same shocked reaction, the slight and sinister chopping movement of the hand. But by this time, as much as we may want and expect the children to escape, our sympathies lie as much with Miss Lee, in the same way that we are as entranced by the outrageous Amazon pirates as we are by the Swallow explorers and, in *Great Northern?*, we will understand the anger of the Gaels when their island is unceremoniously invaded by troublesome 'bairns'.

Boys: Gibber, Roger and Captain Flint

It is Gibber, the master of mimicry, who precipitates disaster. Becalmed between the hundredth port and Swatow (now Shantou), Captain Flint and John take readings with a sextant to ascertain the *Wild Cat*'s position, and Gibber joins in, standing with feet wide apart like Captain Flint and with Susan's scissors to his eye; in the mainmast rigging he becomes a look-out like Nancy, using his curled fingers as a telescope; he copies Roger, asleep. Then, as Captain Flint relaxes with a cigar, Gibber plays his tricks again:

> Everybody was awake by now, and laughed to see the little monkey, so thin, so narrow-waisted, so unlike Captain Flint, copying his every motion, the pull at the cigar, the slow, happy blowing out of the smoke, the little flourish of the cigar when Captain Flint had said 'Come on, then. . . . Anybody else like to lend a hand?'
> 'Gibber would love to,' said Roger.[4]

---

1. *ML*, pp. 3-4.
2. *ML*, p. 204.
3. *ML*, p. 311.
4. *ML*, pp. 17-18.

In the drowsy afternoon heat, the novel lingers over Gibber's comic antics. But when petrol is being shifted from the main tank to the engine room, Gibber steals Captain Flint's lighted cigar, carelessly left in an ashtray on the chart table, and repeats his performance. Now it is no longer funny. After a desperate chase, Gibber decides to hide the cigar in the open filler of the petrol tank. The *Wild Cat* is set ablaze and is lost.

After the Swallows have drifted ashore, Titty and Roger go searching for bananas for Gibber, but, almost inevitably, the monkey is their downfall. As they hide from a row of Chinese workers collecting what turn out to be grasshoppers, Gibber escapes. Finding something else to mimic, he shadows their every movement and follows them more and more closely. Laughter is tempered by the inevitability of his eventual capture, which is itself another bright moment of visual comedy:

> . . . suddenly the Chinese, crouching, searching, hopping, saw the monkey's shadow jerk forward with his own. He looked over his shoulder straight into Gibber's face, screamed, jumped up, dropped his little box and then, seeing what it was, made an angry grab at the monkey.[1]

When Roger dashes to the rescue they are all taken prisoner and there follows Chang's extraordinary donkey procession to meet Miss Lee, with Gibber swinging up on the donkey's tale and riding behind Roger. From now on there is a running commentary in pidgin Chinese, where the dubious humour trumps the seriousness of their plight and Titty can react with masterly and almost unworried understatement:

> 'Tomollow all plisoners see Missee Lee. All eat man fan with Taicoon. . . . Supper. Perhaps tomollow no supper. No heads. No wantee chow.'
>
> Not very cheering, thought Titty, but the Taicoon Chang did not seem to think it mattered.[2]

When, later, Gibber is rescued from Chang and returned to Roger, the grinning ex-cook sums up his antics but, as so often in *Missee Lee*, it is the pidgin English as much as the action which is the centre of the comedy, even if it is uncomfortable for a contemporary audience: '"Numpa one bad monkey," said the ex-cook, grinning. "Him bite. Him

---

1. *ML*, pp. 117-18.
2. *ML*, p. 144.

lun away. Him pull donk tail. Numpa one bad monkey."'[1] It is lucky that in the final moments on board *Shining Moon* Gibber's impression of the counsellor ('solemnly combing with his long fingers the beard he had not got') goes unnoticed.[2]

In *Missee Lee*, Roger is still the mischievous lad of *Swallows and Amazons* and *Swallowdale* and not yet as wilful as he is in *Pigeon Post* and (later) *Great Northern?*. His main role is as Gibber's keeper but, whatever the situation, he is 'less easily dismayed' than the others and his schoolboy ebullience always lightens the mood.[3] He also makes two crucial interventions. First, in the temple, he defaces Miss Lee's Latin grammar by adding an extra line and a gruesome illustration to the rhyme on the flyleaf. Chastised by John and Susan, he quickly regrets it and later pours out an embarrassed apology to Miss Lee. But fortunately for all of them, she is delighted by his addition and retracts her orders to kill them just in time. Moreover, to the chagrin of the others – 'Swot'[4] says Nancy under her breath – Roger becomes the star pupil in Miss Lee's Latin class: 'a lively reading . . . of a bit of Caesar's *Gallic Wars* saved the lot of them'.[5] Secondly, as they attempt their escape, it is Roger who leads their young Dragon in the Dragon festival, leaping and spinning like an acrobat and swinging a lighted lantern around his head. Even his slip in front of the Taicoons in the yamen disarms the murderous Chang who becomes helpless with laughter.

The trio of errant boys is completed by Captain Flint who is again a larger than life character, perhaps even larger than previously, and a further source of rich comedy. As in *Peter Duck*, he plays a central rather than a supporting part. In the opening chapter, he shows irresponsibility and heroism in equal measure: on the one hand are his foolhardy determination to visit the Chinese coast in the face of the harbourmaster's warning and the leaving of his lighted cigar when transferring petrol from tank to tank; on the other are his orderly evacuation of the burning *Wild Cat* and his rescue of Gibber after the falling mast throws him into the sea. But from then on, for at least the first part of the novel, there is a series of comic episodes that cement his reputation as mad and bad: his struggle with the pirates who take him prisoner; his roaring from the perch in his cage at the boys predicting his execution; his gorilla act as he is taken to face Miss

1. *ML*, p. 218.
2. *ML*, p. 400.
3. *ML*, p. 313.
4. *ML*, p. 250.
5. *ML*, p. 215.

Lee for the first time; and his communicating with the Swallows and Amazons through bizarre sea shanties sung at top volume ('Columbia the gem of the Ocean . . .').[1] Above all, his posing as the Lord Mayor of San Francisco in the hope of securing a swift release turns out to have the opposite effect, with Chang seeing the potential for a hefty ransom. The latter leads to a string of amusing moments, not least to the plunging of Nancy and Peggy into early matrimony ('Melican man with two English wives').[2]

In the second half of the novel Captain Flint becomes the comic dunce of Miss Lee's class, but now he takes charge of the situation, insisting on the model behaviour that leads to her neglecting of the Three Islands and her near downfall as she becomes focused only on her students. Finally, with Miss Lee's help, he brings about the daring escape from Dragon Island, although his losing control of *Shining Moon* in the rushing waters of the gorge, with Miss Lee coming to the rescue, means he is not transformed into some kind of melodramatic hero. As Miss Lee gives up her own ambitions and returns to lead the Three Islands and the *Shining Moon* heads for home, it is Captain Flint who offers the barely disguised moral of a moral tale: 'She's got a rum job, but she knows how to do it, and to have a job and know how to do it is one of the best things in life. . . . Miss Lee, twenty-two gong Taicoon, is back in her own place.'[3]

Challenging the Stereotype: Missee Lee, Nancy and Titty

In discussing the *Swallows and Amazons* novels I have alluded to the treatment of the female characters: how, to an extent Susan (like her mother) fits the stereotype of a 1930s wife, mother and homemaker – the mainstay of the family, but in the end deferring to John as the father-figure; how Titty has strengths which make her stand out from the other Swallows and Amazons and so often lead her to save the day – although many of her strengths could be regarded as essentially feminine, she manages to escape the female stereotype; how Nancy and Peggy also defy the stereotype in their pirate games (though more often than not Peggy is an unwilling and subservient accomplice) and parody it when they are dressed up in their party frocks to please Great Aunt Maria. *Missee Lee* sharpens the debate.

1. *ML*, p. 188.
2. *ML*, p. 66.
3. *ML*, pp. 399–400.

Although the Swallows and Amazons are largely ciphers in the novel, Miss Lee herself is Ransome's most developed adult character. The 'bogey' used by Chinese mothers to frighten their children into obedience, and about whom the harbourmaster warns the *Wild Cat*'s crew, turns out to be a 'tiny Chinese woman' wearing 'black silk coat and trousers' and 'gold shoes that rested on a footstool'.[1] But the revolver resting on her knees and the subsequent deference to her shown by the giant Taicoon Chang, tell another story.

Miss Lee, a twenty-two gong Taicoon in a man's world, is a ruthless operator. Chang is convinced that she will chop off the heads of the Swallows and Amazons; she has already once ordered their execution and it is only Roger's mischief and the prospect of her acquiring a class of young scholars that has saved them. She shows no sympathy for Captain Flint: 'If he has lied and Chang cuts his head off it is his own fault.'[2] In her yamen, there is the steady counting of money as prisoners, kept in cages like Captain Flint, pay their dues; the fate of those who cannot pay and are marched straight out of the courtyard is never stated but all too obvious. She is quietly determined in her negotiation with Chang to buy Captain Flint. She has no intention of allowing any of the children to leave and will not let them send a message to their families in England. But there is kindness too in the way she secures the transfer of Polly and Gibber as well as Captain Flint, and it is rare that there is not a smile playing on her lips.

Miss Lee's father was Taicoon of the Three Islands, and had sent her to be educated at an English girls' school before going on to study at Newnham College.[3] But in her first year there her father, now old and sick, summoned her home to learn the pirate business and before his death he appointed her to succeed him, saying 'that it was his whole life that he had put into my hands' and thwarting the pursuit of her own academic dream.[4] Thus Miss Lee's father becomes an invisible patriarchal presence throughout the novel. His grave is the temple where the Swallows spend their first night ashore ('I think my father velly pleased,' says Miss Lee).[5]

---

1. *ML*, p. 183.

2. *ML*, p. 229.

3. Although I have been unable to trace a girls' school at Gleat (sic) Marlow in the early twentieth century, it is possible that Ransome was thinking of Wycombe Abbey School in Buckinghamshire, founded in 1896 just a few miles north of Great Marlow.

4. *ML*, p. 201.

5. *ML*, p. 202.

10. Waiting to Hear Their Fate

Missee Lee turns out to be a 'tiny Chinese woman' wearing 'black silk coat and trousers' and 'gold shoes that rested on a footstool'. But the revolver resting on her knees tells another story.

Although Miss Lee is breaking her father's law by keeping English prisoners (who may bring gunboats and trouble), she believes he would be happy for her to have her own Latin class. However, she tends to use the memory of her father to justify her own wishes. 'Hoc volo, sic jubeo,' she says, which Roger translates as 'She means she's jolly well going to do what she wants.'[1] It is left to her amah (the nurse who accompanied her to England) and her counsellor to warn her that the Latin class is leading her to neglect her responsibilities: traders who have not paid their dues sail past unchallenged while she teaches, so the sailors are angry and, in desperation, the amah steals her books. We are reminded of John's loyalty to his father, Commander Walker, as he is prepared for a career in the Royal Navy, and I wonder whether Ransome is also thinking of his own father, who (in a reverse of *Missee Lee*) once imagined an academic career for young Arthur (a career that lasted a term at Yorkshire College before he followed his own desire to become a writer).

Miss Lee's study, another of Ransome's lovingly described interiors, encapsulates her yearning for Cambridge and how she has been denied her vocation. Only the bamboo pipes and her cartridge belt and pistol holder hanging by the door remind the reader that this is not a room at Newnham College but a pirate's lair in China. Here are an English fireplace; a coloured picture of Cambridge's 'Backs'; photographs of fellow undergraduates; an oak plaque with the College arms; a hockey stick; a team photograph ('Pretty beefy,'[2] murmurs Roger); English tea ('Stlong . . . with milk . . . and plenty of sugar')[3] and a dish of little cakes. Miss Lee's faithful amah struggles with the language, but the children surely recognise her very English greeting: '"How do you do?" said the little old woman. "Velly fine weather."'[4] That evening, the amah chides them for not using their chopsticks properly ('Belong chow-chow China fashion'),[5] but at breakfast the next day, in the Cambridge study, there are knives and forks, and porridge, and fried ham, and toast with (a nice touch) Cooper's Oxford marmalade: 'Evellything Camblidge fashion.'[6] Miss Lee may be a fearsome pirate chief, but Cambridge is where her heart lies. I am tempted to wonder whether her inner circle resents her devotion to English culture as

---

1. *ML*, p. 249.
2. *ML*, p. 193.
3. *ML*, p. 194.
4. *ML*, p. 194.
5. *ML*, p. 210.
6. *ML*, p. 212.

much as her obsession with her Latin class, seeing that those colonised are inevitably changed by their colonisers; remember, too, how Miss Lee's father chose a traditional English education for his daughter.

This internal conflict comes to the fore in the final chapter. It is as much a surprise to the reader as it is to the Swallows and Amazons that, having helped to organise the Swallows' and Amazons' escape, Miss Lee should have stowed away on her own junk; and, just when it seems that *Shining Moon* will be wrecked in the gorge, she comes calmly to the rescue. As Captain Flint shouts above the roaring water, Titty feels 'soft, silent feet': '"Solly. Better let me have tiller, I think," said the voice of Miss Lee.'[1] Where Captain Flint has become helpless, she takes command: 'Aye-aye, sir,' he says, tellingly. She can see in the darkness; she is a skilled seaman as well as an academic; the junk no longer swerves and the whirlpool is mastered; the water becomes smoother. Far from being grateful, Nancy attacks her, believing that she is playing cat and mouse with them and that they are once more her prisoners. However, Miss Lee has decided to escape to England with them. At last she is fulfilling her own desire and 'going back to Camblidge'.[2]

When the wind drops at dawn, she allows a sampan to come alongside, with her signaller, her amah and her counsellor pleading with her to return to the Three Islands. It is uncertain what makes her change her mind. Perhaps it is the counsellor telling her that Chang and Wu are already fighting over who will now be chief, and that she has a duty to her father to stay – '. . . only I, Miss Lee, my father's daughter';[3] perhaps it is the loyalty of her subjects – her signaller, amah and counsellor, and the crew of the pursuing junks who are thrown into confusion when Nancy hoists her dragon flag; or perhaps it is her personal pride as she hears twenty-two gongs ring out for Chang, not her, and sees his flag, not hers, flying over Dragon Town. Whatever her inscrutable thoughts, she comes out of the cabin, wearing her pistol belt and a bandolier of cartridges, and without her books. A pirate again, she is restored to power and the *Shining Moon* sails on without her.

As we might expect, Nancy comes into her own in *Missee Lee*. In *Peter Duck* there were real pirates, but always at a distance. Here, as the Swallows and Amazons wait to learn their fate, the play-pirate meets a 'real' one face to face and their exchange lightens the mood:

---

1. *ML*, p. 379.
2. *ML*, p. 383.
3. *ML*, p. 396.

'I am Captain Nancy Blackett,' she said. 'Amazon pirate when at
home. . . .' She paused a moment to let that sink in.
'Pilate?' said Miss Lee. 'Captain?'
'Rather,' said Nancy.[1]

And later:

Miss Lee looked at John. 'Were you coming here when you lost
your ship?'
'No,' said John.
'We jolly well would have been if we'd known,' said Nancy.
'Why?' asked Miss Lee.
'Well, pirates,' said Nancy. 'Who wouldn't?'[2]

Although on one level Nancy continues with her pirate games in *Missee
Lee*, on another she takes command of the actual situation from the
time the *Amazon* is captured by Chang's men until she and Peggy are
reunited with the Swallows and Captain Flint. After they have been
taken aboard Chang's junk, it is only her decisive intervention which
prevents Captain Flint being thrown overboard: 'Nancy's "No!", a
single, violent, determined word, shouted close beside them, startled
the men. That moment saved him.'[3] Continually reassuring Peggy that
things are not so bad, she is delighted to find a cannon on deck and
by the ensuing sea battle ('"Gosh," said Nancy. "She *is* a pirate. . . ."').[4]
The next morning she forces their way out of the cabin demanding
breakfast, but the junk is deserted and when Peggy fails to make fast
Amazon's painter Nancy manages to paddle the dinghy ashore in spite
of the current which is sweeping them out to sea. Although they are
immediately recaptured and tied up, she stays unfazed: 'Laugh, Peggy,
you goat. Don't let them think we mind.'[5]

Nancy becomes an unwilling Latin pupil, resenting being 'one
time leader but now bottom of the class'.[6] But she loses none of her
feistiness and after the semaphored S.O.S. from Captain Flint hidden in
the parrot food she organises the writing of the ultimatum to Miss Lee
(though in fact it is Titty's subsequent heartfelt intervention and not
the threat of a strike which persuades Miss Lee to buy Captain Flint
from Chang). At the end of the novel Nancy believes that Miss Lee has

---

1. *ML*, p. 187.
2. *ML*, p. 189.
3. *ML*, p. 50.
4. *ML*, p. 62.
5. *ML*, p. 76.
6. *ML*, p. 218.

saved them from shipwreck in the whirlpool in order to keep them as Latin students and so proposes shutting her up in *Shining Moon*'s cabin; but the 'real' pirate is unworried ('You are a blave but foolish child. I am coming with you') and the smile which lights up her face as she admonishes Nancy suggests that she recognises a kindred spirit.[1]

There is little doubt that Titty is Ransome's favourite creation. Throughout the *Swallows and Amazons* novels she displays courage and resourcefulness; she has a remarkable sensitivity to the feelings of others and a particular affinity with nature. Although she may not cross the gender divide in the way that Nancy does, neither does she show any sign of growing into the same domestic mould as Susan. She is adventurous, independent and self-sufficient: it is she who in *Swallows and Amazons* captures the *Amazon* and foils the villains; who in *Swallowdale* finds help for the injured Roger; who in *Pigeon Post* becomes the water diviner and then follows Roger into the disused mine; who in *Secret Water* sets out too late with Roger and Bridget across the Wade and narrowly escapes drowning them all. Always she is even-tempered and unflappable.

Titty's role in *Missee Lee* is a small one, but her emotional depth remains striking. In the first chapter it is she who is most eager to leave port. Though she may lack John's nautical skills, it is she above the rest of the crew who shares his love of the sea and values the escape from the bustle of civilisation that it brings: 'I wish we could just sail on and on for ever.'[2] She revels in the rise and fall of the *Wild Cat*, in the starlit sky, in the romance of harbours like Papeete, 'with palms and houses on the very edge of the quay'.[3] In her cabin, she listens happily to the 'quiet sliding noise of water past the side of the ship' and the 'gentle slap of a rope' and the soothing sounds, recreated in the language, drive away thoughts of Missee Lee.[4]

When Titty and Roger are taken prisoner after Gibber gives them away, it is Titty's shared love of birds with Taicoon Chang that charms their captor and leads to their reuniting with Captain Flint and the Amazons: 'My plisoners. All together. Velly happy. And now we feed my buds. I take you with me . . .' and they engage in delightful conversation which neither understands but which draws them closer together.[5] After they arrive at Chang's yamen, he shows

---

1. *ML*, p. 383.
2. *ML*, p. 7.
3. *ML*, p. 9.
4. *ML*, p. 10.
5. *ML*, p. 124.

his collection of birds to Titty who pleases him further by repeating 'Lovely' at every cage and clapping her hands.[1] At the ensuing pirate supper, another entrancing comic set piece, Titty is given the seat of honour at Chang's right-hand. Following his lead she 'sucked the soup as noisily as she could and licked her lips'[2] (Susan is appropriately horrified) and then allows Chang to feed her with a titbit that she'd rather spit out but instead smacks her lips again and thanks him politely.[3] When they are taken to Tiger Island and become Miss Lee's students it is Titty's impassioned outburst which brings about the rescue of Captain Flint: '"It's the same as if it was Daddy," she burst out. "Think. Think. You couldn't learn Latin if you knew your father was a prisoner. . . ."'[4] But while the others congratulate her on her success, Titty turns away, thinking not so much of Captain Flint, but of her own father, whom they may not see again. Miss Lee is thinking of her own father, too.

In his treatment of the feminine, in *Missee Lee* and in all the novels, Ransome seems to be exploring rather than challenging the patriarchal norm. The norm is Commander Walker as head of the family, with Mrs Walker deferring to him; in the games they play it is John as Captain and Susan as the domesticated 'Mate'. It is Captain Flint and John navigating the *Wild Cat*, using words that the girls 'did not pretend to understand'.[5] Both male and female have their roles to play and the one cannot function without the other, but the female role is ultimately subordinate. However, Titty, who willingly defers to John as Captain, shows not only what we might see as feminine qualities that are as powerful as anything masculine, but also the sort of self-sufficiency and grit which make her stand out from the more usual depiction of girls in children's literature of the time.

Above all, though, it is Nancy's liminality throughout the *Swallows and Amazons* novels which is especially striking, and in *Missee Lee* she comes up against a similarly liminal adult she-pirate who has replaced her father as a patriarch and feels bound by her responsibility towards him in spite of her own scholarly ambitions. Nancy was followed (from 1942) by George in Enid Blyton's *Famous Five* books: like Nancy, though more stridently, George is more of a boy than the boys; like

1. *ML*, p. 147.
2. *ML*, p. 149.
3. In his *Autobiography* Ransome describes enduring a similar experience during his visit to China in 1926-1927.
4. *ML*, p. 229.
5. *ML*, p. 12.

Nancy she changes her name (from Georgina); like Nancy in her 'blue knickerbockers' or 'bathers', George is more at home in her shorts. It is my experience that children find Nancy and George the most appealing characters in their respective contexts: it is their determination to be different that makes them exciting, though they are safer on the page than in real life. While Nancy is pirating, the Walker family, and the Swallows in their games, always offer the security of how things actually are, so while she offers the possibility of escaping the norm, the status quo of the patriarchal family is never really under threat, and in *The Picts and the Martyrs* she is re-inscribed into a more traditionally feminine role. In the fantasy of *Missee Lee*, the mirroring of Nancy (the play pirate) by Miss Lee (the 'real' pirate who faces down the male Taicoons) is a skilful device that suggests that gender stereotypes can be overcome; but, as we have seen, in the actuality of the other novels in the series, John and Susan (at least) find that Nancy's pirating and posturing begin to wear thin.[1]

*

The ending of *Missee Lee* (which is a brief 'afterword' following 'THE END') is something of an anti-climax. We are told that after fleeing from the Three Islands the children simply 'went on with their voyage' as if nothing extraordinary has happened, until the *Shining Moon* finally anchors off St Mawes in Cornwall (the village where Ransome had recuperated after his appendix operation in 1933).[2] But the reality of the Chinese junk anchored at the harbour mouth and the fact that the arrival is reported in the newspapers are calculated to authenticate the adventure as something that has really happened. This is different from the ending of *Peter Duck* where it is clear that time is out of joint and the children make a transition back from a fantasy world to 'real life'.

Missee Lee is the most puzzling of Ransome's novels. It differs even more than *Peter Duck* from the mainstream of the series. The focus is as much on Miss Lee, Chang and Captain Flint as it is on the Swallows and Amazons, and for young readers the political tensions between the Taicoons and Miss Lee's yearning for an academic life can be confusing.

---

1. For a useful discussion of the treatment of the feminine in children's literature, see Judy Simons, 'Gender Roles in Children's Fiction' in M.O. Grenby and Andrea Immel, eds, *The Cambridge Companion to Children's Literature* (Cambridge: Cambridge University Press, 2009).
2. *ML*, p. 401.

As in the other novels, Ransome grounds the fiction of *Missee Lee* in reality; but the reality that he describes with his usual minute attention to detail is the exotic one that he observed as a correspondent in China in 1926-1927.

With the exception of the lengthy explanations of Chapter 13 ('Missee Lee Explains'), *Missee Lee* moves at a tremendous pace. The comedy is perfectly tuned, though some of it is more accessible to adult readers: the Latin jokes are likely to have required a little more knowledge than was expected of most children in the 1940s (young Roger is something of a classical prodigy, even for a preparatory school boy) and are even less accessible today when Latin has all but disappeared from the school curriculum. Other delights are decidedly middle-class as well: for example, the jockeying for position between Cambridge and Oxford universities which leads to Miss Lee's condescending conclusion – 'Better scholars, better plofessors at Camblidge but better marmalade at Oxford'.[1] And how far can a child reader appreciate the sacrifice that Miss Lee feels compelled to make when she finally gives up her desire to become a Cambridge academic in order to save the family business?

In a letter to Helen Ferris, Ransome writes about the dangers of writing specifically for children (a little unconvincingly, since he had a shrewd knowledge both of his primary audience and of commercial success): 'I hate the word "juvenile" applied to my books. 54 is not juvenile, not by long chalks. And they are written for me.'[2] But in *Missee Lee* he does seem at last to be writing for himself, whatever the consequences for his customary readers. Freed from the restrictions of the Lake in the North, he clearly enjoys himself, and it is the unbridled exuberance of the novel that makes it endearing whatever difficulties it may present. The once Bolshevik sympathiser delights especially in the strange morality of Miss Lee herself, the diminutive pirate who is ruthless enough to strike fear into the other tycoons, who defies the British gunboats, who turns out to be more hero than villain, but who is nevertheless a sad figure, unable in the final wrenching scene to escape 'the path of duty'.[3]

---

1. *ML*, p. 213.
2. Letter to Helen Ferris, 20 March 1938, reproduced in *Signalling from Mars*, pp. 254–56.
3. *ML*, p. 380.

11.
The Picts and the Martyrs: 'Imitation and Rehash'?

Opinions differ on *The Picts and the Martyrs* (1943). I have considerable sympathy with those who find it something of a relief after the breathless pace of *Missee Lee*, with its return to the grounded world of the Lake in the North, and I enjoy the scintillating comedy which is its chief characteristic. But in an especially forthright letter, Evgenia – always Ransome's fiercest critic and sometimes a perceptive one – accused him of reusing old and tired material, and worried that his continuing to serve up more of the same would test the loyalty of his admirers and give fuel to his critics:

> If the Swallows & Co are not to be allowed to grow up, if they are put back in the same background with the same means of enjoying themselves as they have done holiday after holidays – they can't help repeating themselves – so the arrival in Rio, the setting up of camp, taking possession of their own boat, are no longer new things done for the first time – fresh and exciting – but pale imitations of something that happened many times before. This feeling of imitation and rehash is continually forced upon one by references to previous adventures in the same places. . . .[1]

This was enough to persuade Ransome not to send the typescript to Jonathan Cape, so there was no Christmas book in 1941. A few months later, however, Ransome's mother applauded the new work: Ransome changed his mind and, to Evgenia's disgust, *The Picts and the Martyrs* was finally published in June 1943; its ironic sub-title, 'Not Welcome at All', teasingly reflects her unabated hostility to the novel. But Evgenia

---

1. Letter to Arthur Ransome, 8 August 1942, reproduced in Roger Wardale et al., eds, *The Best of Childhood* (Kendal: Amazon, 2005), p. 290.

did have half a point and there is no doubt that in *Swallows and Amazons* Ransome hit on a formula which remains largely unchanged throughout the series, even though subsequent novels introduce different settings and characters and take the reader along previously untrodden paths.

To take one example of Ransome's 'rehash', and looking back over the ten novels so far considered, part of the pattern of the *Swallows and Amazons* novels is that each starts with a disappointment to be overcome. The disappointment is not in most cases the moment of crisis or conflict that propels the plot forward. Rather, it is the overcoming of the disappointment that is one of the gateways through which the children enter an imaginary world where they leave the everyday world behind and, to them, their games become real. In *Swallows and Amazons* the disappointment occurs before the story begins, when the expedition to Wild Cat Island is forbidden until Commander Walker has been consulted. So the Swallows are kept in suspense for ten long days until the famous telegram arrives and they can at last set sail. In *Swallowdale*, there are two initial disappointments that threaten the Swallows' planned adventure with the Amazons: the virtual imprisonment of the Amazons by Great Aunt Maria and the wrecking of *Swallow*. At the beginning of *Peter Duck*, the comic mood created by the eccentric procession along the quay is spoiled when the absence of a crewman means that the *Wild Cat* cannot put to sea and the hopes of the Swallows and Amazons are dashed. In *Winter Holiday*, the planned expedition to the North Pole is thwarted by the unseasonably warm weather and by Nancy's case of mumps. At the beginning of *Coot Club*, the D.'s arrive to spend their Easter break with Mrs Barrable aboard *Teasel*, eager to learn to sail like their *Winter Holiday* friends, but there has been a dreadful misunderstanding and the *Teasel* isn't going to leave her mooring. The first twelve chapters of *Pigeon Post* are largely and even tediously taken up by disappointment until Titty finds the water supply and 'Camp Might have Been' becomes 'Can Be After All'.[1] In *We Didn't Mean to Go to Sea* Mrs Walker is reluctant to let her children spend the night on *Goblin* and only agrees when they promise not to sail past the Beach End Buoy. In *Secret Water*, Commander Walker is recalled from leave and the disappointment comes when the planned family expedition to chart the Walton Backwaters is cancelled. In *The Big Six*, the Death and Glories' plan to sail in their newly refurbished ship is thrown into confusion when they are accused of casting off boats, but as the adult world turns on them,

---

1. Arthur Ransome, *Pigeon Post*, 1936. Red Fox edition (London: Random House, 2001), p. 170.

Dorothea uses disappointment to advantage and introduces a different game by setting up 'Scotland Yard'. *Missee Lee* begins not so much with a disappointment as with a literal bang, which sets off the chain of bizarre encounters and escapades.

As well as being the device by which the children achieve their supposed independence, the initial holding up of their adventures helps to control the pace of each novel, creating a tension as time is wasted and ambition denied. Another part of the pattern is the way that this leisurely early progress is countered at the end of each novel by an urgency to make the most of the remaining time before the everyday world, often represented by school, reasserts itself.

In *The Picts and the Martyrs*, as in *Swallowdale*, the initial disappointment centres on Great Aunt Maria. Mrs Blackett, recovering from a bout of influenza, has gone on a cruise with her brother, Captain Flint, leaving Nancy and Peggy, and their guests Dorothea and Dick, to fend for themselves at Beckfoot under the watchful eye of Cook. But when Great Aunt Maria finds out and invites herself to stay to take charge of her apparently neglected nieces, the planned holiday is threatened. To avoid discovery (the D.'s presence as guests in the absence of Mrs Blackett would, in the Great Aunt's eyes, blacken her reputation even further), Dorothea and Dick have to camp secretly in the Dogs' Home, a derelict hut in the nearby woods, which gives them the chance to discover the excitements of fending for themselves and of country living. It is thus that they become the sustained centre of attention for the first time in the series.

There are, of course, myriad other ingredients that run through the *Swallows and Amazons* novels and are part of the 'imitation and rehash' of which Evgenia complains: start-of-the-holiday train journeys, repeated episodes of making camp, cosy cabins and interiors, descriptions of nature, fog, storm, traditional characters and skills, the closed and secure endings. There are also the wider themes that permeate the series: the magic of play, the absent father, the images of a fading empire, the threat to the countryside and its values, and the position of women in a changing world. Many of these are evident in *The Picts and the Martyrs*, too.

This is not to suggest with Evgenia that Ransome was tempted to churn out ever more of the same to keep his publisher and his bank balance happy. Rather, it is to demonstrate how we not only re-enter a familiar world in each novel, wherever it is set and however it is peopled, but also that the pattern and the features of each novel are recognisable to the intended reader. The important half of the point that Evgenia misses is that it is this sameness which successful series fiction demands and which is an important strength rather than a weakness: Victor Watson describes it as 'like going into a room full of friends'.[1] The immediate popularity of *The Picts and the Martyrs* suggests that Ransome's readers knew this, and for them the comfort of sameness was especially important in a world which was now embroiled in the uncertainty of war.

Rites of Passage

Evgenia is also wrong to claim that Ransome's children 'are not . . . allowed to grow up': we have already seen how the Swallows grow and change in *We Didn't Mean to Go to Sea* and *Secret Water*. In *The Picts and the Martyrs* the children also change. Dorothea and Dick, who have turned detective in *The Big Six* to exonerate the Death and Glories, develop further here. Nancy, now aged fifteen, hovers uncomfortably between childhood and adulthood, not as a difficult adolescent, but combining the playing of games with the fierce protection of her mother from the disapproval of the controlling Great Aunt and the looking-after of Dorothea and Dick, now turned Picts. Perhaps she will always be like this: a natural leader (though not always in the right direction) and increasingly alert to the needs of others, but still an irrepressible character, loved and loathed in equal measure.

From the moment the Great Aunt arrives, the narrative divides and we follow the separate existences of the Picts and the martyrs. The narrative of the Picts tells how the D.'s survive, learn and change in the Dogs' Home. These are the 'innocents' of *Winter Holiday* in awe of the Blacketts and Walkers; the greenhorn crew of the *Teasel*, trainees of Tom, Port and Starboard; and the young detectives of *The Big Six*, taking much more of a lead than in *Coot Club* but still firmly protected by Mrs Barrable. But here they have to cope by themselves, in a rite of passage in the woods where, on their first night, 'Dorothea felt suddenly very much alone'.[2] Although the Great Aunt is the cause of their exile, she never impinges on their sylvan existence. They only see her through the gloomy spectacles of Nancy and Peggy or glimpse her from their distant vantage point; they do not meet her surprised face to surprised face until they rescue her from Captain Flint's houseboat at the end of the novel.

---

1. Victor Watson, *Reading Series Fiction* (London: Routledge Falmer, 2000), p. 6.
2. *PM*, p. 69.

Dorothea and Dick's life as Picts is only half a game. They are rather like Mary Norton's miniature Borrowers ten years later:[1] 'Life at Beckfoot was going on without herself or Dick. It was as if they had slipped through a hole in the floor. They had fallen out of that life into another. . . .'[2] Typically, Dorothea tries to turn the whole situation into another story within the story, but she is realising again that life is not as simple as fiction:

> If only it had been a story, things would have been simpler. In a story, villains were villains and the heroes and heroines had nothing to worry about except coming out on top in the end. In a story black was black and white was white and blacks and whites stuck to their own colours. In real life things were much more muddled. Real life was like one of those tangles of string where if you found an end and pulled you only made things worse.[3]

Here Ransome is again enjoying the playfulness of metafiction. 'If only it had been a story,' Dorothea thinks. But of course it is a story, even if it isn't the sort of overblown melodrama which she chooses to write: the 'life' that she finds so muddling is itself a fiction in which she is a central character.

On the second morning the D.'s meet Jacky Warriner, the farmer's son who has been sent with their milk. With his knowledge of country life, Jacky is everything that urban Dorothea and Dick are not, and he becomes their teacher; first with simple lessons in cooking eggs and storing milk and butter away from the summer heat, and then by showing them how to catch trout in the stream by 'guddling' them and how to cook them. The next morning he brings a rabbit he has trapped, which becomes a metaphor for the facing and overcoming of the D.'s fears. 'It looks awfully dead,' says Dorothea, who is disturbed by its dull eyes and cold fur.[4] So cooking the rabbit is put off until the evening, and then a delivery from Cook of pork chops means that it can be delayed for another day. But after they have recovered from the rain leaking through the roof the cooking can no longer be avoided. 'And that rabbit, in the mind of an inexperienced cook, was bulking bigger than an elephant. It had to be skinned . . . and worse . . . and on these vital subjects her cookery book said nothing at all.'[5] In the end, it is

---

1. Mary Norton, *The Borrowers* (London: Dent, 1952).
2. *PM*, p. 73.
3. *PM*, p. 102.
4. *PM*, p. 167.
5. *PM*, p. 206.

Dick who takes the rabbit into the wood to draw its innards, returning 'very green'; then they both struggle to skin it – a 'messy business' which is only achieved with the forgetting of its messiness and their own inhibitions.[1] Finally the stew is cooked and enjoyed 'for its own sake and still more because the Picts were doing the real thing'.[2] They have passed the test.

The other significant metaphor for Dorothea and Dick's growing independence is the way they learn to sail their own dinghy, *Scarab*, which they collect from the boat builder at Rio (if prompted, Evgenia might have pointed out the similarity between this scene and that of the Walkers collecting the repaired *Swallow* from Rio at the end of *Swallowdale*).[3] Dick has been characteristically boning up on the science of sailing since the customary railway journey north in Chapter 2, though it is more by trial and error that they become at least tolerable seamen: at the beginning of Chapter 16 ('On Their Own') they learn how not to lower sail, but by the end of the chapter, when they return *Scarab* to her secret harbour at Beckfoot, 'the whole sail came quietly down into the boat'.[4]

Comedy of Manners

Meanwhile, the Amazons, as martyrs, play out a delicious social comedy, skilfully and outrageously directed by Nancy, with the Great Aunt at its centre. This is a new departure for Ransome, very much in the style of P.G. Wodehouse, whom he greatly admired.[5] Living in awe of the Great Aunt, and manipulated by Nancy, is a downtrodden Lake District

---

1. *PM*, p. 216.
2. *PM*, p. 229.
3. *Scarab* is modelled on *Coch-y-bonddhu*, a dinghy that Ransome had had built for his friend Charles Renold by Francis Crossfield of Arnside, Cumbria, in 1934 (Crossfield had built *Swallow* some twenty years earlier). In the event Renold didn't take to dinghy sailing and gave *Coch-y-bonddhu* back to Ransome. Ransome used her as a tender to *Nancy Blackett* and later enjoyed sailing her on Coniston Water. He owned her until the mid-1950s. In 1992 she was found in a derelict state at a hotel in the West Highlands and was restored by The Arthur Ransome Society. The dinghy is currently on loan to Windermere School.
4. *PM*, p. 199.
5. Ransome was later to name the last two yachts that he owned *Lottie Blossom*, after one of Wodehouse's more flamboyant characters. See also Paul Crisp, 'Great Aunts and Amazons', in Margaret Ratcliffe, ed., *Collecting our Thoughts* (Kendal: Amazon Publications, 2015).

cast: the Cook, the Doctor, the Postman, the Policeman, Colonel Jolys, Mary Swainson, and the hapless Timothy. But underneath the comedy there is always that same sense of the old order fading, as outdated as it may have been glorious. The notion of girlhood, characterised in *The Picts and the Martyrs* by pretty dresses, piano playing and poetry recital, and already challenged in *Missee Lee*, is consigned to the past, though perhaps with just a tinge of regret.

While Dorothea and Dick are throwing themselves into their role as Picts, Nancy and Peggy contend with the Great Aunt. In contrast to the usually measured existence in the Dogs' Home, life at Beckfoot is exaggerated and outrageous. The tone is set by the Amazons' decorating of the bedrooms intended for Dorothea and Dick with skulls and crossbones, and pirate flags – the comedy in *The Picts and the Martyrs* is once more especially visual. Nancy's horror when the telegram arrives from Great Aunt Maria is what we would expect from this least inhibited of pirates – 'Keel haul her. Fry, frizzle and boil her'[1] – but she also has a side to her that we have only glimpsed previously: 'It was clear that in spite of skulls and crossbones, plans, for the present, were for a quiet house-party, with reformed pirates entertaining the most civilized of visitors.'[2] Even when it becomes inevitable that the Great Aunt will invade Beckfoot and foil all their plans, Nancy's concern is only to protect her mother – which means the banishing of Dorothea and Dick, and a week of best behaviour so there is no cause for the Great Aunt to attack her niece's *laissez-faire* approach to parenthood.

Nancy's motive for the chaos she creates is of the best. She would much prefer to play the meanest of tricks on her impossible relative until she flees back home, but she knows that would only make matters worse for her mother. So she chooses the path of martyrdom and takes an almost masochistic pleasure in turning herself and Peggy into malleable models of Victorian propriety. But, as Timothy points out with a weary resignation, 'The trouble with Nancy's velvet glove is that it's usually got a knuckleduster inside it'.[3] The doctor, ambushed by Nancy and dragged into her self-denying game, resents being drawn into Nancy's subterfuge, but is amused too: 'Nancy,' he says, though only half-meaning it, 'I wish you were at the bottom of the deep blue sea.'[4]

---

1. *PM*, p. 9.
2. *PM*, p. 23.
3. *PM*, p. 87.
4. *PM*, p. 100.

Just as in *Swallowdale* the Swallows are appalled at the Amazon
pirates riding in the carriage with the Great Aunt in their best dresses,
the satirising of an old-fashioned idea of how girls should behave runs
through *The Picts and the Martyrs*. As well as the prompt mealtimes
and best table manners, there are the working on holiday tasks, the
learning of poetry, the practice of music, and the knitting. Most of all,
there is more visual comedy as the 'dishevelled savages' become white-
frocked and pink-ribboned young ladies, with Peggy 'idly trailing
a hand in the water',[1] and later on they appear in 'white frocks, pink
sashes, shady white hats' before they discard their femininity in the
Boat House and reappear in an instant as 'two sturdy pirates in shirts
and shorts'.[2] The visual comedy reaches its peak in the thunderstorm
when Nancy leaves her clothes neatly piled on her bedroom chair ready
for inspection, clambers through the window and down the rose trellis,
and turns up in the Dogs' Home 'wet and piebald in the doorway, in
bathing things that glistened in the flickering light of the lantern and
the fire';[3] a 'Visiting Seal'.[4]

It is during this visit to the Dogs' Home that Nancy draws together
the separate strands of the novel and masterminds a joint enterprise
between Picts and martyrs: an enterprise which harks back to *Pigeon
Post*, published nearly seven years before, but which in the chronology
of the series is set only in the previous summer. Timothy, Captain
Flint's 'Squashy Hat' partner in the copper mining company, has to
complete the testing of samples before Captain Flint returns from
the cruise. But, having been spotted by the Great Aunt shinning
over a wall, he is branded a dangerous tramp and feels unable to ask
her for the equipment he needs from Beckfoot. As in *Pigeon Post*,
though more convincingly, Ransome parodies the style of a comic
thriller as Dick is persuaded by Nancy to turn burglar, breaking into
Beckfoot and stealing the equipment. The tension is built up with
deliberate melodrama when the Great Aunt so nearly catches him in
the act: 'Suddenly he heard steps crossing the hall. . . . Steps going
to the kitchen . . . the dining room . . . they would be coming to
the study next. . . .'[5] When Dick makes his escape, the Great Aunt
threatens him with an imaginary gun. As we might expect from
earlier novels, Dorothea neatly parodies the parody: 'Dodging the

---

1. *PM*, p. 121.
2. *PM*, pp. 168-69.
3. *PM*, p. 219.
4. *PM*, p. 229.
5. *PM*, p. 243.

bullets they fled with their dear-won booty. Back in their lair, safe from pursuit, the burglars feasted their eyes on diamond necklaces and golden chains. . . .'[1] Dorothea and Dick may be firmly on the side of Nancy's martyrdom, but the morality is nicely scrambled: John and Susan would never have gone along with Nancy's game, let alone the burglary, whatever the justification. It is just as well that they will only arrive at Holly Howe after the Great Aunt has gone.

The ending of *The Picts and the Martyrs*, about which Ransome worried so much, is a comic triumph. There is the sudden disappearance of the Great Aunt after the 'Rattletrap' runs out of petrol and the unfortunate Billy has hurried off to get more; Cook has a feeling in her bones and thinks she's dead; Jacky is excited at the thought of going in the boat if the police have to drag the lake; Timothy, who despite his otherwise debilitating shyness becomes quietly authoritative (as he does in *Pigeon Post*), sends the children off to the Dogs' Home before contacting the police; Nancy telephones Colonel Jolys and his firefighters. As the search goes on there is a reminder of the detective work in *The Big Six* when Dorothea points out the need 'to get into her mind' and Dick doesn't believe 'they properly looked for tracks'.[2]

As readers we already know that Great Aunt Maria is marooned on the houseboat, having embarked on her own misguided quest for the 'burglars': she is convinced they are the Walker children who, in previous holidays, were guilty of forever making her great-nieces late for meals. But while she waits and sets about clearing up the samples from the mine, the novel turns its attention to the excitements she has left behind.

Chapter 26, 'The Hunt is Up', opens on a light-hearted note despite the fears for the Great Aunt's safety. The cacophony of coaching horns is 'cheerful';[3] the sun is high; the police bring their bloodhound and Jacky's dad brings Jess, the sheepdog; Dorothea imagines yet another story in which Dick, wanted by the police for burglary, 'would have to slip away without giving a name' having effected an heroic rescue;[4] the postman complains (quite rightly) that Nancy 'has you in trouble with one foot, and before you can lift out you're opp to t'neck';[5] Colonel Jolys, the small, self-important man with the big voice, is in his element; the Amazons put on their 'pretties' in case the Great Aunt is found.

1. *PM*, p. 249.
2. *PM*, p. 327.
3. *PM*, p. 330.
4. *PM*, p. 331.
5. *PM*, p. 333.

Meanwhile, it is important that Dorothea and Dick aren't discovered before the Great Aunt goes home, or the whole subterfuge of their existence as Picts, and the complicity of the locals in Nancy's grand strategy, will be revealed. So, in another moment of dramatic irony, Nancy sends them off to the houseboat where their nemesis awaits. Confronted by a seeming stranger aboard the boat, it takes Dick three attempts, and a long sailing lesson from the novel's narrator, to bring *Scarab* alongside without a bump, but the moment of achievement is also a moment of horror as the Picts realise that they – the two people who simply must not meet her – have come face to face with the missing Aunt.

'Boy!'[1] From the Great Aunt's first imperious call to Dick, the comedy builds relentlessly. There are clear similarities between Great Aunt Maria and Bertie Wooster's formidable aunts, and there is also a touch of Lady Bracknell from Wilde's *The Importance of Being Earnest*. The stolen box of scales is placed beside Dick's box of caterpillars, ironically and without comment. The Great Aunt's realisation that it is she who is the quarry of the hunt results in the angry opening of her parasol, which she proceeds to hold erect like a mizzen sail. Then the comic climax comes with her landing on the Beckfoot lawn. All the characters of the novel – all unwilling accomplices in Nancy's plan – are brought together, and each of them fears that their deception will be unmasked, with dreadful consequences. As she steps ashore and the chapter ends, Colonel Jolys begins his face-saving speech, and is cut off almost before he has started:

> Colonel Jolys cleared his throat. He stood all ready to make a speech and at the same time to help the Great Aunt ashore.
> 'Miss Turner,' he began, 'I think I am speaking for all of us when I say ...'
> 'Tommy Jolys,' the Great Aunt interrupted him, 'am I right in supposing that you are the leading spirit in all this foolery?'[2]

All this is seen in Chapter 28 ('Three in a Boat') through the eyes of Dorothea and Dick. But in the opening pages of Chapter 29 ('Great Aunt Maria Faces Her Pursuers') the episode is repeated from a different point of view. Now Nancy is the disguised narrator, criticising the D.'s as 'Mutton-headed galoots' for not staying away as they'd been told. In a neat piece of construction the separate

---

1. *PM*, p. 348.
2. *PM*, pp. 364–65.

narratives come together when we hear the opening of the Colonel's speech again. The Great Aunt's inimitable put-down sets the tone for all that follows.

In recalling the infant Jolys, the Great Aunt pricks his pomposity and humiliates him. At a stroke he is transformed into young Tommy 'lying on the nursery floor howling with temper because your sister had trodden on the tin trumpet you had there': the diminutive 'Tommy' and 'tin trumpets' become belittling refrains.[1] The police sergeant is dismissed as incompetent and the constable is berated for his stupidity. The hapless Timothy is reminded in Wildeian phrase that 'burglary is not usually held to be among the accomplishments of a gentleman'.[2] But the Great Aunt is no fool. She knows that her unjustified quest for the absent Swallows is likely to make her look ridiculous and her bravura performance, backed up by her insistence to leave at one o'clock as planned, with her sandwiches, saves her reputation. So instead of being the object of derision or (worse) of sympathy, she is cheered off by Jolys and the firefighters and it is they who have to cover their embarrassment. Rather than slipping away in shame, she leaves like royalty, preserving her dignity and lapping up the attention by telling her man 'not to drive at more than ten miles an hour'.[3]

The Great Aunt Transformed

However, amidst the laugh-aloud comedy something more serious and much sadder is being played out: perhaps Great Aunt Maria is not just a fairy tale witch after all. In his preliminary notes for the novel Ransome makes it clear that he wants at the end 'to combine with satisfaction that Nancy etc. have come through without disaster, with the realisation of the GA's personal discomfiture (though she must be allowed to save her face) and just the faintest touch of pity for her in the hearts of the young savages'.[4] He goes on to own that he is 'a little sorry' for the GA, who must realise in the end what is happening, and so he is intent on 'preventing the GA from being the bogy she is during the story . . . perhaps Dorothea suspects it fairly early'.[5] It is also worth noticing Ransome's portrayal in profile of the

1. *PM*, p. 371.
2. *PM*, p. 374.
3. *PM*, p. 385.
4. *The Best of Childhood*, p. 281.
5. *The Best of Childhood*, p. 282.

Great Aunt in the illustration 'The Great Aunt Steps Ashore': she is younger than we might have expected, proud but graceful, and there is no trace of spite.[1]

As her disappearance is pondered at Beckfoot, the Great Aunt begins to become human. Even Nancy and Peggy feel that 'a Great Aunt spending time in trying to improve them was better than a Great Aunt who had disappeared'.[2] Dick can't help seeing pictures of her lying with a broken ankle. For all of them, 'The Great Aunt lost was beginning to seem a very different character from the Great Aunt invading Beckfoot in holiday time and having her own way about everything'.[3]

After the D.'s have rescued the Great Aunt and she sits haughtily in their dinghy, Dorothea, always insightful, understands that her anger is little more than an act. Her suspicions of the Swallows and her nieces have turned out to be unfounded and with the hunt out in search of her she knows that she will be a laughing-stock. The metaphor of the stag at bay is entirely appropriate:

> And Dorothea suddenly knew that the Great Aunt herself was afraid of something. Not exactly afraid. Defiant was the word, thought Dorothea, and remembered the picture of the stag at bay on the bedroom wall at Dixon's farm.[4]

Ashore, Nancy looking at everyone waiting for the Great Aunt to disembark at Beckfoot, uses a similar image: she 'felt as she would have felt if she had seen a fox cornered by a pack of hounds'.[5] And when the Police Sergeant begins to berate the Great Aunt, Nancy charges to the rescue: '"She had nothing to do with it," she said. "It was all my fault."'[6] With a look, the Great Aunt shows her gratitude. Throughout the *Swallows and Amazons* series we have seen glimpses of Nancy's sensitivity. In *The Picts and the Martyrs* she shows definitively that, by now, her piracy is a disguise only.

Then Peggy, who throughout the novels is on the receiving end of Nancy's cutting remarks – half bullying, half in jest – makes a striking discovery. As the Great Aunt berates Colonel Jolys, she sees the similarity between her and her sister: 'Peggy, staring at her, suddenly thought that it was very like hearing Nancy calling somebody

---

1. *PM*, p. 370.
2. *PM*, p. 323.
3. *PM*, pp. 328-29.
4. *PM*, p. 357.
5. *PM*, p. 368.
6. *PM*, p. 372.

11. The Great Aunt Steps Ashore

It is also worth noticing Ransome's portrayal in profile of the Great Aunt in the illustration 'The Great Aunt Steps Ashore': she is younger than we might have expected, proud but graceful, and there is no trace of spite.

a galoot.'[1] It is an idea repeated later by Timothy, who suffers as much as anybody at Nancy's hands: 'If you ask me, I think your Great Aunt is remarkably like her Great Niece.'[2] Is this circularity again? Was the Great Aunt also an overbearing pirate in her youth who has been left unloved and embittered? Is this what will happen to Nancy in her turn?

*

There is no arguing with Evgenia that *The Picts and the Martyrs* leaves behind the excesses of *Missee Lee* and returns more closely to Ransome's well established formula, and that after excursions to the East Anglian Coast, the Norfolk Broads and the China Sea he chooses to go back to the Lake of the North where the adventures started. He features many of the characters we have already met in *Swallows and Amazons*, *Swallowdale*, *Winter Holiday*, and *Pigeon Post* (though the Swallows themselves are notably absent). He returns to and reworks familiar themes. But Evgenia's dismissal of the novel as no more than 'imitation and rehash' is as wrong as it is deliberately hurtful ('I am very sorry I am going to hurt you very much').[3] The fact is that in *The Picts and the Martyrs* Ransome is not only doing again what he does best, but he also explores in more detail the characters of Nancy, Dorothea and Dick, and in its final chapters he creates a comic masterpiece. Maybe Evgenia simply didn't understand the novel's very English sense of humour.

Dick especially grows in stature as he manages the gutting of the rabbit and masters the handling of *Scarab*. If we look back over the series we see that in spite of the way he remains distracted by his bird-watching, he has strengths which we have come to appreciate; and though something of a 'boffin' scientist, it is his practicality which increasingly shines through. It is Dick who in *Winter Holiday* rescues the sheep and builds the wind-sledge; it is he who in *Coot Club* engineers the 'breeches buoy' that allows Tom Dudgeon to get the stores to the grounded *Teasel* and who later, in *The Big Six*, sets up and develops the photograph that uncovers the villains; and it is he who in *Pigeon Post* constructs the pigeon alarm and manages the testing of the ore. Now, his quiet triumphs in *The Picts and the Martyrs* – and his unlikely success as a burglar – mean that, like Nancy, he is growing up.

---

1. *PM*, p. 371.
2. *PM*, p. 385.
3. Letter to Arthur Ransome, 8 August 1942, reproduced in *The Best of Childhood*, p. 290.

After the exit of the Great Aunt, there are five whole weeks of summer holiday still to enjoy. Captain Flint is coming home and the Swallows are about to arrive. 'We'll get things moving without wasting a minute,' says Nancy.[1] But Ransome leaves his options tantalisingly open. In the event, he would never share another adventure in the Lake District, and it would be four years until his next and final novel was published.

---

1. *PM*, p. 388.

12.
Great Northern?:
Not Quite a Grand Finale

'Great gaping guillemots!'[1] *Great Northern?* (1947), Ransome's last intriguing novel, is a bird adventure. It stars Nancy (who isn't at all interested in birds) and Dick (who isn't at all bothered about adventures).

Captain Flint has borrowed the *Sea Bear*, a former Norwegian pilot cutter, and with the Swallows, Amazons and D.'s he has been cruising the Scottish Isles.[2] Parents are safely out of the way (in fact, we haven't seen Mrs Blackett since *Pigeon Post* or Commander and Mrs Walker since *Secret Water*). Now it is time to beach the ship on an unnamed island, scrub off the weed and barnacles, and put on a fresh coat of anti-fouling paint before returning her to her owner the following day. While the older children are working with Captain Flint, the youngsters set off to explore. Dick, now the ship's ornithologist, discovers a pair of Great Northern Divers nesting on an inland loch – a historic moment, because this has never been known to happen before, and one that Dick needs to photograph if he is to be believed.

But when Dick lets slip his discovery to Jemmerling, a villainous egg collector on board his motor yacht *Pterodactyl*, it becomes a race to protect the nest and the birds from harm, and the holiday is extended. As a complication, the Gaels – who inhabit the island and protect its wildlife – believe that the *Sea Bear*'s crew is deliberately disturbing their deer and the children themselves become hunted. During the climax

---

1. Arthur Ransome, *Great Northern?* (London: Jonathan Cape, 1947). Red Fox edition (London: Random House, 2001), p. 349.

2. The *Sea Bear* is based on the *Teddy* in Erling Tambs, *The Cruise of the Teddy* (London: George Newnes, 1933). Ransome was to write an introduction to Tambs's book for The Mariners Library edition (London: Jonathan Cape, 1950).

of the story, the Swallows, Amazons and D.'s, together with Captain Flint, are taken prisoner by the Gaels, clearing the way for Jemmerling to steal the eggs and shoot the Great Northerns for his collection. But when the first shot is heard, the Gaels understand who the real enemy is: Jemmerling is captured, the stolen eggs are restored to the nest, and the unharmed birds are able to return.

There are obvious parallels with the theft and retrieval of Captain Flint's trunk in *Swallows and Amazons*; with the race against Black Jake for the treasure in *Peter Duck*; with the protection of the Coots' nest in *Coot Club*; with the mistaken assault on the Death and Glories by the villagers in *The Big Six*, that, if successful, would have allowed George Owdon to get on with the nasty business of egg collecting; and with the imprisonment of Captain Flint and his crew in *Missee Lee*. It is surprising that Evgenia did not launch another salvo of 'imitation and rehash'.

Don't Shoot Myles North

While Ransome was struggling with *The Picts and the Martyrs*, he pondered a fresh attempt at the 'gamekeeper' book which he had intended to write after *Peter Duck*. By May 1943 he had written six chapters, but for whatever reason (probably a 'black spot' from Evgenia) that was as far as he went and, in a letter to his mother that October, he wrote 'Gamekeeper temporarily abandoned'.[1] It was never resurrected. It was also around this time that he toyed with a new *Swallows and Amazons* novel under the working title of *Swallows & Co* (fragments were published posthumously as *Coots in the North*): it was an ambitious idea that would bring together all his child characters for a terrific adventure on the Lake in the North and I will return to it in the 'Afterword'.[2] There is nothing to tell us why Ransome never developed the novel further. Presumably he was unable to find the 'ploy' to fill the three-hundred page gap between the beginning and end that he had drafted. Then in the summer of 1944 he received an unsolicited letter from Major Myles North,[3]

1. Letter to Edith Ransome, 9 October 1943, reproduced in Roger Wardale et al., eds, *The Best of Childhood* (Kendal: Amazon Publications, 2004), p. 304.
2. Fragments of the 'gamekeeper book' and *Swallows & Co* were published in Arthur Ransome, *Coots in the North*, ed. Hugh Brogan (London: Random House, 1988).
3. Major Myles North, a District Commissioner in East Africa, provided Ransome with guinea-fowl feathers with which he made salmon flies.

someone he hardly knew, which included the detailed synopsis for a novel set in the Outer Hebrides.[1] He was immediately attracted by the possibilities of North's central idea and it became the basis for *Great Northern?*

It is arguable that North's letter was a touch unfortunate. If there was to be another *Swallows and Amazons* adventure, what better way of filling those last weeks of the summer holiday after the departure of Great Aunt Maria in *The Picts and the Martyrs* than with a grand finale on the Lake in the North, reuniting almost the whole of Ransome's cast: Swallows, Amazons, Coots and D.'s. If Ransome couldn't make that work – and marshalling so many troops would have been a huge challenge – a different plot to North's, set on familiar 'Swallows and Amazons' territory, might have served him better, especially as *Great Northern?* turned out to be the conclusion to a series which had become synonymous with the Lake District and East Anglia. His readers knew and loved these places and, whatever Evgenia thought, were always anxious to return.

Some Ransome enthusiasts have even been tempted to think that *Great Northern?* isn't a 'proper' *Swallows and Amazons* novel at all, branding poor Myles North as some kind of literary vandal responsible for soiling the purity of the series. But Ransome had often sought help with his plots (usually from Margaret Renold) and he could easily and politely have rejected North's synopsis (as he had done a number of Margaret Renold's suggestions). Here, though, was a nugget that grabbed his attention. Several of North's ideas were dismissed (his letter is annotated with 'No!', 'No!', 'No!') but Ransome transformed the proposal by adding a number of aspects of his own: the borrowing of the *Sea Bear* and the landfall in the fog; painting the *Sea Bear* on the beach; the slow voyage to the unnamed harbour for petrol and the encounter there with Jemmerling and the *Pterodactyl*; Nancy's mutiny; the stealing away from the *Pterodactyl* under cover of darkness and the later game of hide-and-seek along the coast; the introduction of young McGinty; the Pict-house and Roger's discomfiture as the 'Sleeping Beauty'; the deer, the 'decoys', the 'red herrings' and the 'dogmudgeon'; Jemmerling's attempt to shoot the Great Northern Divers; the hiding of the eggs in the heather and their subsequent discovery. Ransome also moved the time of the novel from early August to June. He needed a motive for the Gaels'

---

1. Letter from Major Myles North, 22 June 1944, reproduced in Hugh Brogan, ed., *Signalling from Mars: The Letters of Arthur Ransome* (London: Jonathan Cape, 1997), pp. 314–18.

outrage at the children trespassing on the island: this, he decided, was the disturbing of their deer in the breeding season, and that had to be in the early summer. He knew that a sailing holiday in June raises the question of why the children are not all at their respective schools. There was no solution to this and *Great Northern?* makes no specific reference to the month in which it takes place. In fact, only the key elements of North's synopsis remain: Dick's discovery of the Great Northern Divers and the need to take photographs; the hostility of the laird and his men, leading to the imprisonment of the *Sea Bear's* crew; the problem of the evil egg collector; and the happy ending. The rest is Ransome. The dedication to *Great Northern?* reads:

TO

MYLES NORTH
who, knowing a good deal of what happened,
asked me to write the full story

This double-edged acknowledgement of North's contribution makes clear that 'the full story' is Ransome's alone – with Ransome, in typical fashion, nicely squeezing out any suggestion that someone else may have had a hand in his work.

What we learn from Ransome's development of North's synopsis is that he had lost none of his ability to control the pace of a novel and build suspense, nor his determination to ensure that a sequence of exciting events are driven as far as possible by his characters. *Great Northern?* is not Ransome's most accomplished novel: the plot is unlikely, the characterisation is sometimes thin, and the ending is unsatisfactory; but it also has the usual strengths and is too often undervalued because of its unconventional origin.

In spite of the ornithological detail, it seems that North's idea was for a fantasy sequel to *Peter Duck*: he envisages Flint and his crew sailing on *Wild Cat* (presumably he had not read of her loss in *Missee Lee*). He also has Peter Duck and Bill crewing Jemmerling's yacht: 'This is most useful as they are allies in the enemy's camp, and can provide information.' Ransome's reply to North's letter has not survived, but in a further letter (29 November 1944) North acknowledges 'the distinction you draw between the *Peter Duck*, romantic stories, and the real ones', so we can assume that Ransome had decided on a realistic treatment and was not going to allow Peter Duck and Bill to 'wander in'.[1] The descriptions of the setting are, as usual, meticulous, with

---

1. Letter from Major Myles North, 29 November 1944, reproduced in *The Best of Childhood*, p. 312.

Ransome visiting the Hebrides on a number of occasions to ensure that every detail is exact. (To protect the Great Northerns from any further threat, the precise location is never revealed, but all the evidence points to the Isle of Lewis where Ransome and Evgenia stayed while he researched the novel, with Stornoway as the harbour where the *Sea Bear* puts in for petrol and where Dick meets Jemmerling on the *Pterodactyl*.) There is an absence of such things as pirate ships and a Chinese junk anchored off St Mawes; of murderous treasure-seekers sailing out of twentieth-century Lowestoft and the extraordinary Latin class in Miss Lee's extraordinary 'Cambridge' study.

What we are not told is the year *Great Northern?* takes place. It is unlikely that it is set before *The Picts and the Martyrs* (July 1933): Dick appears older and more assured in *Great Northern?* and the Beckfoot comedy makes no mention of his exploits in the Hebrides. There is also the strong impression in *Great Northern?* that the days of Swallows and Amazons are over and John and Nancy have become 'two old shellbacks, one-time captains of the *Swallow* and the *Amazon*'.[1] Thus it is probable that the earliest date for *Great Northern?* is the summer after *The Picts and the Martyrs*: June 1934. By this time John and Nancy, the eldest, are sixteen and Roger, the youngest, is eleven.

Early in the novel it appears that *Great Northern?*, like *Missee Lee*, may have little connection with the rest of the series. The name *Sea Bear* has no resonance. Titty mentions Nansen, but is not reminded of their polar base – Nansen's ship, the *Fram* – in *Winter Holiday*. Dorothea identifies the Pict-house, but it does not remind her of her very own Pict-house in *The Picts and the Martyrs*. However, almost immediately afterwards, as if Ransome is seeing connections after all, Roger thinks the Pict-house is 'a bit like the igloo'[2] (in *Winter Holiday*) and when Titty crawls through the entrance she remembers their near entrapment underground in *Pigeon Post*: 'Remember the tunnel in Kanchenjunga,' she says.[3] When Roger is criticising Dick for not being interested in exploring, Dorothea, thinking of *Winter Holiday*, asks pointedly, 'Who got first to the North Pole?'[4] Then, when Dick discovers that Jemmerling is an egg collector, 'he thought of his friends of the Coot Club and their long struggle to protect the birds';[5] and Dorothea 'who had shared the adventures of the Coot Club on

---

1. *GN*, p. 272.
2. *GN*, p. 55.
3. *GN*, p. 56.
4. *GN*, p. 69.
5. *GN*, p. 125.

the Norfolk Broads, was the only one of the others who could guess what Dick was feeling'.[1] An author's note explains that McGinty, the name given to the laird to protect his identity, was 'borrowed from Mrs McGinty whom Dick and Dorothea had met at Horning on the Norfolk Broads'.[2] So whatever its beginnings, I believe that *Great Northern?* is very much part of the *Swallows and Amazons* canon.

But if *Great Northern?* is not a fantasy like *Peter Duck* and *Missee Lee*, it is nevertheless, like *Peter Duck*, very much aware of its own status as fiction. Ransome himself intervenes in the brief Preface where he warns off 'Persons who pester the author for more information' and provides intrusive notes in the text explaining the withholding of the names of the harbour and the laird. We are shown how events are seen and recorded by different people in different ways: John writes a nautical log, with all the details of navigation; Titty, the romantic, records her thoughts in a private log; Dick, the scientist, makes a list of birds he has observed, while young McGinty writes his own diary in Gaelic. However, Dorothea, the aspiring novelist, repeatedly turns their exploits into another story within a story in the *Romance of the Hebrides* – her style remains a parody of the worst sort of novels, but even she is aware that the truth (which is itself a fiction) is far more dreadful, and here we see her move suddenly from one register to another:

> 'Life and death,' whispered Titty.
> 'It really is,' said Dorothea. 'Even now the foul murderers are stealing towards their helpless victims. And that beast'll take the eggs and Dick will wish all his life he'd never found them.' Dorothea began with a sentence in her favourite style but ended with the simple dreadful truth.[3]

Setting the Scene

The opening paragraph of *Great Northern?*, set apart as a prelude, introduces the boy in Highland dress, later to be identified as young McGinty. While watching over the deer on his father's island he sees 'a sail far away' but takes no notice of it.[4] We will recall the image of the distant sail when in the wordless ending of the novel, young McGinty watches the *Sea Bear* depart.

---

1. *GN*, p. 138.
2. *GN*, p. 345.
3. *GN*, p. 365.
4. *GN*, p. 1.

Young McGinty, who doesn't feature in North's synopsis, weaves in and out of the story, though as a guardian of the island and a stalker of the explorers, 'decoys' and 'red herrings', he is mainly glimpsed or unseen. When the younger crew members are first exploring the island they see him watching from the tower. Soon after Titty 'got the queerest feeling that they were not alone' and although the others are sceptical, they find themselves hunted by dogs and catch sight of young McGinty on the ridge above them.[1] When they set sail for the unidentified harbour, Roger sees someone fleetingly on top of the Pict-house. The next day, having slipped away from the *Pterodactyl* in the middle of the night, they return to the island and Roger is posted on the Pict-house as look-out. Young McGinty sees him asleep and is angry to discover him occupying somewhere that had always been his own. To let him know that he has been caught, he leaves the mocking message 'THE SLEEPING BEAUTY' which so angers Roger.[2] That evening from the deck of the *Sea Bear* young McGinty is seen spying on the *Pterodactyl*, which is now at anchor nearby, and the following day the 'red herrings' see him again and feel that instead of their simply leading the Gaels away from Dick, they are being pursued themselves and are no longer in control. Watching the deer and the intruders with the young McGinty is the curmudgeonly shepherd – the 'dogmudgeon', as Roger calls him (though his etymology is awry and curmudgeons have nothing to do with curs or dogs). At first it is only the dogmudgeon's lingering tobacco smoke that gives him away, and at night it is noticed from the *Sea Bear* that ashore 'someone was lighting a pipe'.[3]

For the moment, though, the focus shifts from Young McGinty to the yacht whose sail he glimpses: the *Sea Bear*, closing on the island with Nancy at the helm. Nancy is very much in charge in *Great Northern?*, as she has been in *Missee Lee* and *The Picts and the Martyrs*. It is she who persuades Captain Flint to beach the *Sea Bear* on the island for painting instead of going into the busyness of the harbour (Flint, a captain in name only, agrees 'rather reluctantly').[4] When the fog closes in and Captain Flint thinks it will be safer to head for the harbour after all, Nancy persuades him otherwise: '"All right, Nancy," he said. "You win."'[5] In Chapter 10, 'Mutiny Aboard', it is Nancy who (with the unintended help of Jemmerling) makes sure that the cruise is extended so Dick

1. *GN*, p. 69.
2. *GN*, p. 271.
3. *GN*, p. 106.
4. *GN*, p. 3.
5. *GN*, p. 16.

can photograph the Great Northern Divers. It is Nancy who devises the plan to distract the Gaels and thwart Jemmerling, so Dick can take his photographs without being discovered; and after the 'decoys' and 'red herrings' are taken prisoner she becomes the spokesman as she has done in *Missee Lee*. When Captain Flint tries to persuade old McGinty, the laird, to set them free from the storeroom-prison, Nancy rudely interrupts to impress on him the urgency of the situation: 'Don't waste time being polite,' she says.[1] It is an effective intervention, but smacks of an imperial arrogance.

So, although in command, Nancy does not become all responsibility in this final appearance. Aged at least sixteen now and no longer a pirate, she still has the same unbridled enthusiasm for life and is able to add some bird humour with her delightfully changed exclamations: 'Great Auks and Guillemots!';[2] 'Peewits and Puffins!';[3] 'Great Gannets and Guillemots!';[4] 'Great Auks for ever!';[5] 'Great Auks and Albatrosses!'[6] And when Jemmerling attempts to persuade Captain Flint to disclose the whereabouts of the Great Northerns, she observes drily, 'The *Pterodactyl*'s cooking his own goose.'[7] After the younger crew members claim to have been chased by Gaels and the *Sea Bear* leaves the island for the first time, Nancy laments that 'If they're really hostile it's an awful pity we'll never be seeing them again';[8] and although for her the rare Great Northerns are 'Just like other ducks. . . . Bit big perhaps',[9] she still sees them as the perfect excuse for some fun. As in the earlier novels, Nancy's abandon is set against and emphasised by Susan's 'native' caution: when stirring up mutiny, Nancy says to her, 'Don't go native just when things really matter.'[10]

While the *Sea Bear* is closing on the island, the fog descends (just as it has played a significant part in *Swallowdale*, *Peter Duck*, *Coot Club* and *We Didn't Mean to Go to Sea*): here at least Captain Flint displays masterly seamanship as the novel describes the edging towards the shore, the taking of soundings and the laying of anchors. But with the fog, 'The whole feeling of the day had changed,' and there are enough clues that another

---

1. *GN*, p. 374.
2. *GN*, p. 161.
3. *GN*, p. 163.
4. *GN*, p. 200.
5. *GN*, p. 243.
6. *GN*, p. 397.
7. *GN*, p. 152.
8. *GN*, p. 106.
9. *GN*, p. 197.
10. *GN*, p. 141.

adventure is about to begin.[1] The children feel that so far the holiday cruise has gone too much to plan for there to be any excitement, but when the next morning the *Sea Bear* is beached Titty assures us that, 'It's the sort of place where something's simply bound to happen.'[2] All the colonial imagery of the series is reawakened. 'Don't get into trouble with natives,'[3] warns Susan as the younger children go ashore and become 'explorers in a strange land'.[4] Using their chart they take control of the island by naming it ('Just putting in those few names on the chart made the valley seem almost their own')[5] and the diary they find hidden in the Pict-house 'belongs to one of the natives. . . . A savage Gael'.[6] As they explore further, Dorothea, imagining another episode in her story, turns the day into a game of smugglers, but seeing the Gaels' cottages, Titty, still an explorer, declares, 'Native settlement'.[7] Dick is not at all interested in games and is obsessed only with discovering Black-throated Divers, which is how he discovers the Great Northerns' nest and how the troubles start.

Different Perspectives

Dick's disastrous meeting aboard the *Pterodactyl* sparks the main action of the novel. Jemmerling is a suitable villain for a thriller. He has the red hair that North suggested and, Ransome adds, 'clever eyes . . . a long, narrow nose, and a straight, thin lipped mouth'.[8] Dick is horrified by the racks of dead blown eggs and the shot Great Northern which looked 'like a feathered balloon from which the air had escaped', but in his need to prove himself right he gives away the presence of the nesting birds and puts them under threat.[9] Jemmerling's subsequent attempts to bribe Captain Flint to reveal the whereabouts of the nest finally convince Flint that Dick has stumbled across something important. Plans to return the *Sea Bear* to her owner are delayed and under cover of darkness they slip their moorings and sail back to the island. But when Dorothea thinks she may have seen something in the distance and then there is 'a long white splash' far out at sea, it is clear that the *Pterodactyl* is close behind.[10]

---

1. *GN*, p. 19.
2. *GN*, p. 37.
3. *GN*, p. 47.
4. *GN*, p. 47.
5. *GN*, p. 56.
6. *GN*, p. 58.
7. *GN*, p. 65.
8. *GN*, p. 123.
9. *GN*, p. 128.
10. *GN*, p. 184.

The main action of *Great Northern?* takes place over the course of a few hours on the following day. Dick waits for his photographs, Nancy and John become 'decoys' to lure Jemmerling's sailor-spy away from the nest, the younger crew members become 'red herrings' to mislead the Gaels, Roger goes off to confront young McGinty, and the Gaels determine to round up all these intruders on their island. In a series of chapters (from Chapter 20, 'The Decoys', to Chapter 25, 'Roger's Dull Day') the novel views the situation from each of their points of view, drawing the different narrative strands together as one by one the Gaels imprison their enemies.

When Dick is safely installed in his hide, Nancy and John set off as 'decoys', with John dressing up somewhat unconvincingly as Dick (his spectacles are drawn on with burnt cork). With Nancy in charge, the mood is comic. 'Can't you see it?' she shouts to John, pointing to an imaginary albatross so they can look back to see if the sailor has been tricked into following them; and then, one assumes *sotto voce*: 'Pink with green wings. And there's another, speckled gold and purple.'[1] They revel in leading the sailor from one irrelevant loch to another, all the time taking him away from Dick and his birds. To their delight, he sinks into marshy ground and has to stop to empty water from a sea-boot. But they become overconfident. When they rest for lunch John wipes his face and smudges away his spectacles, and the sailor manages to get close enough to find out that he has been beautifully tricked and John isn't Dick at all. Soon afterwards, they catch sight of the 'red herrings' who have not yet realised that they are being surrounded by Gaels. Waving a handkerchief, Nancy sends a message in Morse code: short – short – long, a warning of danger.

Meanwhile, the 'red herrings' are on their own mission to draw the Gaels away from Dick. A shrill whistle reassures them that they have the unseen Gaels in tow, but as the day goes on the atmosphere alters, and they sense that they are being hunted more than stalked: 'In a queer way, the whole desolate valley seemed astir.'[2] Susan, with her customary caution, wants to go back. Then she worries that they are trespassing on someone else's land and that Roger is missing. She sees Nancy signalling from the other side of the valley: short – short – long, 'You are standing into danger'. But it's too late to escape and her loud apologies are useless: the Gaels speak no English.

While all this excitement is going on, Dick watches the Great Northerns, their movements described in exact detail. This is the real thing. The pace slows, but for Dick time passes in an instant. He doesn't for a moment

1. *GN*, p. 285.
2. *GN*, p. 309.

think of the others. Hour after hour he waits, until the sun moves round and he can take his photographs. One after the other, worried that the click of the shutter may disturb them, 'setting the aperture at its widest and the speed at one hundredth of a second', Dick is patient, meticulous, and scientific.[1] His work done, he rows the folding boat carefully back to the shore, only to be met by the dogmudgeon, who lays a hand on his collar and leads him up to the growing convoy of prisoners.

Roger, meanwhile, has hatched his own plan to get even with young McGinty. Roger's character changes in *Great Northern?*. He has always been full of mischief (as well as of food and chocolate) and is at the centre of many of the light-hearted moments in the series. But he is growing up now, and full of insecurities and perceived slights. Hazel Sheeky shows how in *Great Northern?* Roger distances himself from the group, resenting his treatment as the youngest member of the ship's crew, with no responsibility apart from the engine and where there is 'always a Captain somewhere or a Mate to tell him what to do'.[2] He thinks that the others blame him for falling asleep and not spotting the *Pterodactyl* searching for the *Sea Bear*, and with her the Great Northerns: 'He sat back on his heels, hating everybody'.[3] Back at the Pict-house, 'He had a pleasant feeling of badness, to which he was well accustomed'.[4] While for Dick time is passing quickly, for Roger, waiting by himself, it could not pass more slowly. Young McGinty comes – and goes: Roger is hiding and misses his chance, emerging just as his enemy is running away from the Pict-house and towards the prisoners – 'decoys', 'red herrings', and the ship's ornithologist – being marched away. Part of him is rather pleased and 'he planned to do a little gloating himself':[5] he is, after all, 'the only one uncaught'.[6] But the sailor has done his job well. He has seen Dick on the loch and he and Jemmerling are heading for the Great Northerns, armed with a gun. Forgetting his private feud, Roger becomes a 'Sea Bear' again, a rescuer, discovering the storehouse-prison and tapping gently at the door. 'Tap . . . tap . . . tap,' and from inside the prisoners listen. 'It's Roger,' exclaims Susan with relief.[7]

---

1. *GN*, p. 334.
2. Hazel Sheeky, 'The Politics of Sailing in Swallows and Amazons', in *The Arthur Ransome Society, Transcripts from the Twelfth Literary Weekend* (Kendal: The Arthur Ransome Society, 2015), p. 51.
3. *GN*, p. 225.
4. *GN*, p. 351.
5. *GN*, p. 359.
6. *GN*, p. 360.
7. *GN*, p. 364.

Young McGinty and the dogmudgeon have a different perspective: here we see the action from the point of view of natives threatened by colonisers. The novel unobtrusively introduces them to the reader as friends, using their names: young McGinty is a sandy-haired boy called Ian; the dogmudgeon is an old shepherd called Angus. On the *Sea Bear*'s first visit to the island they see the children apparently chasing their deer and frighten them off. The next day, though, they see the intruders return, followed by more troublemakers in a motor cruiser. The laird's instructions are clear: 'Lay hold of the bairns . . . and we will soon ken who put them up to it.'[1] Sure enough the children come ashore and are clearly up to mischief, careless of their surroundings and frightening the deer from their breeding grounds. Enlisting the help of the ghillies, Ian and Angus track them and round them up, holding them in the storehouse for the laird to deal with. Angus reflects with satisfaction that 'His had been a successful day'.[2]

As the five separate narratives converge in the storeroom-prison, Jemmerling is left free to shoot the Great Northerns for his collection and steal their eggs. The mood is lightened for a little while as Roger attempts to speak to the laird and in doing so fells the piper. The prisoners roar and scream to attract attention. Amidst the chaos, Susan worries about iodine for Roger's grazed knee. But it is the gunshot that changes things. Enemies become allies, and young McGinty and the dogmudgeon, the real protectors of the birds, are instrumental in trapping Jemmerling and his sailor-accomplice in the obligatory 'nick of time'. Susan, whose exaggerated 'native' attitudes have turned her into a figure of gentle fun, worries that Titty and Roger have wet feet.

'Farewell to the *Sea Bear*'

The ending of *Great Northern?* is something of a mystery. While the captured Jemmerling argues with old McGinty, he sees the children searching on the lake shore for the box he has hidden which contains the stolen eggs. A triumphant yell tells everybody that it has been found. It is Titty, so often the hero of the series, who discovers it hidden in the heather, just as in *Swallows and Amazons* she discovers the treasure on Cormorant Island. Dick, whose determination to photograph the nesting birds has led to the whole escapade, has throughout the day sat motionless in his hide, oblivious to the dramas being played out around him; but now he is beside Titty in an instant. Titty and Dick take the

---

1. *GN*, p. 225.
2. *GN*, p. 344.

folding boat and as quickly and quietly as possible set out to replace the eggs on the nest, hoping the Great Northerns will be brave enough to return before the eggs go cold. If they succeed, Dick will have his place in history; if they don't, his interference will mean that the eggs will never hatch. With the eggs back where they should be, Dick becomes the narrator as he looks through his binoculars and describes first one bird and then the other swimming for the shore. Then: 'It's on the nest. . . . Here, you look. . . . What's the matter?'[1] But Titty, both brave and sensitive to the last, whose hands and arms are bloodied from the search in the heather, is for a moment overcome: 'It really was dreadful, the way her eyes would weep when there was nothing whatever to weep about.'[2]

It is Ransome's usual practice to round off each novel by tying up the loose ends and giving the reassurance that everything, like the eggs, is safely back in its rightful place. But that doesn't happen in *Great Northern?* where, after Titty's sentimental tears, Dick's joyful 'Gosh! Oh Gosh!' are the last words. Aware of Ransome's customary closed endings, Myles North had included in his synopsis the details for a neat conclusion: Dick's writing his account for British Birds; Dorothea including a Jemmerling-like villain in *A Romance of the Hebrides*; Old McGinty watching the Divers escorting their 'two fine young' on his loch; and (since North was on a roll) Nancy opening up the possibility for the next novel: 'Shiver my timbers. What's coming now?' But Ransome ignores all that and for the first and only time signs off with no more than a full-page illustration, 'Farewell to the *Sea Bear*', in which the young McGinty is placed in the foreground on the island cliff, holding binoculars to his eyes and seeing the *Sea Bear*, no more than a white speck of sail, disappearing over the horizon. Jemmerling, like Owdon in *The Big Six*, is forgotten altogether.

Perhaps this is enough. The young McGinty, who in the first sentence of the novel watches the distant *Sea Bear* approach the island, now watches her depart; the island, its people, its deer, and the Great Northern Divers can return to their peaceful and untroubled existence. The colonial explorers have moved on and the native Gaels, like the Great Northern Divers, are left to get on with their lives. But as readers we look over young McGinty's shoulder and perhaps we too are seeing the Swallows, Amazons and D.'s for the last time: 'Farewell' not only to the *Sea Bear*, but to her crew as well. Or perhaps even Ransome wasn't

---

1. *GN*, p. 409.
2. *GN*, p. 409.

12. Farewell to the *Sea Bear*

*As readers we look over young McGinty's shoulder and perhaps we too are
seeing the Swallows, Amazons and D.'s for the last time: 'Farewell' not
only to the* Sea Bear, *but to her crew as well.*

altogether sure where the *Sea Bear* and her crew were heading – to the adult world and the end of childhood stories, or off to new adventures if he could just summon up the energy. Did he sense that it really was 'farewell' to the characters who had become his constant companions for seventeen years since he had first brought them to life in *Swallows and Amazons*? Or did he deliberately leave open the possibility that they might just come back to bother him and share in another story?

Afterword:
A Sense of Endings

So, for the moment at least, it is time to return the *Swallows and Amazons* novels to the shelf. It has been a pleasure to read them once again, and to share that reading with you, but they are complex books which display as many differences as similarities, and I offer no neat conclusions. The settings range from the Lake in the North to the South China Sea. There are accounts of explorations and conquests, pirate fantasies, travelogues, thrillers, detective stories and domestic comedies. There is an array of characters from country and town, from the professional classes to boat-builders, from old to young, from colonial to savage. There are heroes like Titty and John; there are transgressors like Nancy and Captain Flint; and there are not always convincing villains like Black Jake, George Owdon and Jemmerling. It is through Ransome's skill that the children grow and change, and from time to time they surprise us, as even old friends do. But we come to know them perhaps too well, and in the later novels they begin to slip into caricature.

However, we have seen a clear movement from the innocence of the early novels, through the unease of *Pigeon Post, We Didn't Mean to Go to Sea, Secret Water* and *The Big Six*, to the prevailing comedy (begun in earnest in *The Big Six*) of the final books. We have observed constants in Ransome's skill as a story-teller (though it is unkind to call them 'rehash'): the clarity of his prose; the exactness of his descriptions of place which ground even *Peter Duck* and *Missee Lee* and make them believable; the remarkable insight into his developing characters that he conveys almost without our noticing; his sense of pace (which is arguably more suited to an age which had the luxury of time); his manipulation of narrators and narrative form; the space in both writing and illustration which he leaves for the reader's imagination to fill; and, yes, a similar underlying pattern in each novel, one which is reassuring and which works.

We may also have been surprised that in the *Swallows and Amazons* novels Ransome is not altogether the champion of Empire and all it represents that he is often held to be, although inevitably that is how his first readers saw him – not least because of their own belief in the Empire. Contemporary adult readers would have recognised his depiction of their carefully structured world, and his imperialist imagery and tone, and seen no problem with his assigning stereotypical female roles to Mrs Walker, Susan, Peggy, and (to an extent) Dorothea, or with John's seeming mastery of Susan in the storm-tossed *Goblin*. Middle-class readers in the post-war period would have read Ransome in much the same way, revelling in the nostalgia, as a dwindling band still does. But that is to miss so much of the novels' irony; it is to miss the complexities and contradictions of Ransome's own make-up, which are reflected in the characters he creates: he is as much, if not more, in Dick, Captain Flint and Admiral Barrable as he is in the skipper of the *Cachalot* and the serious, rather self-righteous Captain John; it is to miss his revelling in the piracy of Nancy and the Death and Glories; it is to miss his recognition of Titty and Dorothea, in particular, as disguised narrators helping to create and control the novels through their imagination; it is to miss his fondness for savages and his amused rejection of the behaviour insisted on by Great Aunt Maria. We should note that it is Nancy, the Amazon pirate, who is placed firmly at the centre of his last three novels, *Missee Lee, The Picts and the Martyrs* and *Great Northern?*

This is not to say that Ransome did not value, above all, the traditional qualities displayed by his characters: leadership, courage, endurance, honesty, care for one another, initiative, common sense, good humour, service. Nor is it to deny his belief in the patriarchal family, which for him had been so cruelly cut short. Nor is it to say that he did not have a lingering pride in Empire and the stability that it represented. It is to say, rather, that in the *Swallows and Amazons* series all these things are balanced by an innate radicalism that challenges the status quo, authority and convention, and that Ransome explores the relationship between them with understated skill. In the novels, the stability is a safety net for the transgressors, but before long it would become a mould to be broken, not necessarily for the worse.

Throughout the series there is also an inescapable sense of endings: of childhood, of the idyll of rural England, of Empire. The paradisal innocence and freshness of *Swallows and Amazons* is juxtaposed with the experience of colonial adventure.[1] The Swallows are never the same

---

1. Watson suggests that 'Eden lies within this story. The children are like Adam and Eve naming the beasts and the flowers.' Victor Watson, *Reading*

after the terrifying sea passage in *We Didn't Mean to Go to Sea*, and in *Secret Water* they move away from play and 'savagery'. In *Coot Club*, the Hullabaloos, who are representative of a new urban and selfish culture, may be repelled, but we know they will return. In the Lake District, in Suffolk and in the Hebrides, the colonial imagery is central, even as the Empire starts its inexorable decline. In *The Big Six*, the comedy and excitement of the detective story never mask the unease of a world in crisis, where bullies threaten and the mistrusting adults turn quite wrongly on the children, not least because of their class. All may seem secure in the novels' comfortable endings, but when in the Postscript of *The Big Six* the old fisherman sees the size of the pike caught by the Death and Glories, a chill irony mingles with the boys' optimism and the humour of his closing words:

> 'Poor lad,' said the old man. 'Poor lad. . . . So young and with nothing left to live for.'
> 'Let's go and catch another,' said Pete.[1]

It is also the case that Ransome's own life intrudes on the *Swallows and Amazons* novels. He draws on and transforms his personal experiences, the people that he knew and the places that he loved; but, because he transforms them, we must avoid the temptation to make connections that are too exact. He confronts his ambiguous relationship with his father; and he escapes from his miserable schooldays, his often unhappy personal life, the treadmill of his journalism and his years in Russia as an apparent Bolshevik sympathiser and a spy. There is, then, one more way in which the novels offer to the reader the sense of an ending, although it is not altogether a happy one: an ending of sorts to the momentous and very personal voyage of Arthur Ransome.

Coots in the North

Before taking final leave of the 'Swallows and Amazons' novels I want to touch on *Coots in the North*, the grand finale to the series that was never completed. The first four draft chapters are typical of the preceding Norfolk adventures. It is August 1933 (in Ransome time), the year after *Coot Club* and *The Big Six*. The peace of the Norfolk rivers is shattered by holidaymakers, even if they are not behaving quite as wildly as the Hullabaloos:

Series Fiction (London: Routledge Falmer, 2000), p. 13.
1. Arthur Ransome, *The Big Six* (London: Jonathan Cape, 1940). Red Fox edition (London: Random House, 2001), p. 424.

There was a noisy crowd of holidaymakers going to and fro between their boats and the little shops across the green. More and more boats kept coming up, looking for a place, finding none, and bumping in to tie up to the boats early moored there. It was the second week in August and every boat-letter on the Broads had let every boat he had.[1]

Jonnatt, the Horning boat-builder featured in *The Big Six*, has built a motor cruiser, the *Bonnka*, for a customer in the Lake District.[2] The lifting of the cruiser onto the lorry that will take her on the journey northwards is recounted in typically minute detail, both the process and the unfounded nervousness of the workers. Then a casual remark from Mrs Barrable puts it into Joe's head that the three Death and Glories might make the voyage in the *Bonnka* to the Lake in the North where Dick and Dorothea are staying at Dixon's Farm. Tom Dudgeon, Port and Starboard are conveniently on holiday, but it seems from a discarded opening as if Mrs Barrable will be invited to join the Callum family in Cumbria.

Thus the three boys stow away on board and soon the cruiser is speeding through the night with its secret crew. The description of the boys 'steering' the boat along its land voyage, romancing the road trip into a nautical adventure, is the equal of anything that Ransome ever wrote. The language is simple yet compelling: the contrast of light and dark, the shifting shadows, and the vastness of the land and sky beyond 'the outposts of their world', are captured absolutely; the cockpit is transformed into the bridge of an ocean liner; the Death and Glories come alive in their Norfolk dialect. His powers had not deserted him:

> On either side of them was the dark of the fields. Overhead was starry sky, broken now and then by the roadside trees. Ahead of them, the tremendous headlights of the lorry swept the road, lit up tree trunks that grew bigger and bigger and suddenly vanished into blackness.
>
> 'Old "Death and Glory", she never go as fast as this, not with a full gale blowing stern,' said Bill. . . .
>
> 'Starboard your hellum,' shouted Joe. Pete steadied, and with hands trembling on the spokes, steered as carefully as if at the wheel of a liner. The cruiser answered her helm as the big lorry took the bend in the road.[3]

1. Arthur Ransome, *Coots in the North*, ed. Hugh Brogan (London: Jonathan Cape, 1988). Red Fox edition (London: Random House, 1993), p. 126.
2. 'Bonnka' is Norfolk dialect for a strapping young woman.
3. *CN*, p. 158.

When the lorry reaches the Lake, the Death and Glories disembark just before the end of the journey (perhaps to escape discovery when the cruiser is unloaded). But they accidentally leave Joe's white rat aboard, and before setting out to find the D.'s they have to locate the cruiser at its final destination and rescue the pet. The boat's owner looks kindly on them, allows them to stay, and points them to Dixon's farm. As the Death and Glories are rowing to the farm, they see a dinghy capsize. Their salvaging instincts take over, and in effecting the 'rescue' they meet the piratical Nancy:

> 'Got her,' said Joe. 'She's a strong one.'
> Slippery with water, the victim twisted under his hands. He lost grip for a moment, but got her by the hair. 'Do I bat her one?' he said. 'Never hold her else. She's gone. . . .'
> The drowning sailor had twisted over and dived like a seal. Kicking feet showed above water. Pete got hold of one in both hands.
> 'Look out! You'll drown her!' There was a shout from one of the other sailing boats and then, 'Dick! Dick! It's the Coots.'
> 'Ow!' Pete saw stars. Something enormous hit him on the nose. The next moment a head showed above water a yard or two from the boat.
> 'Shiver my timbers!' said an angry voice. 'What are you playing at? Tearing my hair out by the roots. Hullo! Did I get your nose? Good.'[1]

This robust meeting between the Lake pirates and the Norfolk pirates-turned-salvagers is full of possibilities for the development of the novel and continues the comic mood of *The Big Six, Missee Lee*, and *The Picts and the Martyrs*.

The Norfolk Coots are at the centre of these opening chapters of *Coots in the North* and we know that Ransome intended them to function as the disguised narrators (just as Titty and Dorothea had been disguised narrators in the earlier books):

> That ploy and the other children [are] seen throughout, like the lake, hills, etc., through the eyes of the three Norfolk boys.[2]

In a post-war world, which had seen many of the vestiges of privilege wiped away, they were the right heroes for a new age. Although Ransome accepted that 'all the others, Roger, Titty, Nancy, Susan, etc.

---

1. *CN*, pp. 174–76.
2. *CN*, p. 177.

must be given a chance', he never decided what that chance might be. It was now the turn of the masses rather than the classes to make sense of the peace. If the Death and Glories' moral code was less rigid than the Swallows' ('Bill sat firmly on his conscience, Pete forgot his, and Joe, in the warm glow of his idea, seemed never to have had one'), it was still rooted in rural tradition, and for Ransome there could be no better model for civilised behaviour.[1]

Ransome also made notes on a possible end to the novel in which, significantly, it is the Death and Glories who take charge of the Swallows and Amazons to salvage Captain Flint's houseboat when the anchor chain parts. As reward, Captain Flint pays for their journey home, with salvage money for each of them besides, and the familiar closed ending implies that as usual all will be well: 'Geewhizz!' says Joe as the train pulls out of the station and we bid our last farewell to the Norfolk Coots. 'Salvage ain't so bad after all.'[2]

Packing Away

In the garden at Holly Howe, and in Tom Dudgeon's shed, rather sadly, the dressing-up clothes are now being folded (by Susan, naturally) and put away for the last time. Inconveniently, Titty can't stop her eyes from weeping again. What games and adventures the Swallows, Amazons, Callums and Coots have enjoyed, but they are growing up now and it is time to progress in life's journey. As in *We Didn't Mean to Go to Sea*, where the sea is a metaphor for the adult world, they are both exhilarated and afraid. They know that some of the clothes belonged to their parents, who 'once upon a time' played the same games; and one day perhaps their own children will follow in their footsteps. But for now other adventures are beckoning.

John Walker will follow his father into the Royal Navy. Susan, like her mother, will become 'the best of natives'. We can't be sure about Titty, though in her quiet way she will most likely break with convention: perhaps she will become an artist. Roger, with his penchant for oil and greasy rags, will become a naval engineer (unless, with his prowess in Latin, he is encouraged to follow Miss Lee to Cambridge). We know that their precursors, the Altounyans, followed different paths, but the Swallows have become people in their own right and have independent lives to lead.

Nancy Blackett – she will never revert to Ruth – will one day become the mistress of Beckfoot where there will never be a dull moment; we

1. *CN*, p. 154.
2. *CN*, p. 179.

must hope that life treats her well and that she does not in the end, after a string of heartbreaks, become sad and controlling like her Great Aunt. Once out of her sister's shadow, Peggy will flourish.

Dorothea will at last become an author in the real world instead of being an author in other people's stories, but although she will write romances, she will have to learn (as Ransome did) to curb the excesses of her style. Dick will be a scientist, of course. In Norfolk, Tom Dudgeon will be expected to train as a doctor or lawyer, but he will still enjoy a pint with Joe, Bill and Pete, boat-builders like their fathers, in the Swan Inn on the bend of the river in Horning.

All of them will be amazed by the speed at which the world will change around them, but they will remember the simple pleasures of their childhood and the moral compass that their parents have given them. Whenever the chance arises, they will return to the countryside, and to the lakes, rivers and seas.

And although they will not know it, all of them will remain loved by millions of people they will never meet, who will read about their exploits in some of the finest novels for youngsters of every age that have ever been written. Inevitably, readers in the twenty-first century will see Swallows, Amazons, Coots and D.'s, on the surface at least, as historical figures from a different era, although, once they have made that jump, they will find them no less credible and exciting. Introduce mobile phones, for example, and the plots would fall flat (and that is a lesson in itself about children and independence); but, as the cliché has it, human nature itself doesn't change that much.

Ransome, who, in spite of all his insecurities, could be an arrogant man, would not have been surprised that the novels in which his characters come and stay alive have never been out of print in hardback fifty years after his death. No longer up-to-date, they nevertheless provide links with a now distant past, and with a way of life that in many respects some find better than the present. As his myriad readers would have it: Swallows, Amazons, Coots and D.'s for ever!

Select Bibliography

Ransome's *Swallows and Amazons* Novels
(In order of first publication)

Note: *All references in* Swallows, Amazons and Coots *are to Random House 'Red Fox' editions, 2001*

Swallows and Amazons (London: Jonathan Cape, 1930. Red Fox edition, London: Random House, 2001)

Swallowdale (London: Jonathan Cape, 1931. Red Fox edition, London: Random House, 2001)

Peter Duck (London: Jonathan Cape, 1932. Red Fox edition, London: Random House, 2001)

Winter Holiday (London: Jonathan Cape, 1933. Red Fox edition, London: Random House, 2001)

Coot Club (London: Jonathan Cape, 1934. Red Fox edition, London: Random House, 2001)

Pigeon Post (London: Jonathan Cape, 1936. Red Fox edition, London: Random House, 2001)

We Didn't Mean to Go to Sea (London: Jonathan Cape, 1937. Red Fox edition, London: Random House, 2001)

Secret Water (London: Jonathan Cape, 1939. Red Fox edition, London: Random House, 2001)

The Big Six (London: Jonathan Cape, 1940. Red Fox edition, London: Random House, 2001)

Missee Lee (London: Jonathan Cape, 1941. Red Fox edition, London: Random House, 2001)

The Picts and the Martyrs (London: Jonathan Cape, 1943. Red Fox edition, London: Random House, 2001)

Great Northern? (London: Jonathan Cape, 1947. Red Fox edition, London: Random House, 2001)

Coots in the North and Other Stories, ed. Hugh Brogan (London: Jonathan Cape, 1988. Red Fox edition, London: Random House, 1993)

Other Books by Ransome
(In order of first publication)

The ABC of Physical Culture (London: Henry J. Drane, 1904)

The Stone Lady (London: Brown Langham & Co Ltd, 1905)

Bohemia in London (London: Chapman and Hall, 1907)

A History of Storytelling (London: T.C. and E.C. Jack, 1909)

Edgar Allen Poe: A Critical Study (London: Martin Secker, 1910)

Oscar Wilde: A Critical Study (London: Methuen, 1912)

Old Peter's Russian Tales (London: T.C. and E.C. Jack, 1916)

On Behalf of Russia (1918) in Arthur Ransome, *In Revolutionary Russia*, with Introductory Essay by Paul Foot (London: Redwords, 1992)

Six Weeks in Russia in 1919 (London: George Allen and Unwin, 1919)

The Crisis in Russia (London: George Allen and Unwin, 1921)

Racundra's First Cruise (London: George Allen and Unwin, 1921)

Rod and Line (London: Jonathan Cape, 1929)

The Autobiography of Arthur Ransome, ed. Rupert Hart-Davis (London: Jonathan Cape, 1976)

Arthur Ransome's Long-Lost Study of Robert Louis Stevenson, ed. Kirsty Nichol Findlay (Martlesham: Boydell, 2011)

Letters and Notebooks

Brogan, Hugh, ed., *Signalling From Mars: Letters of Arthur Ransome* (London: Jonathan Cape, 1997)

Crisp, Paul and others, eds, *Ransome Broadside* (Kendal: Amazon, 2005)

Wardale, Roger and others, eds, *The Best of Childhood* (Kendal: Amazon Publications, 2004)

Biography – People and Places

Brogan, Hugh, *The Life of Arthur Ransome* (London: Hamish Hamilton, 1985)

Chambers, Roland, *The Last Englishman: The Double Life of Arthur Ransome* (London: Faber and Faber, 2009)

Griffiths, Maurice, *The Magic of the Swatchways* (London: Edward Arnold, 1932. New edition, London: Adlard Coles, 1977)

Hardyment, Christina, *Arthur Ransome and Captain Flint's Trunk* (London: Frances Lincoln, 2006)

——, *The World of Arthur Ransome* (London: Frances Lincoln, 2012)

Jacks, M.L., 'Education for Tomorrow' in *The Headmaster Speaks* (London: Kegan Paul, Trench, Trubner & Co., 1936)

Lockhart, Robert Bruce, *Memoirs of a British Agent* (London: Putnam, 1932)

Miller, Douglas, 'The School and the Community' in *The Headmaster Speaks* (London: Kegan Paul, Trench, Trubner & Co., 1936)

Smith, Michael, *SIX: A History of Britain's Secret Intelligence Service, Part I: Murder and Mayhem 1909-1939* (London: Biteback, 2010)

Wardale, Roger, *Arthur Ransome and the World of Swallows and Amazons* (Skipton: Great Northern Books, 2000)

——, *Arthur Ransome's East Anglia: A Search for Coots, Swallows and Amazons* (Wilmslow: Sigma Press, 2001)

——, *Arthur Ransome: Master Storyteller* (Skipton: Dalesman Press, 2010)

——, *In Search of Swallows and Amazons: Arthur Ransome's Lakeland* (Wilmslow: Sigma Press, 2006)

——, *Nancy Blackett: Under Sail with Arthur Ransome* (London: Jonathan Cape, 1991)

——, *Ransome at Sea* (Kendal: Amazon Publications, 1995)

Criticism, Imperial History
and Works by Other Authors

Barrie, J.M., *Peter Pan* (1904)

Bogen, Anna, 'The Island Come True: Peter Pan, Wild Cat Island and the Lure of the Real', in M.S. Thompson and C. Keenan, eds, *Treasure Islands: Studies in Children's Literature* (Dublin: Four Courts Press, 2006)

Booth, Wayne, *The Rhetoric of Fiction* (Chicago: Chicago University Press, 1961)

Brantlinger, Patrick, *Crusoe's Footprints: Cultural Studies in Britain and America* (New York: Routledge, 1990)

Byrd, Max, ed., *Daniel Defoe – Twentieth Century Views* (Englewood Cliffs, NJ: Prentice Hall, 1976)

Defoe, Daniel, *Robinson Crusoe* (1719)

Dusinberre, Juliet, *Alice to the Lighthouse* (Basingstoke: Macmillan, 1999)

Edwards, Owen Dudley, *British Children's Fiction in the Second World War* (Edinburgh: Edinburgh University Press, 2007)

Faulks, Sebastian, *Faulks on Fiction* (London: BBC Books, 2011)

Fisher, Margery, *The Bright Face of Danger* (London: Hodder and Stoughton, 1986)

Froude, J.A., *History of England from the Fall of Wolsey to the Defeat of the Spanish Armada* (London: 1856-1870)

Genette, Gérard, *Narrative Discourse* (Oxford: Blackwell, 1972)

Golding, William, *Lord of the Flies* (London: Faber and Faber, 1954)

Green, Martin, *Dreams of Adventure, Deeds of Empire* (London: Routledge & Kegan Paul, 1980)

Hawlin, Stefan, 'The Savages in the Forest: Decolonizing William Golding', *Critical Survey*, 7 (1995), pp. 125-35

Hunt, Peter, *Approaching Arthur Ransome* (London: Jonathan Cape, 1992)

Inglis, Fred, *The Promise of Happiness* (Cambridge: Cambridge University Press, 1981)

Kennedy, Alan, 'Titty and the Hazel Wand – Reflections on *Pigeon Post*', in *Mixed Moss 2016* (Kendal: The Arthur Ransome Society, 2016)

Knight, E. F., *The Cruise of the Alerte* (1890; reprinted London: Granada, 1984)

Lingley, Janice, '*Bevis* and Arthur Ransome's *Swallowdale*', in *The Richard Jefferies Society Journal*, No 23 (2012)

Mabey, Richard, *Dreams of the Good Life* (London: Allen Lane, 2014)

Nansen, Fridtjof, *The First Crossing of Greenland* (London and New York, Longmans, Green & Company, 1890)

——, *Farthest North* (London: George Newnes, 1898)

Norton, Mary, *The Borrowers* (London: Dent, 1952)

Phillips, Jerry, and Ian Wojcik-Andrews, 'History and the Politics of Play, in T.S. Eliot's "The Burial of the Dead" and Arthur Ransome's *Swallows and Amazons*', *The Lion and the Unicorn* 14 (1990), pp. 53-69

Ransome, Cyril, *Our Colonies and India: How We Got Them and Why We Keep Them* (London: Cassell, 3rd edition 1887)

Ratcliffe, Margaret, ed., *Collecting our Thoughts* (Kendal: Amazon Publications, 2015)

Seidel, Michael, '*Robinson Crusoe': Island Myths and the Novel* (Boston: Twayne, 1991)

Sewart, Dave, *Illustrating Arthur Ransome* (Kendal: Amazon Publications, 1994)

Sheeky Bird, Hazel, 'The Politics of Sailing in *Swallows and Amazons*', in *Transcripts from the Twelfth Literary Weekend 2013* (Kendal: The Arthur Ransome Society, 2015)

——, *Class, Leisure and National Identity in British Children's Literature, 1918 – 1950* (London: Palgrave Macmillan, 2014)

Simons, Judy, 'Gender Roles in Children's Fiction' in *The Cambridge Companion to Children's Literature*, ed. M.O. Grenby and Andrea Immel (Cambridge: Cambridge University Press, 2009)

Smythe, Frank, *The Kanchenjunga Adventure* (London: Gollancz, 1930)

Snow, C.P., *Death Under Sail* (London: Stratus, 2000)

Stevenson, Robert Louis, *Treasure Island* (1883)

Tambs, Erling, *The Cruise of the Teddy* (London: George Newnes, 1933. Mariners Library Edition, London: Jonathan Cape, 1950)

Wardale, Roger, *Ransome the Artist* (Kendal: Amazon Publications, 1998)

Watson, Victor, *Reading Series Fiction* (London: Routledge Falmer, 2000)

Westerman, Percy F., *A Mystery of the Broads* (Glasgow and London: Blackie and Son, 1930)

——, *Sea Scouts of the Kestrel* (London: Seeley, Service & Co., 1930)

Wheeler, Roxann, '"My Savage", "My Man": Racial Multiplicity in *Robinson Crusoe*', *ELH*, vol. 62, no. 4 (John Hopkins University Press, Winter 1995)

Index

The Arthur Ransome Society

Enjoy the books. Rediscover the Ransome magic.

- Regional events – hiking, sailing, camping, exploring, literary, historical
- International annual general meeting
- Biennial literary weekend
- Extensive library
- *Mixed Moss* – the Society's annual journal, with articles on all things Ransome
- *Signals* – a regular round-up of Society activities
- 'Red Slipper' research fund

For more details, go to www.arthur-ransome.org.uk

Arthur Ransome Trust

Putting Ransome on the map

The Arthur Ransome Trust exists to help people discover more about Arthur Ransome's fascinating life and works. The Trust's main goal is to establish a public centre in the Lake District. Whilst working towards a centre, ART arranges exhibitions, displays and lectures. The Trust is also working to develop teaching materials, for use in schools, and virtual materials for use by visitors to the Lake District.

To find out more, please visit us at:
www.arthur-ransome-trust.org.uk